THE HORSES OF MY LIFE

RICHARD DUNWOODY

THE HORSES OF MY LIFE

JOHN BLAKE

Published by John Blake Publishing Ltd,
3, Bramber Court, 2 Bramber Road,
London W14 9PB, England

www.blake.co.uk

First published in Hardback in 2005

ISBN 184454 140 1

British Library Cataloguing-in-Publication Data:

A catalogue record for this book is available from the British Library.

Design by www.envydesign.co.uk

Printed in Great Britain by CPI Bath

1 3 5 7 9 10 8 6 4 2

Papers used by John Blake Publishing are natural, recyclable products made from wood
grown in sustainable forests. The manufacturing processes conform to the environmental
regulations of the country of origin.

Every attempt has been made to contact the relevant copyright-holders, but some were
unobtainable. We would be grateful if the appropriate people could contact us.

For my father, George.

ACKNOWLEDGEMENTS

The authors would like to thank James de Wesselow and Gary Millard, whose meticulous research of form helped jog the memory. We would also like to thank Weatherbys for similar research.

CONTENTS

PREFACE

I N DECEMBER 1999, I WAS FORCED TO RETIRE FROM HORSE-RACING ON MEDICAL GROUNDS. I always knew, of course, that I wouldn't go on riding forever but I had hoped to go on for a few years more at least. Though I had ridden my luck over the years no one fall had kept me out for too long but the cumulative effect had begun to damage the nerves in my neck. I make no excuses, I've found retirement from the saddle frustrating like many before me and, no doubt, many who will retire in the future. I still miss the camaraderie of the weighing room and daily adrenalin rush of race-riding and was still contemplating a return to the saddle in 2005 but specialists put an end to those ideas.

Several of the 18 horses featured in this book have sadly passed away, like old West Tip, who died in 2001 through the ravages of old age. Desert Orchid still goes on, amazingly, as an ambassador for jump racing, as popular as ever. He does fewer and fewer parades and is led rather than ridden but he is still as popular and as recognised as ever.

The most tragic ending befell One Man, three weeks after his greatest moment. In the chapter on One Man I recall the rides I had on him in the Gold Cup and how, rounding the bend, he had been travelling like a winner and how, going to the last, he emptied of all energy and staggered home like a drunk. His trainer, Gordon Richards, who died shortly after this, reckoned he did not quite see out the three and a quarter miles of the Gold Cup. I thought that maybe something was hurting him internally.

Subsequent events may have proved Gordon right and me wrong though I still maintain something may have hurt him in the later stages of a longer run race. That One Man's strongest suit was a strongly-run 2-mile chase over a stiff course was proved when winning the 1998 Queen Mother Champion Chase. That was one race I was destined never to win. I won races on Klairon Davis, Viking Flagship, Remittance Man, Katabatic, Martha's Son, Deep Sensation and One Man but none of them ever in the Champion Chase.

That season, One Man had run a terrible King George at Kempton and I couldn't ride him at Ascot when he dropped back in trip for the Comet Chase. Besides I was told afterwards by Norman Williamson, who was beaten five lengths on Strong Promise over the two and half mile trip, that One Man would never win a Champion Chase! I was, nevertheless, committed to Klairon Davis for the Champion Chase. Tony Dobbin was injured on the first day of the 1998 Festival and Brian Harding stepped in for the ride. Though delighted for Brian who had spent a year out with a head injury I was, naturally, upset with myself for making such a bad decision. It was a scintillating performance. One Man travelled strongly all the way and beat Or Royal four lengths. I could only watch him power away up the hill a further 10 lengths back in fourth.

His death, on the eve of the Grand National at Aintree three weeks later, was one of the saddest events I have witnessed. One Man hit the first in the back straight hard, and died in the subsequent fall, a premature end to a career that had for a long time perplexed but had its moments of pure brilliance.

THE HORSES OF MY LIFE

WEST TIP

MOST SUCCESSFUL JOCKEYS CAN PICK OUT ONE HORSE, AND OFTEN ONE PARTICULAR RACE ON THAT HORSE, THAT DID MORE THAN ANY OTHER TO GIVE THEIR FLEDGLING CAREERS A LIFT OFF THE GROUND. This is the horse that, so to speak, got the jockey's name changed from chalk to paint on racecourse number boards. The horses are not always famous nor necessarily brilliant. For John Francome it was a little black horse trained by Fred Winter called Osbaldeston, with whom he won seventeen races. The first really good horse Peter Scudamore was associated with was the hurdler Broadsword; but Scu believes his career was helped on its way by a horse called Rolyat, trained by Toby Balding, who also gave a number of other successful jockeys, including the starter Brian Reilly, their first winners. For it was Rolyat who had the distinction of being the first horse – point-to-pointers apart – to carry Scu past the winning post in front. Adrian Maguire, who was already establishing a name for himself in Irish point-to-points, came to the attention of the British and indeed wider Irish racing public when he rode Omerta to victory in the Fulke Walwyn/Kim Muir Challenge Cup Chase for Martin Pipe at the Cheltenham Festival in 1991. For good measure he rode Omerta in the Irish National at Fairyhouse a month later, beating the Irish champion jockey Charlie Swan and Cahervillahow a short head, which launched his career. Tony McCoy believes it was a couple of wins over fences on the former champion hurdler Beech Road as a conditional jockey that really began to establish him as a name to be reckoned with in National Hunt racing. The fact that Toby Balding had let such an inexperienced jockey loose on the horse, who had never been as smooth or as successful a chaser as he had over hurdles, was advertisement enough for the young McCoy's talents.

Looking back, the first horse that really set me on the way was West Tip. I was asked to ride him at the tail end of his novice season in 1984 when he ran in the Midlands National at Uttoxeter. He went on to jump 172 Aintree fences (142 with me on board), falling at just one of them – when he was leading over Becher's Brook on the second circuit in 1985, the first time he ran in the race. His Grand National Record – a win, a second and two fourths in six runs – is a remarkable one and makes him the most successful Aintree horse since Red Rum a decade earlier. What is more, he was so clever I don't think he ever returned home from Aintree with a scratch or cut on him. It would have been a thrill to have ridden West Tip at any stage of my career, but to a young, naïve professional, just out of the amateur ranks and still pretty wet behind the ears, he was a real gift.

The West Tip story nearly came to an end before it had truly started. One foggy morning he was out at exercise from the yard of his trainer Michael Oliver at a village called Elmley Lovett, about ten miles north of Worcester. The weather had delayed the arrival of Philip Hobbs, who had been coming to school West Tip and a number of other horses, and Michael told the string to take a turn in the lane. The conversion of an old RAF base nearby into a trading estate had brought a lot of heavy traffic to the roads around Michael's yard at the time, and at this point a lorry came past the horses too fast. At the tail of the string the young West Tip, having seen others in front of him spook at the fast-moving vehicle, whipped round. The hooks underneath the bed of the lorry ripped into his near-side rump.

2

It was a horrific injury. Michael describes it as 'looking like a rump steak' hanging off the horse. 'I really thought it was a shooting job,' he recalls. When Philip Hobbs arrived he said he could see the bones of West Tip's pelvis and that there was a 'hunk of flesh' hanging from the horse's quarters. 'I really thought he had no hope,' he said. The local vet Peter Thorne (whose brother John rode Spartan Missile to finish second in the 1981 Grand National behind Aldaniti at the grand old age of fifty-four) was there within the hour and, using Michael's wife Sarah as his assistant – Michael was squeamish at the best of times – they inserted numerous internal stitches and eighty externally. The triangular scar and indentation remained with West Tip throughout his career and is clearly visible on photographs of him jumping taken from his near-side. Remarkably, though, there was no muscle damage.

The accident had taken place in the October of West Tip's five-year-old season. On 29 December 1982, the same year, he ran in his first race, the Bob Cratchit Novice Hurdle at Warwick, and won it as a 50–1 outsider.

West Tip, by Gala Performance out of a mare called Astryl, had been bred in Ireland by Thomas Haynes and named after a hurling team, the West Tipperary. I think in fact he is mis-spelt as they are known as the West Tipps and I remember Andy Easton, his lad, wearing a West Tipp supporter's baseball cap. He was first bought by Paddy Prendergast Junior as a potential bumper horse but had proved not much faster than a carthorse at home – a characteristic that stayed with him throughout his career: he was never willing to over-extend himself away from the racecourse – and he had ended up in the hands of Tommy Wade, who is one of the shrewdest judges of a young jumper in Ireland. In his youth Tommy had been one of the first civilian riders in the Irish show-jumping team and is still remembered in those circles for his legendary partnership with the little show-jumper Dundrum, a mere 15.2 hands high. Tommy bought West Tip cheaply from Paddy Prendergast in order to send him point-to-pointing. However, every time they arrived at the track with West Tip he would invariably pull out of the horsebox lame. Neither Tommy nor any vet ever understood the reason for the lameness, but the upshot of it was that, unlike so many chasers whose careers began in Ireland, he never ran in an Irish point-to-point.

Michael had quite a good line in point-to-pointers which he often sold on ready to run for a number of clients, and if he ever wanted a horse from Ireland he'd go to Tommy. On one of his visits Michael was shown West Tip and told about the lameness. He thought that, for a big horse, West Tip was extremely light on his feet and bought him for IR£1,700. Peter Luff, a businessman involved in the construction industry in whose colours West Tip ran throughout his career, bought the five-year-old unseen from Michael – he liked the name.

When West Tip was despatched to Warwick for his first outing in December 1982, the going was heavy, and Anthony Webber was confident of victory on a hotshot called Up Country. It was also Peter Luff's birthday. Philip Hobbs, who is now one of our leading jump trainers based at Bilbrook near Minehead in the West Country, was in the saddle. Though he was surprised at how little time his mount had taken to recover from the accident with the lorry, and although the horse jumped well at home, he held out little hope of winning over two miles. Up Country, as expected, took up the running at half-way, but at the last West Tip jumped past him and galloped away. 'It was hard to believe after what we had seen at home,' recalls Philip. 'We never thought he'd be fast enough to win over two miles.' However, if you ask some trainers what they would look for in an Aintree horse they would tell you that a potential National winner should have had enough speed to win a two-mile hurdle at some stage of their career.

For his second outing West Tip went to Chepstow for the Rabbit Novice Hurdle on 10 January 1983. This time he started a 4–1 shot but was still not fancied enough to be favourite. Philip was in the plate again and rode a similar sort of race, hitting the front at the second last and beating Les Kennard's Sutton Prince by seven lengths. Sutton Prince went on to become a prolific point-to-point winner later in his career but at this stage Les was worried he'd bought a horse that might not be as good as it had been cracked up to be. 'Ooh, arghh,' he huffed and puffed to Philip Hobbs about West Tip, ''ow good is 'e, boy?'

4

His next four runs saw him placed. At Wolverhampton he went back to two miles and finished a close third to Celtic Cracker. He paid his first visit to Cheltenham – a place he was to love as much as Aintree – at the end of January and, anchored by penalties which saw him carrying 12st 6lb, was beaten into fourth place, again over two miles, by another horse who went on to become something of an Aintree specialist: Lean Ar Aghaidh (who also became known as Lean on the Aga because of the difficulty the British had in pronouncing his Gaelic name). Lean Ar Aghaidh never won a National, but he finished one place ahead of West Tip in the 1987 running, when they finished third and fourth respectively behind Maori Venture, and in 1990 won the Aintree Foxhunters. West Tip seemed to be acquiring a habit of coming up against horses that would go on to much greater things, for at Stratford, at the end of February, he was second to Michael Dickinson's Delius, another good horse in the making. Delius was partnered by the then amateur Dermot Browne, who subsequently went on to become racing's most wanted man – not, I might add, because of his undoubted talent as a jockey. The following week, back over two and a half miles, he finished third, again carrying over 12st.

If one race was needed as proof that West Tip was not slow, it came in that season's Sun Alliance Novices' Hurdle, the first race run on the middle day of the Cheltenham National Hunt Festival. Remarkably, West Tip was to make a record nine consecutive visits to the Festival, which is a huge tribute both to the horse's durability and to his trainer's methods. He never disgraced himself at the premier meeting, and rarely had worse than an each-way chance, whatever the race he was run in. This first outing at the Festival was also the first sign that the horse would raise his game for the big occasion. Indeed, towards the end of his career the only places that really inspired him were Cheltenham and Aintree.

In 1983, the Sun Alliance Novices' Hurdle was a race the Irish and the in-form yard of Michael Dickinson – who the following day would send out the first five home, headed by Bregawn, in the Gold Cup – were expected to dominate between them. Ballinacurra Lad was favourite, Stag Hill second favourite, and Lettoch from the Dickinson stable third favourite. Graham Bradley, who was due to partner Bregawn in the Gold Cup, was on a less fancied Dickinson horse, Sabin Du Loir. In the immediate aftermath of a race like the 1983 Sun Alliance Hurdle it is hard to judge the quality of the contest. One never knows what novice hurdlers will go on to do and, to a certain extent, one can only guess at the time. This year's race stood up as one of the best Sun Alliances not only of that decade but probably in the whole history of the race.

Dawn Run led for much of the way before Brad took over on Sabin Du Loir at the eighth of the twelve hurdles. He couldn't shake off Paddy Mullins's game mare and as they turned into the home straight West Tip, who had been hard ridden through the field by Philip Hobbs, was close on their heels. Ballinacurra Lad had been off the bridle and was now retreating. Noble Heir and Lettoch both had chances; but it was Sabin Du Loir who ran on best of all, beating Dawn Run, who went on to become the only horse ever to win a Champion Hurdle and Gold Cup, three lengths with West Tip two and a half lengths back in third. It was, on reflection, a hell of a run.

5

His eighth and last race of that first season was at Aintree where he ran in the Hen Harrier Novice Hurdle, again over two and a half miles. The Mildmay course there is fairly sharp for a big galloping horse like West Tip and he concluded his campaign with his first unplaced outing, finishing sixth behind Fulke Walwyn's Noble Heir, the horse who had finished fourth in the Sun Alliance at Cheltenham.

After a deserved summer off, the following season West Tip made his chasing debut at Ascot on 29 October in the two-and-a-half-mile Embassy Premier Chase (qualifier) – the same day that Desert Orchid had his first win over hurdles. You could never accuse Michael Oliver of wrapping West Tip up in cotton wool and not running him. It was the first of eleven races he had as a novice chaser. At Ascot, after a dry autumn, the ground was fast enough for the six-year-old West Tip's chasing debut. He had schooled well at home but you never know how well they will jump fences until you get them on the racecourse. A little bit backward but jumping immaculately, once more under Philip Hobbs, West Tip chased the leader and hot favourite Homeson. He gave Homeson a fright and his jockey Paul Nicholls (now another top West Country trainer) had to throw everything at the favourite to get him home by a length and a half. It was, everyone agreed, a satisfactory start for West Tip.

That could not be said of his second outing, when he fell at Sandown. It was the first of just three falls in his career. Leading for much of the way, he was in third and still with a good chance when he came a cropper at the seventeenth, one of the 'railway fences', in the Crowngap Novice Chase. The race was won by Nick Gaselee's good old servant Duke of Milan.

The following week he went to Cheltenham for the Fred Withington Novice Chase on Tripleprint Gold Cup day (it was called the Kennedy Construction Gold Cup in those days), where he was beaten two and a half lengths by that season's subsequent Sun Alliance Chase winner A Kinsman. Philip's brother Peter, a student at the Royal Agricultural College in Cirencester, was third in the race on Membridge. Staying on well up the Cheltenham hill at the end of an extended three miles, and much stronger than he had been the previous season, West Tip showed that his stamina was now beginning to come to the fore.

6

For his first victory, however, the team surrounding West Tip had slightly changed. According to Michael, a photo had appeared in *Horse and Hound* of Philip sitting back on West Tip in one of his previous races. It was suggested to Peter Luff by a friend – you're never short of advisers when you have a half-decent horse – that this was unstylish and, for one reason or another, Philip was replaced by the amateur John Weston. Philip was pretty philosophical about it. John, a popular horseman in the Midlands, and West Tip were odds-on when they went to Wolverhampton just after Christmas. Though it wasn't a great race it was back over two and a half miles, and he duly won with John only having to push him out to beat Royal Norman by four lengths. The others were a distance away.

The fifth outing took him to Haydock in January. Outside of Aintree, Haydock's fences were the biggest in the country then. Again a short-priced favourite and ridden by John Weston, West Tip was always handy and this time, back over three miles, won even more comfortably. A week later he went to Ascot for the Embassy Final, where Ballinacurra Lad, who had travelled over from Ireland again, this time got the better of him; West Tip finished ten lengths away in second, and but for Greenwood Lad and Hywel Davies falling at the last he would have been third. Against this level of opposition it was becoming increasingly clear that West Tip now needed at least three miles.

His only run during February saw him finish third to Hy-Ko and Paul Barton in a three-and-a-quarter-mile novice chase at Uttoxeter. Three weeks later he went to Newbury for the Steel Plate and Sections Young Chasers Novice Chase qualifier. The race was won by Fred Winter's Aces Wild, ridden by John Francome. Only two horses finished and the other wasn't West Tip. At the fourteenth fence Aces Wild and Linawn were disputing the lead; just behind them Palatinate and Boots Madden fell, and the effect was domino-like. Behind Palatinate Aramoss went down; behind him West Tip and John found themselves with nowhere to go and were brought down in the mêlée.

March 1984 saw him back at Cheltenham for the National Hunt Festival, again by invitation of Sun Alliance, this time for their novice chase – the race that, all things being equal, should throw up a future Gold Cup winner. This year came close, though the favourite, Forgive'N Forget, who won the Gold Cup the following year, could only finish second to West Tip's old adversary A Kinsman. West Tip, who had always struggled to go the pace, was seventh and finished as close as he had been at any stage of the race. Then came his second visit to Aintree, which proved more successful than the first. Partnered for the first and only time by John Francome, he finished a creditable six lengths second to Baron Blakeney, a horse who was doing great things for the reputation of a small West Country trainer called Martin Pipe, ridden by Oliver Sherwood, then the leading amateur rider and assistant to Fred Winter. Forgive'N Forget, reunited with Mark Dwyer, ran no sort of race at all and was eighteen lengths behind West Tip in fifth.

7

Michael worked quite closely with his brother Martin Oliver. If I was ever round there schooling, the chances were that Martin would call in at some stage. It is Martin who takes the credit for alerting Michael to an up-and-coming amateur whom he had spotted riding an old chaser called Ballydonagh for Lady Eliza Nugent the previous year at Ludlow. I think Martin had also been at Hereford when I had ridden a four-timer as an amateur there in March. The long and the short of it was that I was already riding a few for the yard at his suggestion. The first was a good old handicapper called Bashful Lad, a horse who usually made one dreadful mistake in every race, but was otherwise a great ride, and a mare called Free Choice belonging to Michael's wife Sarah. I ended up riding a lot of winners for the Olivers including Von Trappe, on whom I had some of the hairiest moments of my career but also my first Festival winner. A good horse on his day – but could he get low at a fence! I have some great memories of riding him; he was brilliant and lethal in roughly equal measure.

West Tip's eleventh and last race of that season was the Midlands National at Uttoxeter. Nowadays it is always run before Aintree as a National trial, but in 1984 it was a week after Aintree. Michael wasn't in the habit of running novices over such an extreme distance, but this horse seemed to be an out-and-out stayer. My claim had been reduced to 4lb by now, but Michael thought that would also be a help and I was asked to ride West Tip for the first time. At that stage of my career he was un-questionably the best horse I'd sat on. When we got to Uttoxeter the ground was much firmer than Michael had anticipated, and he had grave reservations about running. Peter Luff had said he would be at the meeting but never made it; however, he was expecting the horse to run and, unable to discuss his worries about the going with the owner, Michael decided West Tip should take his chance.

West Tip never really got into the race on that ground. Michael had told me he was hard work and that I should keep pushing. I was just about with the main pack but when they quickened I couldn't go with them. The race was won by Mr Mole, trained by John Webber and owned by Sally Gill. Sally had a bad fall out hunting afterwards, ironically on a horse that had doubled up for Aldaniti in the film *Champions*, and, from her wheelchair, did tireless work and fund-raising for people with spinal injuries. She was a good fun owner, and in that respect it was a great result. West Tip eventually finished ninth, just behind Little Polveir who went on to win the 1989 Grand National. He also finished sore, and when he returned home to Elmley Lovett he had not just one but two bowed tendons.

From the day after Uttoxeter West Tip never took another lame step during his career. Everyone has ideas about how tendon injuries should be treated, whether they should be 'fired', injected, split, strengthened with implants or just left alone. Vet Peter Thorne's theory is that it is not the length of time you give a horse off following a tendon injury that counts, it is what you do before the rest that is important. It is, he believes, essential that the tendon is cool and hard before it is fired. Firing is an old practice – banned for a while but subsequently reinstated – whereby hot bars or acid are put on the horse's legs, in theory to increase the blood supply to the tendon. The Midlands National had been in early April; by June West Tip's tendons were cool and hard, and he was acid fired. He was ready to run at Ascot's autumn meeting that same year.

On the subject of West Tip's health it should also be mentioned that at some stage during the early part of his career he had developed a heart murmur. A horse up for sale can fail its veterinary examination if a heart murmur is diagnosed, but West Tip's was only noticed when he was much later given a 'medical' for insurance purposes. Some humans have heart murmurs and some horses have them; it made no difference to West Tip, who went round Aintree six times with his. Mind you, had I known at the time I might not have been quite so keen to approach a fence like The Chair on a horse whose heart was probably missing a beat more often than any jockey's.

Though he was ready to run at Ascot in the autumn the ground was firm and connections were wary of risking damage to his recently fired legs, so it was not until 14 December that I had my second chance to ride him, in the Stoneleigh Handicap Chase. I was now professional – but not very: I still had a lot to learn about racing and about West Tip, who was clearly doing less at home as he began to get older and wiser. He needed this race. However, he ran well for a long way with Sam Morshead and the front-running Run And Skip setting a good gallop. I don't think anyone got near Run And Skip that day, who beat Port Askaig by ten lengths. West Tip got tired from about the fifteenth and faded into sixth place, but after his leg problems we were just happy that he should finish sound, and once he began to flag I pretty much looked after him.

9

We went to Newbury for our next outing. Michael couldn't go for some reason and Sarah was in charge. I was still getting to know West Tip and I'm not sure whether he thought I was a soft touch or not, but by the cross fence about five furlongs out we were twenty lengths off the pace and going nowhere fast. Turning into the straight I gave him a crack and he took off, not quite like a rocket, but shifting up into overdrive. In fact, he flew with me. He had plenty of weight and was giving over a stone to the first two, Sommelier and Greenbank Park. We were beaten less than two lengths and the speed with which we finished made it look embarrassing. I'm sure that if I could ride that race again now I would win on him. As it was, it very nearly cost me any more rides on West Tip. When I came in, Peter quite rightly had words to say. Sarah, who knew I was young and quite inexperienced, looked horrified; she and Michael had done as much as anyone at that stage to nurture my career, and a bollocking for me was, as far as she was concerned, a bollocking for her.

Anyway, we seemed to get over that problem, and I partnered the horse again a week later in the Anthony Mildmay/Peter Cazalet Memorial Handicap Chase at Sandown, a traditional Grand National trial over three miles and five furlongs. This event is run in memory of one of the most famous amateur riders of all time and his great friend and trainer Peter Cazalet. Ironically, Lord Mildmay, who died taking his daily swim in the sea, had several celebrated near misses in the National. In 1936 he had landed in front over the second last on 100–1 shot Davy Jones when the buckle on his reins came undone, leaving him unable to steer; the horse ran out, scattering the crowd, at the last. A dozen years later in 1948, several months after breaking his neck in a fall at Folkestone, he was attacked by a crippling cramp which rendered him virtually immobile, little more than a passenger on Cromwell for the last mile. It was remarkable that Cromwell even managed to finish third behind Sheila's Cottage.

The morning of the race was very cold and we'd had a sharp frost: the ground was hard and white and I thought there was very little chance of racing going ahead. And to tell you the truth, after the ride he'd given me at Newbury and the bollocking I got after it, I wouldn't have minded if it hadn't. Even in those days, when I was sharing a cottage in Kingston Lisle with Chris Nash (from where Charlie Morlock now trains), I was struggling to do 10st and put up 1lb overweight at 10lb 1lb. But West Tip ran a totally different race. Much more interested, probably fully fit now, and getting nearly two stone from Canny Danny, he shared the lead with Lean Ar Aghaidh and Bold Yeoman, then landed in front over the Pond Fence; after that, Canny Danny and Mark Dwyer could never get to us. We beat them by a length. I was very impressed with how he had stayed on up the hill and, at that stage of my career, pretty impressed by the five-figure first prize (£10,329). He wasn't immediately made favourite for the National but Michael was now keener than ever to enter him.

At the end of January, safely entered in the National and his season now geared to that one race, we went back to Cheltenham for the Holsten Distributors Chase over three miles and a furlong. There were only four runners: Ardent Spy, the favourite, fell at the eighteenth, I slightly lost my position and Richard Rowe took it up on Door Latch, another very classy horse on his day. West Tip never really travelled this day, at any rate not like he had at Sandown, until he landed over the second last. Door Latch was only giving us a couple of pounds and turning in I thought he would take some catching, but West Tip relished that hill like few other horses I have

10

ridden. He would take a look at it, take a deep breath, put his head down and gallop. He caught Door Latch half-way up it and beat him a length and a half. Now he was ante-post favourite for the National, and by dint of these two wins he had become 'my' ride. All this in my first season as a professional – and this race had come on the day that I was having a joint twenty-first birthday party with Martin Bosley.

The plan now was to give him a month off, then bring him back to Hereford at the beginning of March to get his eye in for Cheltenham, where he would run in the Ritz Club Handicap Chase. Though he needed the race and Run And Skip was in opposition, I don't think West Tip has ever travelled as well as he did for me that day at Hereford, a track he liked almost as much as Cheltenham and Aintree. He was always going well, and for once I wasn't having to kick and boot him along. We went to the front three out and he ran on well to beat Run And Skip, who was taking a similar route to Cheltenham via Hereford, by three lengths. The race put both horses spot-on for the Festival.

In 1985 the Ritz Club (or William Hill Trophy Handicap Chase, as it was some-what unromantically renamed in 2005) was run after the Gold Cup. By The Way, trained by Mrs Monica Dickinson following Michael Dickinson's switch to the Flat, was favourite. West Tip was 6–1 second favourite on the strength of three straight victories. There were twenty runners in all, including Acarine, The Ellier, Hardy Lad, Broomy Bank, West Tip's friend Lean Ar Aghaidh, Run And Skip and Maori Venture – a good collection of staying chasers. At this stage of my career there was nothing better than Cheltenham. Forgive'N Forget and Mark Dwyer had just won the Gold Cup and there was a big buzz in the changing room, particularly that corner occupied by the northern jockeys. Towards the end of may career, I didn't enjoy riding at the Festival as much as I should have – it was all pressure. In those days, though, before I became cynical and battle-weary, it meant everything to me; and this was also the day after I'd had my first winner there on Von Trappe, also for Michael. Cheltenham was a drug I couldn't get enough of at the time. Riding a winner there had the effect of making you feel taller, it put a spring in your stride as you came to weigh in, it made your face ache from grinning.

West Tip was happy doing his own thing in the middle of the field. In the Ritz you shouldn't have to worry unduly about bad jumpers. This is a race for sensible, experienced handicappers and National types who might perhaps lack the class of the Gold Cup contenders or, as in West Tip's case,

11

don't want a desperately hard race three weeks before Aintree – which he would undoubtedly have had in the Gold Cup. Maori Venture was the only faller on the first circuit and I began to get West Tip in a decent position going down the hill away from the stands for the second circuit. If possible it is always better to give your horse a breather up the hill at the back of the course than be off the bridle there trying to catch up.

He never felt quite like he had in the Mildmay or even at Hereford: I felt he just wasn't travelling. At the top of the hill I was upsides Dermot Browne, who was riding Prince Rowan for Mrs Dickinson. Though I hadn't wanted to get after the horse up the hill, I had little option if I wanted to hold my place so I gave him a smack going to the sixth last, the open ditch, about a mile from home. As I connected, my stick broke in half. The actual rod of a whip is usually bound in something, nowadays padding, but in 1985 just thick cotton. My whip was now in two halves, still attached to each other by string. The one half got wrapped round Dermot's head and the half in my hand was basically just the handle. There wasn't much I could do with that, so I threw it away. From there on it was going to be hands and heels and as much rein as I could slap him with. I was pushing and slapping him either side of his neck with the reins. I think he was ignoring me but, as he did at Cheltenham, he picked up of his own accord turning into the straight. Acarine led us over the last and our other danger, Run And Skip, had really thrown his chance away with a mistake at the eighteenth, although he too ran on up the hill. We pretty soon had the measure of Acarine, and West Tip galloped all the way to the line. I was shattered, absolutely exhausted, too much so to enjoy the moment. Looking back on it I think there have probably been only half a dozen times when I have been as tired at the end of a race. But it was my second winner in two days at the Festival! I left Cheltenham that night thinking I was the bee's knees.

The build-up to a Grand National was something I had jealously watched but until now never experienced. Now, aged twenty-one, on board the joint favourite but never having ridden over the course in either the Foxhunters or the Topham Chase, I was to be the focus of some of the pre-race attention. I travelled up with Brendan Powell for the meeting. The season had gone very well so far and now I was about to realize a childhood dream – something I'd thought about every time I'd jumped a drop fence out hunting in Ireland on my pony – by riding round Aintree, surely the greatest challenge for any National Hunt jockey. Of all races, the

12

one I missed riding in more than any other was the Grand National. It was so different from any other.

My first ride round Aintree was not on West Tip but on Run To Me for Richard Mitchell in the Topham, two days before the National. I was going well when he was brought down five out. One always wants to win, but I was gutted about having failed to complete the course, desperately disappointed – and that was only in the Topham. I was going to be inconsolable if I fell in the big one.

National day came. Conditions were perfect for West Tip. Michael had him looking a picture and I rode him out in the morning. Your first National is very exciting, it's hard this long afterwards to remember everything in detail, the extra nerves and excitement. The race, as it proved in the 'bomb scare' year of 1997, is a British institution, and for twenty-four hours is the focus of attention for the sporting nation. I didn't really feel much pressure, even though I knew I had a good chance of winning: so many things happen in the race that often no one really blames you if you get brought down or don't win.

The thing I remember most about the start of the 1985 Seagram Grand National is having in my mind two horses that I would want to be as far away from as possible: Solihull Sport and Dudie, two very suspect jumpers. I since learned to get myself in a small group of reliable jumpers at the start – although, as 1985 proved, that doesn't always work. Hallo Dandy, the previous year's winner, fell at the first, and you'd have backed him at least to get round. Nevertheless, I was preoccupied with Dudie and Solihull Sport when the tapes went up. Crossing the Melling Road going to the first there were forty of us, and who should come sailing past me but Sam Morshead, on the runaway Solihull Sport, who was fighting for his head with a better view of the sky than an astronomer. I don't think he can have seen the first fence. He went into the obstacle just in front and to the right of me, veered violently left on take off, cut straight across my bows and landed upside down on his head in the process of a well-executed forward roll. I should think West Tip put his front legs between Solihull Sport's. I know it was close. We were lucky not to be brought down and join Sam on the deck with Graham Bradley who had come down on Hallo Dandy, Graham McCourt who was already in the habit of getting no further than the first, having fallen there on Michael's other runner Bashful Lad, and Anthony Webber, who had also gone at the first on Talon.

Every year you get someone on a no-hoper who cuts out the early

running – mainly, I think, to get a slice of the glory and a few good photos for the mantelpiece and to give their owners a thrill. Every year Robert Stronge rode in the race he seemed to be the one. This year he was bowling along on Rupertino and, to be fair to Robert, he actually went on to run a huge race and finish seventh, having made much of the running. For the first circuit we were just behind the leaders. West Tip had in a funny sort of way given me confidence when he stepped round Solihull Sport at the first. Good Aintree horses – Red Rum, for example – have the inbuilt radar which tells them where to put their feet. West Tip had adapted immediately to the fences which are so different from those anywhere else and he was relishing the challenge they presented, measuring them and making my job easy.

14

We moved into third passing the stands, where the race begins in earnest. He was loving the fact that the race was being run at what he considered a suitable pace. Rupertino and a loose horse were with me going down to Becher's for the second time. I was running away: West Tip had never been going like this at any stage of any race. We had decided beforehand that it would be better not to hit the front until we had jumped second Becher's. In those days there was a grandstand on the landing side, with a crowd of people in it, and as you swing left-handed when you land, it must seem to a horse coming to the fence that he's going to jump over it into the stand. There are cameras clicking, loudspeakers blaring out commentary, and a lot of distractions. I arrived at the fence upsides in front – but he just didn't get high enough. I'm convinced he was looking at the grandstand. He certainly wasn't paying attention because I have lots of photos of him with his head touching the floor and his ears still pricked. Though I had the other two horses with me I think it was pure lack of concentration – things had been going almost too easily for him. He was used to struggling in his races. He had got into this great rhythm but the stand, the television gantry, the cheering people, all distracted him. What he wanted was a good hoick in the mouth to get him on his hocks and make him think about it, but because he had been jumping so well and because of my inexperience in such a situation I let him be. It was an elementary mistake, really.

I have rarely felt worse, emptier or more distraught. I know 'gutted' is an over-used word in sport these days, but I don't think there is a better one to explain how I felt. I let the field pass – very lucky that I wasn't injured by Broomy Bank, who stepped over me while I lay on the floor – and got up to go to an ambulance. I think I'd have been just as annoyed at the end of my career if the same thing happened, even having won it twice. I felt I had it in the bag, most other people felt I had it in the bag and West Tip was running away – with 10st 1lb I think he thought he was loose. Obviously we were still a long way from home and anything could have happened, but I think his other runs in the race back up my argument that we would probably have won. Falling when you have such an important race within your grasp is hard to describe to anyone who has never ridden in the race; for me, at that stage of my career, sitting, drenched in self-pity, on the landing side of Becher's, watching the other runners sail on was like seeing the train to my future leave the platform without me. I don't know about character building; it just about broke mine.

Hywel Davies went on to win the race on Captain Tim Forster's Last Suspect. He sprinted from the last and caught Mr Snugfit and Phil Tuck close to home. Phil must have felt like I did, as he too had looked to have it in the bag. At the time I was second jockey at the Captain's to Hywel, and the disappointment hit me again the next day when I had to go to the yard in Letcombe Bassett to welcome home Last Suspect. He was an old character; the next season I even won on him. At the time, though, you don't know for sure that you'll ever get another chance like that. For all I knew West Tip could have had a leg injury the following year.

15

He had one more run that season, in the Whitbread Gold Cup, won by By The Way. West Tip ran a good race; though he only came fifth, the ground was way too fast for him and he was off the bridle for most of the way, finishing closer than he had been throughout. And though the fall in the National clouded our season together, it had in fact been a pretty successful one, with two important wins – with luck, he would be an improved horse the following season.

But the 1985–6 season began badly. West Tip had done himself well during the summer and was getting harder to fitten up at home, and it was November before he reappeared at Warwick. That first run of the term was a poor one. As was now West Tip's custom, he needed that first race and blew up badly, finishing a tailed-off last of the seven runners behind Run And Skip, who beat Arctic Beau a comfortable three lengths. The next time he ran I couldn't ride him – Captain Forster required me to ride Lefrak City at Sandown – so Anthony Webber took over in the Rehearsal Chase, a warm-up for the Welsh National. He had clearly come on a great deal from his first race, physically and mentally, and he put up one of the best performances. If the Sun Alliance was his best effort over hurdles, this was not far off his best over fences formwise. Making most of the running, he finished between Burrough Hill Lad, who eighteen months earlier had won the Gold Cup, and Wayward Lad, who went on to win the King George VI Chase at Kempton on Boxing Day. At the last fence it still looked like as if Anthony might win, especially as Burrough Hill Lad had made a mistake at the second last; however, his class got him home by half a length from West Tip with Wayward Lad, who looked like he was coming to win the race three out, two and a half lengths further back in third. It was a hell of a run from West Tip, getting just 6lb from the winner and 4lb from the third.

We then went to Ascot for the SGB Chase; we started favourites, but Door Latch beat us quite easily by eight lengths. We had every chance turning in, but he just couldn't quite quicken as Door Latch could when he was on song. Nevertheless, we weren't despondent; Burrough Hill Lad was back in third this time, and behind us too were The Tsarevich, Castle Warden, Corbiere and Ballinacurra Lad, who was now being trained by Martin Pipe.

I thought West Tip would run very well in the Welsh National that year: three and three-quarter miles and a good test of stamina was about ideal for him now. However, his run at Chepstow disappointed me. He ran well for three miles but then, instead of staying on, seemed to weaken. The race was won by Run And Skip who made all the running and had seemingly not stopped improving for John Spearing. He beat Golden Ty, ridden by the amateur Andy Orkney, an optician who went on to become a professional jockey, combining the two careers. In the mornings he would fix old ladies up with specs in Leyburn, and in the afternoon he would get covered in mud at somewhere like Sedgefield. He was one of the few jockeys with a degree and one of his great claims to fame was to ride Golden Ty without irons from Becher's to the finish in the Foxhunters at Aintree. No mean feat, although a degree probably wasn't much good to him over the last seven fences. West Tip finished seventh, just behind Peaty Sandy, who had been one of the best staying chasers in the north at the height of his career, and just in front of Corbiere, a previous Grand National winner, and Rhyme 'N' Reason, a future National winner. I don't think, on reflection, that he was actually right that day. He was beaten a long way and it was just not his run. He might have had some bug on him, or perhaps he was suffering from a few quick, hard runs.

His next outing was not much different. About a month later he went to

Haydock for the Peter Marsh Chase – different course, same result. Beaten a distance by Combs Ditch. I felt Michael might have left him a bit short that day because he was training him for the National during the second half of the season. For that reason and because of the weather – we lost most of February's racing in a freeze-up – he didn't run again until Cheltenham, nearly two months later. Having won the Ritz Club Chase the previous year we were now lumbered with joint top weight of 11st 7lb, and I went there with one aim: to get round safely and ride him with one eye on the National in three weeks' time. Half an hour before West Tip's race I had my first ride in the Gold Cup on Von Trappe for Michael and was buried at the nineteenth. Amazing that we got that far.

West Tip needed the race, but wasn't beaten too far by Charter Party and Peter Scudamore, to whom we were giving 11lb. We finished seventh and the horse that finished eighth was a nine-year-old called Young Driver. I was happy with that, though. In 1996 there were a lot of complaints that, because of the date of Easter, the National followed on only two weeks after Cheltenham. A lot of trainers reckoned it didn't give those horses who had run at the Festival sufficient chance to recover. Rough Quest proved them wrong, but they must have forgotten West Tip. By now Michael Oliver knew the horse inside out and he was not happy, after the weather problems of February, that West Tip would have been fully tuned up by Cheltenham. A racecourse gallop wouldn't have been much good to a horse like West Tip, although it is probably what a trainer would do now.

17

One of Michael's masterstrokes was to run him again between Cheltenham and Aintree. With such a careful horse as West Tip it could hardly have been described as a gamble – he was sure to come home without a nasty cut or some such injury that might keep another horse out. Several trainers I've ridden for would wrap a horse up in cotton wool at this stage, but Michael really understood West Tip and sent him to Newbury nine days after the Ritz for a three-mile handicap chase. It was ideal. He won the race – his first win of the season – which was good for my confidence, Michael's and the horse's, and proof, if we needed it, that he was a spring horse. He lost his place down the back but stayed on up the straight, as he tended to do at Newbury, beating Beau Ranger two and a half lengths. I have it down in my rides file that he 'dossed': he didn't do a tap, but it must have put an edge on him and when he went to Aintree on 5 April it was for his third run in three weeks.

The Aintree meeting got off to a good start when I won on Glenrue for the late Terry Casey in the Topham Trophy: my first winner over the Grand National course. He was a horse who tended to break blood vessels but he jumped faultlessly and ran on strongly. A year later he fell at the third in the National and smashed Brendan Powell's wrist.

On National day, my first ride was the big one. It was an overcast day and the ground was on the soft side. At seven o'clock in the morning there had been snow lying on the course. On the strength of his second in the race last year and, according to the *Sun*, the sexual fantasies of a million or so housewives (who'd probably never given it a thought until they read the paper), Mr Snugfit was the 13–2 favourite. West Tip was second favourite. With Corbiere, Hallo Dandy and Last Suspect in the line-up there was a good cast of previous winners.

The one horse I wanted to stay clear of this year was a Czechoslovakian stallion called Essex. I was right to be wary of him: he set off at a million miles an hour, pulling the arms out of his rider Vaclav Chaloupka and throwing himself at the fences. He was also running around, which meant wherever you were you ended up behind him at some stage: you just prayed it wasn't going into an obstacle. He eventually ran out of steam and was pulled up before The Chair.

Charlie Mann made most of the running for the first circuit on Doubleuagain. Characteristically, we lost Graham McCourt at the first on Port Askaig, and Richard Rowe came down in sympathy with him on the third favourite Door Latch. Uncharacteristically, we lost Corbiere at the fourth. Last Suspect was towards the back – this time hating the experience, although I wasn't aware of it at the time. Plundering and Simon Sherwood went at the Canal Turn. Classified, Sommelier, Monanore, Rupertino, Kilkilowen and myself were all prominent in behind Charlie, who was giving Doubleuagain an inspired ride.

It was at the seventeenth fence, the first on the second circuit, that Doubleuagain was jumped into and knocked over by a loose horse. That was the nearest we came to being undone. I was quite close to Charlie at the time and without a slice of luck we could easily have been taken out. That left Kilkilowen and Kevin Morgan in front, and this time I was determined to get a lead over Becher's. It always remained a bogey in my mind and, while I was riding I wouldn't lead the field over Becher's on the second circuit – even though they removed the stand and levelled off the drop on the landing side.

West Tip was jumping faultlessly and, unlike some of his other races this season, had no intention of dropping himself out. He loved the pace of the National, and landed over one fence looking for the next. Coming back on to the racecourse with two to jump it had developed into a two-horse race, with Christ Grant on Young Driver leading us. I'd been going very well since Becher's second time and could have taken up the running at any stage, but we'd planned that, if possible, I'd get a lead to the Elbow. If he was in front too long, we thought, he might idle.

We actually got to the front a bit earlier than the Elbow, and when we got there the old horse pricked his ears at the roar of the crowd. All I could remember was the previous year's race when Hywel had come with a late run on Last Suspect. I thought, if something comes to me West Tip will respond, but if it comes very wide like Hywel did last year he won't see it and won't pick up. Luckily Young Driver kept pretty close to us, and at the line we beat him two lengths. It was the first of three seconds Granty was to ride in the race. Classified was twenty lengths back in third.

Watching in the stands Michael Oliver, usually a bundle of nerves during a race, was as calm as you like. 'It was like it was planned,' he recalls now. 'For once in my life I was confident, and unless we had dreadful luck in running I thought we would win.'

19

The moments after you win a National are hard to describe. It is an emotional mixture of relief and immense satisfaction. A lot of people patting you on the back and wanting to shake your hand, faceache from smiling too much, being carried by policemen from the winner's enclosure to the scales. I was just in a haze. You get such a buzz from riding and completing the course anyway. You appreciate that some great jockeys have gone through whole careers without a decent ride in the race, and here I was at twenty-two having achieved something I'd dreamed about since I was a child. Everything is a rush: an interview here, a presentation there; that year they drove me down the course in an open-top car. The fact that everything was a haze was one of the reasons I so much wanted to win it again, just so I could take it all in.

That night we celebrated with a few friends and our girlfriends at the Dragon Inn in Burford, which was just about on the way home. The next day I went to Michael's for the 'welcome home' party.

Grand National day 1986 was the biggest in West Tip's career. A wonderful, intelligent horse, he was, naturally, clobbered by the handicapper for much of the rest of his racing days. From then on he saved his best for Cheltenham and Aintree. Now that I was riding for David Nicholson (the 'Duke'), getting off to ride him was always going to be a problem. I managed to ride him for all of the next season until matters came to a head in the 1987 Gold Cup, when I was claimed to ride Charter Party – who gave me a crunching fall. Michael thought that as West Tip had given me a National win I should ride him in the Gold Cup. The Duke thought there was a Gold Cup in Charter Party and wouldn't let me off. You could see both their points of view – but Michael said that whoever rode the horse in the Gold Cup would ride him in that year's National. Sarah Oliver has a photo of the story on Ceefax. 'Dunwoody will never ride for me again – Oliver.'

There was a snowstorm during the afternoon of Gold Cup day and the start was delayed an hour and twenty minutes. Richard Linley was booked to ride West Tip but dislocated his shoulder riding a finish on Gala's Image to win the Arkle and was replaced by Peter Hobbs. West Tip ran his best race in the Gold Cup to finish fourth, just over four lengths behind The Thinker, against a white backdrop. He had given a fantastic performance and not surprisingly was favourite to win his second National three weeks later. For that I managed to get back on him – somehow. Ultan Guilfoyle was doing a BBC documentary on me, and much of it was to focus on the build-up to the National. At one point it looked like I wouldn't have a ride. Again he ran a blinder. He had every chance at the third last, but I think 11st 7lb found him out over the last half-mile. Maori Venture and Steve Knight won it; the Tsarevich was second with John White, a quiet horseman who had a great record round Aintree – in fact he had the misfortune to 'win' the void National on Esha Ness in 1993; Lean Ar Aghaidh and Guy Landau, who had been near or in front for much of the way, were third and subsequently went on to win the Whitbread. It was still a great thrill to finish fourth, and we were only beaten thirteen lengths in all. I had to ride West Tip quite hard for the first circuit and I wonder now if his run in the Gold Cup might just have taken the edge off him. It's one of those things we'll never know. His last race that season was in the Golden Miller Chase later that April at Cheltenham, where he finished a good second to Golden Friend. He hadn't won in nine outings but he had put in some good performances.

20

Getting off to ride him was even more difficult the next season, and a variety of jockeys rode him including Ned Buckley and Richard Rowe: but the understanding with Michael was that I would ride him in the National. Micky Hammond rode him to finish sixth in the Gold Cup behind Charter Party, who got it right this year. In the 1988 National he gave me another great ride. Brendan Powell won it on Rhyme 'N' Reason, who'd made a terrible mistake at Becher's on the first circuit and injured himself in the process, but in the heat of the race hadn't felt the injury. Again, coming back across the Melling Road for the last time I found myself with every chance. However, this time West Tip just galloped on one-paced to finish fourth – and it was still a great thrill. You can't expect to win the race every year, and I was still having some great rides in the race. The one thing you knew with West Tip was that you were safer riding him round Aintree than most people sitting in an armchair at home watching the race on television. He never lost the touch, nor that sixth sense good Aintree horses have for avoiding fallers and trouble.

My fifth and last National ride on West Tip was in 1989. Michael had decided, now that the horse was having to carry 12st every time he ran in a long-distance handicap and running too well too often to come down much in the weights, to run him in hunter-chases. He also decided that my co-author Marcus should be let loose on him, first out hunting and then in a hunter-chase. The hunting went well until half-way through the afternoon when West Tip stopped at a small post and rail under which there was some pig wire. The wire got caught between his shoe and hoof and wedged there. Now, a lot of horses would have pulled back, ripped the shoe off along with a large chunk of hoof and panicked further when the fence came with them. Not so West Tip. He stood there with his foot up in the air for twenty minutes while Andy Easton, who looked after him through all his years with Michael, went off in search of wirecutters.

21

In their first hunter-chase together, at Huntingdon, West Tip rose less than a foot at the first fence and turned a somersault. A great start to the new partnership. He then turned in a normal performance at Nottingham next time: off the bridle for much of the way, with Marcus pushing and shoving and eventually coming back blowing harder than the horse. However, the ploy worked when West Tip ran at Hereford on 4 March 1989 and won his first race since the 1986 Grand National. Hunter-chase it may have been, but he had beaten the odds-on favourite Stearsby; despite spooking half-way up the run-in like a green youngster, the twelve-year-old West Tip had got his head back in front and that, with his fifth crack at the National a month away, was a huge bonus. After their great start it also did something for the confidence of his new partner.

Although he had won one hunter-chase, you have to be placed first or second in two to qualify for the Christies Foxhunters at Cheltenham, which would have been the ideal race for West Tip at this stage, at level weights against mostly average horses. As it was, however, there was little alternative but to run in Desert Orchid's Gold Cup. It was desperate ground. Desert Orchid beat Yahoo a length and a half, with Charter Party and I not far away in third. There was a distance back to Bonanza Boy and another distance back to West Tip, who was pulled up by Peter Hobbs going to the last. He'd been tailed off, but Ten Plus and Ballyhane had come down three out, Cavvies Clown had refused at the last and only four had finished, so Peter turned West Tip back into the last and crossed the line in fifth – to pick up £2,393.

The 1989 National gave me one of the biggest thrills I've had outside of winning the race. I'd been told by everyone what good form West Tip was in after his hunter-chasing, and it was easy to ignore that extraordinary Gold Cup. I remember clearly being near the front and going out for a good time. West Tip was one of those horses who would respond to that sort of attitude. He'd won it, been fourth twice and was as safe as houses: you could throw caution to the winds on him round Aintree now. Brendan Powell was on Stearsby and we were just remarking on what great rides we were having as we went into the eleventh, a big ditch. We spoke a fence too soon: Stearsby, whose jumping was never amazing, put his front feet in the ditch and it was goodnight Brendan. He got absolutely smothered.

We were always in front or near the front in that race. West Tip was giving me a tremendous ride. Carl Llewellyn was going very well on Smart Tar – in fact so well that it reminded me slightly of West Tip in 1985 when he was unseated at the twentieth. Jimmy Frost on Little Polveir joined us in front over the water as we set out for the second circuit and from there on he always seemed to be going just a shade better than us. When the pace quickened three out West Tip just struggled to go with the leaders, but he began to stay on and I still thought I'd nearly win at the last, although Little Polveir, who had never shown much of a liking for the place before, was staying on even more strongly. Still, when you're beaten seven lengths that's fair and square and I knew there was nothing else we could have done to beat Jimmy. It was such a thrill, though, to have finished second on the old horse again for Michael and Peter Luff.

The National put the horse straight for Marcus in the Howard E. Perry Hunter Chase at Cheltenham a couple of weeks later. 'He should have been an odds-on shot for that,' recalls Michael Oliver. 'He must have been the biggest certainty there has ever been that day, not a 9–4 shot. It was, after all, one of his favourite courses.' He beat Drops O'Brandy fifteen lengths, in the last race he ever won.

He ran in the Whitbread at the end of that season, finishing fourth, and the following season he again went hunter-chasing, starting off at Nottingham where he ran his typical first race of the season into third place. The next time Jamie Railton rode him at Wolverhampton in a handicap chase before he went to Leicester for another hunter-chase. Then it was Cheltenham, for the penultimate time. Now aged thirteen, he ran a blinder in the Christies Foxhunters. He jumped the last upsides Call Collect and Old Nick, the runner-up, and was beaten less than five lengths. Had it not been fast ground, I believe he would very nearly have won the race.

In 1990, for the first time in six Nationals, I couldn't ride West Tip, being claimed for Brown Windsor by Nicky Henderson. The ground was firm for the first time since the war, and though his age wasn't a problem West Tip was always going to be struggling to go the pace on it. Nevertheless, in his own time, he jumped round to finish tenth of the twenty finishers, while up front Mr Frisk, chased home by Durham Edition, smashed the course record. It was a fine end to a wonderful Aintree career, and when he popped over the last it was the 172nd Aintree fence he had jumped.

The following season he ran in three more hunter-chases: on his last run, fittingly at Cheltenham, he finished sixth in the Foxhunters behind Lovely Citizen. West Tip, the best horse around Aintree since Red Rum, was then retired and given to the vet John Williams, a partner of Peter Thorne, who had put him together following the collision with a lorry all those years before. He led an active retirement eventing in a small way, hunting and participating in promotional events. At a motor show in Birmingham he was was the star attraction at the Saab motors stand, ridden by me and accompanied by TV commentator Des Lynam. No doubt it was the lights, the photographer and the crowds which spooked him, but West Tip stepped squarely on to Des's foot, breaking a toe. His appearance provoked much press coverage after the event – though not necessarily for the right reasons. Michael Oliver retired from training, moved from Elmley Lovett and concentrated on selling on his Irish point-to-pointers.

23

DESERT ORCHID
2

D ESERT ORCHID WAS ALREADY THE BIGGEST NAME IN RACING BY THE TIME I CAME TO RIDE HIM AT THE START OF THE 1989–90 SEASON. Books were being written about him, he'd already won two King Georges and a Gold Cup and, Red Rum apart, he was the only racehorse with a fan club. His phenomenal success, his instantly recognizable grey-getting-whiter colour and his legs of iron that meant he never missed a season made him, without question, the most well-known horse in the country.

25.

During his career he had three regular jockeys, Colin Brown, Simon Sherwood and me. Towards the end of the 1988–9 season, after he had won an amazing Gold Cup at Cheltenham, Simon, who had won nine out of ten races on Dessie, announced his retirement and his intention to build a yard at Summerdown in East Ilsley and to train. A new jockey would have to be found for Britain's most popular horse. In the view of the media it was a two-horse race, so to speak, between Graham Bradley and me.

David Elsworth, who trained Dessie so well throughout his career, asked me a couple of times if I'd be interested in riding the horse. He was, at any rate, keen for me to ride. Around the end of April 1989, one of Dessie's owners, Richard Burridge, asked me if I would like to ride him. It was the official popping of the question. *Like* to ride him? I'd love to. It was like being invited to spend the weekend with the Royal family – you'd have to have a fairly good reason to turn it down. I needed only to clear it with David Nicholson (the 'Duke'), who retained me at the time. He was pleased about it and, certainly for the first season, didn't think he had horses that would clash with Dessie. We wrote Dessie into my contract.

The first time I sat on Dessie was a fairly hair-raising experience and left me clear about one thing – never sit on this horse anywhere other than on a racecourse. I think he was having fun at my expense. I knew that Simon had not particularly liked schooling or riding Dessie at home because he was so strong, and that Rodney Boult, David's head lad, was almost the only man in the world who could stop Dessie running away. The horse was not terrified like some who run away, nor was he malicious: this was pure, undiluted enthusiasm for his equine athleticism. It was a wonderful autumn Sunday morning, down at Whitsbury at David Elsworth's gallops on the edge of the New Forest, when new jockey met old pro. I had flown back from America the previous night after the Breeders' Cup Steeplechase. I was tired, and I was greeted by more cameras than you find at Aintree on National day. Richard Burridge was there too. Dessie, on home ground, pricked his ears. I'm a showman, he thought. Here's a crowd, I'll give them a show – it doesn't matter whether it's Richard Dunwoody or Fred Bloggs on board.

2 6

The idea was that Dessie would canter round the all-weather woodchippings gallop a couple of times to warm up before schooling over David's five practice fences. As we cantered around, Dessie became stronger and stronger, and I began to struggle to hold one side of him. I knew that on the open Downs up above Whitsbury it's possible to go quite a long way without a hedge or fence to stop you. I began to think of the good people of Salisbury, queuing up for the cathedral, seeing this white horse galloping down the street towards them and thinking that the good Lord has arrived a trifle earlier than anticipated. (Have a look at the Book of Revelations if you don't know what I'm talking about.) Brendan Powell had tipped me that David used to take Polo mints with him when Simon was schooling Dessie, and when he wanted Simon to pull the horse up, he would step out on to the circular canter, put out his Polos-laden hand, and Dessie would stop. Sure enough, here came David, proffering Polos. Well, Dessie was motoring at this stage. An athlete enjoying full training as much as this is not in the mood for Polos. A bowl of gently bruised Canadian oats or other such gourmet equine tidbits would not have stopped him. The cameras were on me, and I didn't want it to look like I was being carted. So I did everything I could do to stop him, short of extracting his back teeth with the bit, and we ground to an uneasy halt a circuit later. Time for the practice fences.

'If he jumps them well,' said David, 'don't pull him up, just work up over a mile with Paul Holley who will give you a lead over the fences.' I felt a little comforted. My aching arms could not have pulled Dessie up again. We set off. Paul must have been riding something pretty fast because we didn't hang around. As for Dessie, he hardly touched the ground, let alone a fence. He was standing off miles and landing just as far out the other side. By the time we landed over the last, Dessie was off. We worked up over a mile. After a good, searching piece of work like that, most horses will pull up. As soon as I stood up in the irons, Dessie, realizing his morning's fun was over, pulled up like a gentleman. Riding him on a racecourse was not going to be a tenth as difficult or hair-raising as riding him at home. (One of the last times I sat on Dessie, at a show where he was parading after he had retired, he ran away with me, cornering like a motor bike, and carted me out through the collecting ring.)

That great career began, where it was eventually to end, at Kempton in the Walton Novice Hurdle on 21 January 1983, some six and a half years before I became associated with the horse. It was an inauspicious start. A lanky, darker grey, but up against juveniles who had mostly run on the Flat, he was behind when he fell at the last with Colin Brown. A month later, against novices of all ages, he went to Wincanton, his local track, and finished down the field in a race won by John Francome on Raise The Offer. Even our Marcus Armytage managed to finish in front of him that day, on a mare called Rostra who went on to win eight races. Things got better the following month when he was a neck second to Diamond Hunter at Sandown and opened his prize-money account with the grand sum of £347.20, but on heavy ground at Newbury he struggled in a slightly superior novice hurdle. His first season came to an unsuccessful conclusion although it gave his connections plenty of hope for the future. A summer on his back would help him fill his frame.

He returned the following October at Ascot. The firm ground had kept away much of the opposition but Dessie had been going well at home and came to the race as second favourite. He was now a bit keener and Colin let him bowl along in front. He made all and won unchallenged. The same happened in a three-horse race in November, but similar tactics just failed at Sandown where, after leading all the way, a couple of mistakes caught him out and he was collared up the hill by Catch Phrase. David then dropped him back to two miles, at Kempton on Boxing Day, for the

Foodbrokers Armour Hurdle. This time ridden by Richard Linley, he got very warm beforehand but it made little difference. He kicked the third out of the ground but otherwise made all the running. By the time John Francome set off to try to catch him on I Haventalight, he was gone, kept going and beat him fifteen lengths. The dashing, front-running grey was beginning to win admirers.

Now that his team had found the way to ride him, Dessie was galloping his opposition into the ground. He added the Tolworth Hurdle, the Datchet Hurdle and Kingwell Pattern Hurdle to his already smart record as an outstanding novice. In the Kingwell Pattern Hurdle, a recognized Champion Hurdle trial, he had the good mare Stans Pride, Janus, Very Promising, Prideaux Boy and Admiral's Cup all behind him. At the Champion Hurdle itself, with Dawn Run taking him on he did not find it so easy to dominate and the only time he could get to the front was between the third and fourth flights. He finished down the field. The season, a tough one for a five-year-old, had probably taken its toll.

28

The following season, 1984–5, was always going to be difficult. Handicaps were virtually out of the question, he was still young enough to go chasing yet, and in condition hurdles he was going to find the opposition consistently tough. Ra Nova beat him first time out, See You Then beat him at Ascot, and although he beat See You Then in the Christmas Hurdle at Kempton he found Browne's Gazette too good. In the Irish Sweeps Handicap Hurdle, anchored by 12st, he led to the last but weakened quickly. He did get on the scoresheet at Sandown when he made all to win the Oteley Hurdle, but he was pulled up in the 1985 Champion Hurdle behind, once again, See You Then.

The 1985 Champion Hurdle was the first time I rode against Dessie. In fact, it was my first ride in the race at all. I was on Northern Trial for Paul Kelleway. In the paddock he said: 'See that grey horse, Desert Orchid? He'll want to make the running – don't let him. However quick he goes, I want you to go quicker.' At the top of the hill I was still about four lengths clear (I watched the race on television afterwards and got a real buzz when Peter O'Sullevan said: '. . . and it's Northern Trial five lengths clear . . .') but Northern Trial hit a wall after the second last and fell heavily at the last. He broke his back or his neck and had to be put down. Not a happy start to my Champion Hurdle record.

Until then I'd only really noticed Dessie because his half-brother, a horse called Ragged Robin, was at Capt Forster's yard and had buried me on the schooling ground one day. I'd also ridden Ragged Robin once on the racecourse and he had done the same thing there. They say you can choose your friends but you can't choose your relations, but none the less I was wary of Desert Orchid because of his brother.

On a recovery mission Dessie was pulled up by Colin in the heavy ground at Chepstow in the Welsh Champion Hurdle behind Browne's Gazette and for his final hurdle of the season went to Ascot for the Trillium Handicap Hurdle. Carrying 12st again he was in front when he took a heavy fall and very nearly broke his neck. He was already flamboyant and would stand off some of his hurdles ridiculously far. Although hurdles are small, they still need some respecting. A slight misjudgement and you catch a toe just under the crossbar of the hurdle, and it can flip you straight over. After that fall he had his only run in a Flat race, when Brian Rouse rode him in the Sagaro Stakes over two miles at Ascot. He trailed in beating only one. His return to hurdling the next season again ended up on the floor, this time at the second last in the Captain Quist Hurdle at Kempton. The race was at his mercy but once again his lack of respect for hurdles cost him. It was not only costing him races, it was going to cost him his life sooner or later. The only alternative was to send him chasing, where he might find the bigger fences more of a challenge and treat them with less disdain.

He made an immediate impact. He won his first four chases. 'Made all. Unchallenged' was the succinct description of those novice chases and, more important, after his final two hurdles he only made one mistake in those four races. His fifth chase in January, however, saw him unseat Colin at Ascot in a three-horse race won by another useful novice called Pearlyman. Dessie came up from nowhere and didn't quite make it though he just about remained on his feet. At Sandown, a difficult course for a novice, he again jumped a clear round but found the useful Berlin half a length too good. He reversed that form in that season's Arkle Challenge Trophy but for the third time he had showed an apparent dislike for Cheltenham when he could only finish third – albeit a very respectable third – to Oregon Trail and Charcoal Wally, whom he had beaten earlier. His season which had begun with such promise then tailed off a little with defeats by Clara Mountain at Sandown, and Repington back at Ascot in April when he ran as if he was over the top. He was also giving a lot of weight away.

His first race of the 1986–7 season saw him taking on me and Very

29

Promising in the Holsten Export Lager Handicap Chase at Sandown Park. Dessie was getting very nearly two stone, set off like a rocket, and though he only beat me seven lengths my horse blew up that day. It is hard for me to make an assessment of Dessie's performance that day. When I was race-riding I was so focused on my own mount, and in those days it was difficult to make an accurate judgement of others'. He was then beaten in a vintage H. & T. Walker Chase at Ascot by Church Warden. He won the Frogmore Chase at Ascot over two miles, beating his old adversary Charcoal Wally and again making most of the running, and David was keen to give him a crack at three miles for the first time in the King George VI Chase. At the same time David had another good chaser in his yard, Combs Ditch, though he hadn't run this season. He had a good record in the race and had been second in it twice, once to Burrough Hill Lad in 1984, and once to Wayward Lad in 1985. Now in 1986 Colin had the unenviable task of choosing between the ten-year-old Dessie and his seven-year-old stable companion. Colin's choice was under-standable but it was the only time Dessie was ever rejected by a jockey – except in his retirement by people who didn't want to get run away with round showrings or during racecourse parades.

I had been approached by David to ride whichever Colin rejected but in the end the Duke sent me, of all places, to Huntingdon. Simon Sherwood came in for the spare ride. Again it was a case of 'Made all. Unchallenged'. Simon let him bowl against the best of horses of the time: Forgive'N Forget, Wayward Lad, Door Latch, Bolands Cross, Von Trappe and Western Sunset. None of them had an answer for Dessie. It was his first King George VI Chase and Dessie's popularity was growing rapidly.

There followed two more good wins, in the Gainsborough Chase at Sandown Park and Jim Ford at Wincanton, before the Queen Mother Champion Chase for which he was second favourite behind Pearlyman. This was a great race: Dessie led to the second last, where I took it off him on Very Promising, with Pearlyman taking it up at the last. Dessie kept on well under Colin and though I was only beaten a neck in a titanic scrap he was just three lengths away in third. Three weeks later he won again carrying 12st 4lb at Ascot but after a few mistakes Colin pulled him up in Lean Ar Aghaidh's Whitbread Gold Cup over three miles five furlongs. Dessie was suffering from his corns that day.

The following season, 1987–8, he won the Terry Biddlecome Chase by a distance, then a trial at Kempton for the King George. But reverting to two miles he had to give Long Engagement and myself all but two stone. He ran an extremely good race to go down by three lengths. In the King George VI Chase, for which he was evens favourite, Colin was taken on by Peter Scudamore on Beau Ranger. The pair of them went very fast, too fast, alternating the lead. Beau Ranger was the first to crack but the race had taken its toll on Dessie too and at the third last he was just about cooked. He was passed by the 25–1 French challenger Nupsala (François Doumen's horses have rarely been allowed to start that price again). Forgive'N Forget was beaten and tired when he fell at the last. Dessie, heroically, stayed on to finish a distant second. I managed to beat him again in the Gainsborough Chase at Sandown in February. I was on Charter Party who was in cracking form that season and went on to win the Gold Cup so it was brilliant form from Dessie's point of view. He was third beaten just over eight lengths but he was giving me 17lb. Rhyme 'N' Reason, who went on to win that season's Grand National, was second. At Wincanton, though, Dessie was beaten by Kildimo in the Jim Ford but he put up a great effort to finish second to Pearlyman, beaten only marginally further than he had been the previous year in the Queen Mother Champion Chase. He beat Very Promising this time. It was his fifth visit to the Festival and he still hadn't won.

At the Festival Colin Brown announced his retirement from riding. He had had a long and successful career and had ridden Dessie during the horse's formative years. He deserves a lot of credit for the making of Desert Orchid. Colin encouraged his flamboyance and raised no objections if Dessie wanted to go long. Colin suited his style of racing, found the key to him – which was his front-running – and was unlucky not to have won a King George on him. So, for his second last race of the season, a new and even more golden era began for Dessie. Simon Sherwood, who had won his first King George on Dessie sixteen months earlier, was reunited with him. For the second time together they never saw another horse, making all to win the Chivas Regal (now Martell) Cup by eight lengths to Kildimo. That was two out of two for Simon.

Dessie was already massively popular and his last outing of the season in the Whitbread Gold Cup did much to increase his popularity. Making most of the running he was briefly headed at the Pond fence by Run And Skip but Simon knew Dessie by now, didn't panic, and was soon back in front. Dessie ran on really strongly up Sandown's tough hill to rapturous applause from the big Sandown crowd. He may not be a champion at two miles but here was a horse who could live the best over

that trip and still win over nearly twice as far. He was getting whiter and he was appealing to non-racing folk as a horse they could instantly recognize. Since the retirement of Red Rum, jump racing had been starved of a real hero who turned out without fail season after season. Dessie was capturing their imagination.

After a summer off, that partnership began to flourish again. Come December with two major wins to his credit, Dessie had another tussle, similar to the one he and Simon had had in the Whitbread, to win his second King George VI Chase at Kempton. There Dessie was becoming a standing order. I rode Charter Party that day and I think it was a bit firm for him; he finished last of the five runners.

Dessie's win in the Victor Chandler Chase at Ascot where he had reverted to two miles was one of the season's epic races. He and Panto Prince, to whom he was giving 22lb, fought out an incredible duel up that famous hill. Panto Prince was a popular horse himself and from the last it was ding-dong all the way up the hill. Only strides before the line Dessie got his grey head in front. That day was all about courage. A month later he tackled three miles to win the Gainsborough Chase at Sandown Park, his Gold Cup prep race. This time it was Pegwell Bay who put up the stiffest opposition and it was only in the dying strides that Dessie asserted his authority.

The Gold Cup was a race full of emotions. It had rained very hard and the ground was desperate. In some places, water was pumped off the course, in other parts helicopters were used as giant hairdryers. It was 'shall-we-shan't-we' in the Dessie camp. They had a difficult decision to make. They had a four-legged national institution on their hands, half the crowd had come to see him run in the Gold Cup, and the course was as soft as it had ever been in the last decade. What if he slipped and hurt himself? He had never really liked Cheltenham like he had Kempton, Sandown and Wincanton. I remember borrowing a pair of galoshes and walking out on to the course where the water gushed in over the top. Stewards, trainers and jockeys stood about in small groups discussing the ground, Richard Burridge wore a damp overcoat and had wet, bedraggled hair; David Elsworth wore a pensive look. If the whole thing had been cancelled you'd never have got the crowd back. It had to go ahead, and no one who was present that day will forget it.

It was one of the most memorable Gold Cups of all time. It was way up there with Red Rum's third National, Bob Champion's victory on Aldaniti at Liverpool after he'd recovered from cancer, and Dawn Run's Gold Cup. I rode Charter Party who ran a good race to finish third, giving me one of the best seats in the house for the duel between Yahoo, who seemed to have Dessie's measure going away from the last, and Dessie, driven by Simon back past him three-quarters of the way up the hill. Often in a race you don't really hear the crowd. The roar when Dessie hit the front opposite the people-packed grandstands was the loudest I've ever heard anywhere.

Yahoo's jockey Tom Morgan must have thought he'd won it after going about two lengths up on the run-in. When you come that close you are so disappointed. The crowd were going mad as we walked back to the winner's enclosure, whooping, cheering, throwing hats into the air. A tide of people followed Dessie crossing the paddock, cheering the horse and Simon. Yahoo and Charter Party were just extras on a filmset. Dessie was the big lead who'd just flown in from Hollywood. It was one of the few times I've seen an English horse accorded an Irish-style reception. The only other time I have seen the place go wild was when Dawn Run won the Gold Cup in 1986. I had fallen at the fourth last on Von Trappe. All I remember hearing was a loud cheering from the stands – then suddenly deathly silence. Dawn Run had been headed briefly by Wayward Lad. Then, just as suddenly, a tremendous roar broke from the crowd as she got up to win. It was a very special moment for me as a relative newcomer to top-class racing.

In the weighing room there were other emotions. Kevin Mooney had been travelling very well on Ten Plus, Fulke Walwyn's last good horse. A lot of people within racing would have loved to see him win but the horse, who was in the lead and travelling well, fell at the third last and broke his leg. Simon was on cloud nine, Kevin was at rock bottom. The second, third and fourth favourites had all fallen. If people hadn't heard of Dessie before, they had now.

Desert Orchid had established a record at the top level second to none in my memory. He was exciting to watch as he bowled along in front, putting in flamboyant leaps at his fences and galloping his rivals silly. Simon Sherwood had won nine races out of ten on Dessie – the exception was the Martell Cup at Liverpool when Dessie fell – and he even called his biography *Nine Out of Ten*. When I came to ride Dessie he was effectively unbeaten at the highest level for two and a half seasons. That creates a bit of pressure in itself. No horse, especially one who has no option but to run in some handicaps, is going to remain unbeaten for ever. The sooner we got that first defeat out of the way, the better.

33

My first ride in a race on Dessie was at Wincanton on 9 November 1989 in a two-horse race for the Silver Buck Handicap Chase. It was a few days after that enjoyable – in the end – schooling and getting-to-know-you session at Whitsbury. Roll-A-Joint was the other runner – he was later killed in that season's Grand National when he fell at the Canal Turn. A two-horse race should be no problem, but the pressure was definitely on. A large crowd had come to Wincanton just to see him run – Dessie could always put quite a few thousand on the gate. He was responsible for the record King George crowds on Boxing Day and must have introduced goodness knows how many people to the sport. I was trying to put the pressure out of my mind and to focus on the race. Ian Lawrence, the chirpy character who was riding Roll-A-Joint, was laughing at me down the back straight. Dessie and I won very comfortably.

Our second outing together was at Sandown in the Tingle Creek Chase the following month. The Duke had a runner in the race, Long Engagement, who had 2st less than Dessie. David Elsworth had given me orders just to pop away and not to go a crazy gallop. So I did just that, went a nice gallop without going mad. Long Engagement, ridden by Brendan Powell, himself on the wrong end of some great duels with Dessie, came past us at the last and, up the hill, I wasn't able to quicken. He beat me two and a half lengths.

The press went crazy. You'd think I'd murdered the horse. I was slated for not going fast enough, not setting a good enough gallop. I think they overlooked the weight I was giving Long Engagement, a fair horse on his day, and the time was good enough on fairly fast ground. They may have been right that if I'd gone a bit faster I might have stood a slightly better chance, but to be beaten two and a half lengths is fair and square in my book.

So we went to the King George VI Chase in 1990 with one win and one defeat to our credit. There were only six runners, among them David's former two-mile Champion chaser Barnbrook Again, but I regarded Pegwell Bay as my biggest danger. I also knew, having ridden him, that Norton's Coin was pretty useful if Sirrel Griffiths had him fit. Yahoo, Dessie's old adversary from the Gold Cup, was in the race but hadn't been showing the same form this season. His trainer John Edwards also had Bob Tisdall in but I didn't regard him as a danger. Dessie's races at Kempton had always seemed to follow a pattern. You'd be in the shake-up turning out of the back straight, he'd take a blow round the bend and as you straightened up for the third last he just took off again.

We took a little time to warm up but were soon going a good clip. I'm sure Dessie knew that it was his place, his race. He made a couple of mistakes, one at the penultimate ditch where a photographer perched on a ladder probably distracted him, but these were only blemishes on an otherwise perfect third King George VI for Dessie and first for me. I did not have to quicken him up – he did it on his own. By the time he had jumped the third last the race was already won. It was all over. He won very easily. Barnbrook Again and Brendan Powell were second and Yahoo third. Norton's Coin had travelled extremely well until blowing up turning into the straight, which would give Graham McCourt grounds for optimism in the Gold Cup.

It was the first really big reception I'd had on Dessie. The crowd, many of whom came out from London to see Dessie as a Christmas ritual, went mad with cheering. I should think most of them had backed him.

In February he had a dolly round Wincanton and won extremely easily, beating Bartres and Mick Bowlby, before going back to Kempton for the Racing Post Chase. Even in the paddock, given a leg-up by David Elsworth, I was always impressed by the feeling of power Dessie gave off underneath me and by the strength of his neck. No other horse has given me such a feeling. Carrying 12st (12st 3 lb on this day) meant nothing to him. Some horses don't carry big weights at all – Mr Frisk was a typical example: he always ran his best races carrying a low weight against better horses rather than a big weight against lesser horses – but Dessie had incredible strength. I don't think 13st would have anchored him. In the 1990 Racing Post Chase he was giving 2st to Delius, a very good horse on his day, 2st 2lb to Ballyhane and 2st 6lb to Seagram, who went on to win a Grand National fourteen months later.

35

The race followed a similar pattern to the King George although Luke Harvey on Solidasarock led for much of the second circuit before getting tired – the cost of taking on Dessie. We passed him at the third last when Dessie just picked up on his own accord and flew up the straight. The race was run in very fast time and in a matter of strides he put clear water between himself and the struggling opposition. Delius was eight lengths away and Seagram sixteen. At 1lb a length, it made Dessie 50lb better than the following year's National winner.

I will always maintain that that was his best run for me. David who had him so well wished it had been Gold Cup day. That came three weeks later and was won by Norton's Coin at 100–1. I led, went a nice gallop, and then

Ten of Spades took me on at the middle one down the back, about six out. He got the inner and I had to pull out round him. I gave Dessie a breather, and then was carried a bit wide by Kevin Mooney coming into the straight. Norton's Coin and Toby Tobias got a good run through up the inner. I was beaten four and three-quarter lengths. The real battle had been between Graham McCourt on Norton's Coin and Mark Pitman on Toby Tobias. A couple of little things went wrong for me but nothing major. They had not cost me the race.

Some people said Dessie never really acted round Cheltenham. (They also said the same of One Man but I think there was a lot of rubbish written about it.) He jumped a little right at times and with Cheltenham being a left-handed track it didn't help. He preferred Kempton and Sandown. But I agree with David. Had Dessie been as spot-on for the Gold Cup as he was for the Racing Post Chase three weeks earlier, then I think he might have won this one too.

We went on to Fairyhouse for the Irish National. If there is one country in the world where a good steeplechaser is appreciated, it's Ireland. Even before the race people were trying to touch and pat him and some were trying to pull hairs from his tail. Rules as to who is allowed into the paddock are a bit more lax in Ireland than they are in the UK. But far from upsetting Dessie, I think it had the opposite effect. Some horses like to show off. You often find with National winners that when they are thrust into the limelight and start opening fêtes and getting in front of the cameras they love it, and act up to the occasion. Well Dessie was an old hand at performing for the crowd by then and he loved every moment in Ireland.

36

I'd had a fall in the previous race from Charlie Brooks's Arden who had unseated me at the first hurdle in the Jameson Gold Cup Hurdle. Arden had then disappeared off the course into the Meath countryside – with my saddle. I had to borrow one off Declan Murphy for Dessie. Again Dessie had 12st which was 2st more than any other horse, except Have A Barney who was only getting 26lb from him. Over three and a half miles I thought it might be hard going, especially at the end of another tough season. We bowled along in front, taken on by Bold Flyer who had won a Galway Plate. That meant we were going a tremendous gallop. It was a hell of a performance. Only between the last two fences did his action seem to go a bit and it says something for his strength that he managed to keep going. As his action had gone I didn't commit myself at the last. I didn't want to go too long on him and risk decking him but at the same time I suppose I was not that definite with him about going short. In the end he launched himself out of my hands and virtually ended up straddling the fence. He wasn't ever going to fall but it was what they call a 'big moment' in motor racing. For the first time I felt he was tired and leg weary – but he had galloped everything else into the ground and had won easily. The reception we got as we came into the winner's enclosure matched anything we had ever known at Kempton.

His well-deserved summer holiday was spent, as usual, on the North Yorkshire Moors at the home of Richard Burridge. 1990–1 was to be his last full season. He reappeared in the Plymouth Gin at Devon And Exeter and was beaten six lengths by Sabin Du Loir. We were favourite but we never headed Peter Scudamore and Sabin Du Loir. The Duke had let me off Waterloo Boy for the Plymouth Gin but, after Jamie Osborne got unseated on him, I was not to be let off for the Tingle Creek Chase at Sandown. David and the Burridges were understanding – after all the race, over two miles, was really just prep for his attempt at a record fourth King George. Graham Bradley rode him, he had top weight, and he finished a well-beaten fourth behind Young Snugfit, Sabin Du Loir and myself on Waterloo Boy. He didn't run a great race.

The King George attracted a good-looking field of nine, including Sabin Du Loir, who had become something of a thorn in Dessie's side this season, a five-year-old from France called The Fellow, Gold Cup runner-up Toby Tobias who was having his first run of the season, and Celtic Shot, a previous Champion Hurdler. Sabin Du Loir set off at a furious gallop with the intention of disappointing Dessie. For the first time in a race I felt Dessie wasn't enjoying it. Kempton was his place and he liked to dominate round there. I wasn't going to make the mistake of taking on Sabin Du Loir and busting Dessie in the process, however, so we had to sit and suffer. At the thirteenth, Sabin Du Loir fell, leaving us in front. Immediately Dessie's ears pricked and he was happy again. He took a breather round the bend, as usual, then picked up and galloped to the line from the third last to beat Toby Tobias twelve lengths. He had slaughtered a good field and the reception was tremendous. It really was quite a handy little Christmas present to have had the ride on Dessie for those couple of years.

In the Victor Chandler Chase at Ascot later that season we were messed about by a loose horse and were only beaten six lengths by Blitzkrieg into

37

fourth. Again he was giving lumps of weight away to the best two-milers in the country. Katabatic, who went on to win that season's Champion Chase, was getting 24lb from Desert Orchid, now a mature twelve years old. The Agfa Diamond Chase was next. It was one of the bravest races he ran for me. We had a memorable tussle up the hill with Nick The Brief, who headed me jumping the Pond Fence. I looked beat, but Dessie flew the last and really battled to the line to beat Nick The Brief three-quarters of a length. It was to be his last win and it typified everything about the horse.

In the Gold Cup everything went well until about half-way when we were headed, a bit like the previous year. This time, however, I completely lost my place. Dessie, unlike a lot of horses who would have given up on you at this stage, rallied and kept battling so much so that he eventually finished third behind Garrison Savannah and The Fellow, who were separated by a short head. Remember that he was getting on in years by now and maybe he wasn't quite on song.

The following season, 1991–2, he had just three runs, starting off with his own race, the Desert Orchid South Western Pattern Chase at Wincanton in which Sabin Du Loir beat us. It was an odd race because although Sabin Du Loir broke the course record – no mean feat at Wincanton which has played host to some very useful horses over the years – the third horse, Shannagary, finished only three and a half lengths behind Dessie in second. Shannagary, who was only getting 8lb this day, was rated 59lb below Dessie on their respective handicap marks. In the Peterborough Chase at Huntingdon, Sabin Du Loir, who was also twelve but enjoying a resurgence in his form, beat us again but Norton's Coin split us.

The build-up to the King George centred on whether I would ride Remittance Man or remain loyal to Dessie, who had already provided me with two King Georges. I opted for Dessie. I led for a little bit early on, made a mistake at halfway, and was struggling. Dessie was tired and I went very long on him at the third last. He came up for me, stepped on the fence and turned over. There was a hush in the stands as the crowd waited for him to get up. Ahead of us, The Fellow was getting the better of the brave little horse Docklands Express. Remittance Man, who had been cantering into the straight, looked like he failed to get the trip. I felt slightly sorry for The Fellow – the best reception was reserved for Dessie as he cantered, loose, with his reins dangling, past the stands. Not the end we had hoped for but the end nevertheless. A week before his thirteenth birthday Dessie was retired from racing.

Dessie likes being centre-stage. He is a huge attraction at fund-raising occasions and he can still put thousands on the gates at events.

Dessie's toughest fight was saved for his retirement when vets gave him a 20 per cent chance of recovery from a colic operation. During his recuperation he received a get-well card from Australia, addressed: Desert Orchid in his warm stable, England. It found its way to Newmarket where he was being looked after by vets.

Dessie is now a snow-white 25-year-old, and Richard Burridge is rightly strict about how much he does. I was privileged to ride him. I was still in nappies when the great Arkle was racing and I don't remember him but since his time only two horses have caught the public imagination in the same way. Desert Orchid is one of them, Red Rum the other. We've got tough, brave and brilliant horses in this book, but Dessie had it all.

39

CHARTER PARTY

C HARTER PARTY WAS PROBABLY THE MOST UNDERRATED OF ALL
MY BIG WINNERS. A lot of people did not rate the 1988 Gold Cup
as a vintage one but he won it by six lengths and I have yet to see
a bad Gold Cup, and never rode in one. On his day he was an exceptional
horse and on that particular occasion he was as good as any I have ever
ridden. As we walked round the paddock Tommy McGlinchy, his lad, had
told me that the horse was in cracking form: 'He hasn't taken a lame
step all day.' That remark tells the story: Charter Party was very good but
plagued with navicular – a crumbling of the bones in his feet – which
made him difficult to train and hard to keep sound.

The Duke (David Nicholson) told me that his father, Frenchie, who was a
great trainer of jockeys as well as horses, used to come and look round his
intake of young horses every autumn. When he saw the young Charter
Party he told the Duke that the horse would win the Gold Cup one day. How
he knew I'm not sure but he was a great judge of a horse and six years later
was proved right. The Duke himself began to believe he had a fair
performer after Charter Party's first run in a novice hurdle at Towcester in
December 1982. He finished eighth after making a mistake three out but
the Duke turned to his owners Raymond and Jenny Mould, who owned him
in partnership with Colin Smith, and told them they had a racehorse.

The following season he showed a little more promise as a novice
hurdler. Ridden in the early stages by the Duke's then jockey Peter
Scudamore, he was second first time out at Nottingham, progressed to
win at Haydock, was second at Newbury, and was fifth at Liverpool in a

race which also included another future Gold Cup-winner, Forgive'N Forget. He ended the season by stumbling and unseating Scu when ten lengths clear in the Haig Whisky Novice Hurdle Final at Newcastle in the heavy. Throughout his career he preferred a good cut in the ground, no doubt because it cushioned his sore feet.

Nor did he make an immediate impact as a novice chaser. From the start his jumping was a little bit hit-and-miss. His first run was at Lingfield, which before they put in an all-weather track was a lovely course to introduce a horse to chasing. He was well beaten by the Fred Winter-trained Carved Opal, ridden by John Francome, over two miles which would have been too sharp for him. He came second at Leicester, and at Ascot he never got into the race, which was won by the tearaway Cyrbandian and Jonjo O'Neill. His first win was at Worcester, when he was stepped up to two and a half miles. He was placed again behind Donegal Prince at Stratford and in March, which always seemed to be his month, especially if it wasn't too dry, he won at Sandown and Newbury. However, he ended the 1983 season by taking a crashing fall at Ascot's third last with Scu. Both horse and jockey lay there for dead for some time. Both lived to tell the tale, but there were a few anxious moments. I remember Scu that day; he was badly concussed and didn't know whether he was Arthur or Martha, whether he was at Ascot or Aintree!

Charter Party's first season as a handicap chaser started with a place at Sandown and another fall at Ascot in the H. & T. Walker Chase. He won his first handicap chase at Worcester but was not desperately impressive. That spring, though, he had two wins at Newbury, the second of which was given in the stewards' room after Solid Rock bumped him up the run-in. Sandwiched between those two wins was another heavy fall in the Kim Muir Chase at the Cheltenham Festival, when he buried Tim Thomson-Jones, then the leading amateur. Happily, his return to his local track in April was more productive, and he finished a good second to Aces Wild.

By now he had already developed feet problems, but he was slowly and surely working his way up in the handicap. With Scu still in the saddle, he fell again in the Hennessy Cognac Gold Cup at Newbury, which was won by Mark Dwyer on Galway Blaze. I pulled up a horse called Don Sabreur in that race. Charter Party won at Kempton Park, on Boxing Day, but a mistake once again very nearly cost him the race. After a disappointing performance in January at Windsor he didn't run again until the Ritz Club National Hunt Chase. I rode West Tip, and Charter Party wasn't really

fancied. He became the Duke's second ever winner at the Festival. Charter Party then demonstrated his liking for Cheltenham with an even more convincing win in the Golden Miller Chase in April with top weight.

At this stage Scu left the Duke to ride for Fred Winter and I came in. The only horse of the Duke's Scu was keen to keep the ride on was Very Promising and he didn't seem to mind not riding the inconsistent jumper Charter Party, who had just come good at the end of his last season there.

The first year I rode him I never thought he was quite right and I too managed to end up on the floor twice with him. Sometimes I think horses are bred bad jumpers and unfortunately Document, Charter Party's sire, had so few other runners it is hard to compare him with any of the others. He wasn't the most athletic horse, despite his ability to gallop, and at a fence you had to be very positive with him. If you wanted to go short you had to make sure he got the message, and likewise if you were a bit long at one and wanted him to come up for you you had to make sure he knew about it by squeezing him or giving him a kick in the ribs. Once I realized this I was more confident about his jumping but it was hard always to get it right.

On our first outing together he finished fourth to Broadheath, beaten about sixteen lengths, at Wincanton. In the 1986 Hennessy, which Broadheath won, I pulled him up. He was third to Maori Venture in the Mandarin Chase at Newbury with top weight and fell when tiring in the Gainsborough at Sandown behind Desert Orchid in February. At Nottingham he was disappointing behind Mr Frisk on good ground but since he was giving the winner all but two stone he might have deserved more credit.

For the 1987 Gold Cup I got off West Tip to ride Charter Party for the Duke. I had no option. This was when I was told I would never ride West Tip again though I'd won the National on him eleven months earlier. The connections thought I should remain loyal to the horse that had won me a National and perhaps I should have done but the Duke retained me and he wanted me to ride Charter Party although he was a 25–1 shot. This was the day with the snow on the ground – The Thinker's famous Gold Cup. We got down to the start. It was snowing so hard and balling in the horses' feet and we were called back to the stables. The race, meant to run at 3.30, didn't start until 4.50, by which time we were soaked and freezing because we hadn't been let back into the changing room to keep warm.

43

The course and fences were covered in snow when it began to rain. Some snow melted and they tried to blow the rest off with helicopters. The course was multi-coloured. You'd go through wet snow, across a patch of green and then out of the murk would appear the orange rails on the fences. Charter Party wasn't going to like this. Nor was I in my most positive frame of mind having already had one fall off him. We got as far as the fifth before crashing out. I came back in a Landrover and watched the rest of the race from the last fence. West Tip was running a stormer and finished fourth, beaten just over three lengths by The Thinker, another horse I'd ridden earlier that season: in the Rowland Meyrick at Wetherby when Ridley Lamb had been injured. I thought then there'd be a Gold Cup in him.

I pulled up Voice of Progress in the next race – it wasn't my best day at a Festival. The only luck I had that day was running out of petrol on the way home 100 yards short of the only petrol station on a 30-mile stretch of the A40. My year of getting to know Charter Party was not a tremendous success.

His 1988 Gold Cup season started with a defeat at Lingfield. First time out in the mud he was a bit thick-winded. He improved to finish second to Sun Rising at Kempton on Boxing Day carrying a prohibitive 12st 4lb. It was a good effort to go down by half a length on ground slightly better than he'd have preferred. He was then part of a three-timer I rode at Sandown in early February 1988. Long Engagement and Celtic Chief also won for me so it was a fair afternoon but we were particularly pleased with Charter Party who ran on really well to beat Rhyme 'N' Reason eight lengths. Desert Orchid was third and Run And Skip fourth. He always travelled really well and it was the first time I'd won on him. It was also the first time that I thought he had a serious chance in the Gold Cup if the ground came up right for him.

About eight days before the Gold Cup, the Duke took his Cheltenham horses to use Henry Candy's gallops at Kingston Lisle, near Wantage. The Duke was keen to put an edge on his horses by taking them somewhere different and Henry, who has some of the best gallops in the country, kindly obliged. I didn't know this at the time but the Duke insisted I ride another horse in the piece of work and he instructed Willie Humphreys, who was riding Charter Party, to remain two or three lengths behind the last horse so that I couldn't see him. Charter Party was quite crippled at the time and the Duke knew that if I saw him moving badly I might go out for the Gold Cup in a negative frame of mind. He was playing a bit of a game. After

44

Willie, prompted by the Duke, had raved about Charter Party, Tommy, his lad, did his bit in the paddock before the race. The Duke, meanwhile, had lined the floor of his box with rubber to insulate it and take any possible jar out of it. Earlier in the day I'd won on Kribensis so I was in good form and I thought we had a good each-way chance in the Gold Cup. Playschool, the Hennessy winner, was a very warm favourite. I was 10–1 and also ahead of me in the betting were Kildimo, Cavvies Clown, and Nupsala, the King George VI Chase winner.

I jumped off and from the word go things went unbelievably well. He was travelling well and I was able to help him a lot more at his fences. Beau Ranger gave me a good lead and going to the second last I managed to get upsides Simon Sherwood on Cavvies Clown. There was a gap on his inner and I took advantage as soon as I saw it. Cavvies Clown walked through the second last. I have a vivid memory of Simon with no reins and Cavvies Clown with his head nearly on the floor! By that stage it had become a two-horse race – Playschool had been pulled up and they thought he had been doped after an inexplicably bad run – and that mistake would hand me the race on a plate providing I jumped the last. Charter Party galloped up the hill to beat Cavvies Clown six lengths. I don't enjoy watching the video of this race. If the same race were run today, I would have received a deserved whip suspension. I was in the wrong being so punishing on the old horse. However, it sealed my second season with the Duke and provided me with one of my greatest thrills at Cheltenham. For me this unforgettable day was only equalled in excitement by my two winning Grand Nationals. It became a blur. Fortunately I was able to enjoy a smashing party hosted by my good friends John and Sylvia Bosley.

In the following season and, indeed, for the rest of his career, his problems overtook him. After blowing up he finished last of five in the Rehearsal Chase at Chepstow on his first run the following season – it is tradition that the previous season's Gold Cup winner gets beaten in this race – and last of five in the King George VI, although he wasn't beaten that far by Desert Orchid on fast ground. He was also last of four, beaten a long way, behind Desert Orchid again in the Gainsborough at Sandown. He jumped slowly early on and gurgled towards the end of the race. He must have been very wrong. We took him to Ireland for the Vincent O'Brien Irish Gold Cup. He was going very well when I went too long on him at one and ended up putting him on the deck at the eleventh. The race was won very easily by the seven-year-old wonder horse Carvill's Hill.

45

Charter Party then went back for his third Gold Cup in 1989, and ran a cracking race. It was desperately heavy but he travelled well, jumped a lot better and still had a great chance at the third last before staying on at the one pace behind Desert Orchid and Yahoo in a memorable race. It was a real slog after the torrential rain. You couldn't see much through your goggles and the reins slipped through your hands. But just to walk back down past the crowd with Simon Sherwood on Desert Orchid was something I will never forget. Later, at Liverpool, both Simon and I ended up on the deck at the same fence in the Martell Cup. It was down the back straight at the twelfth. Dessie fell and Charter Party came down so steep that I was unseated. Two Gold Cup winners down at the same obstacle. I have a picture of Dessie on the ground and me coming off. The Duke asked: 'What d'you fall off for?' Being unseated was one of his pet hates – mine too! Charter Party had actually been running a good race that day and was second, behind Dessie, at the time. Yahoo went on to win it. He deserved to win a decent race after his efforts in the Gold Cup.

The Golden Miller Chase provided me with one of the most embarrassing moments of my career. I think I was lucky not to be sacked off the horse but the Duke was always very loyal to his jockeys. He was running a good race with top weight and went to the fourth last, the one at the top of the hill, and put down on me. He didn't make much of a mistake and it didn't really stop him but, expecting him to be turned sideways by the fence, I went to the buckle end of the reins, the sort of thing you do once a race, and for some reason I let go. Sometimes a fall can seem to take for ever. I remember that I kept going backwards while he simply cantered out from beneath my legs. It was such a simple mistake I had to laugh about it. Even the Duke grinned. His owners would have been quite within their rights to jock me off for the Whitbread after that performance but they stuck by me. Carrying 11st 6lb Charter Party put up one of his best handicap performances to finish just over three lengths third to Brown Windsor and Sam Da Vinci. The first seven horses in that year's Whitbread were running off 10st apart from the eleven-year-old Charter Party. His last five runs of the season had seen him finish third in a Gold Cup and a Whitbread and fall or unseat me three times. It was an eventful season.

At Haydock the following season Charter Party had another run but he pulled up lame and the Duke decided with his owners to call it a day. This was a real gent of a horse – so kind that you could have slept in his box

46

without a worry. He went hunting for a while but wasn't suited to it and was retired to Jenny Mould's Guiting Grange in the Cotswolds and, sadly, neither owner nor horse are still with us. Jenny died of cancer while, in racehorse terms, Charter Party lived to a great age and is buried in a field at Guiting.

47

VERY PROMISING

WHEN YOU RIDE SIX OR SEVEN HORSES IN AN AFTERNOON, FIVE OR SIX DAYS A WEEK, IT IS HARD TO GET TO KNOW AND TO LOVE THEM ALL, ESPECIALLY IF THEY HAVE CARRIED YOU ONLY AS FAR AS THE FIRST OBSTACLE THROUGH WHICH THEY HAVE CRASHED. The trainers and even more the lads are the ones who get attached to their horses. Jockeys, however, despite our all-too-brief liaisons, do nevertheless become attached. Very Promising was one of the loveliest horses I've ever had anything to do with and I think if you ask anyone else who knew him they'd agree.

If there had been a two-and-a-half-mile Champion Chase in the eighties, Very Promising would surely have ruled it. During a distinguished career he was so sound that he was never fitted with a bandage and he never bit or raised a hindleg to another horse in anger. He ran equally well whether on soft or fast ground. He was also a great mate.

His life, like so many in this book, began in Ireland where he was bred by D. O'Keefe. He was by the popular jumping sire The Parson who tended to have more influence on stamina than speed, which was indeed this son's forte. His dam, No Hitch, never ran. He was bought privately by the trainer Michael Hourigan, and was given his name when a local owner down the road asked Michael how the young horse was going. 'He's very promising,' he said, and it stuck. He ran in one bumper, at Mallow (now renamed Cork Racecourse), which he won before he was bought by Mercy Rimell, wife of the late Kinnersley trainer Fred Rimell who won the Grand National four times with ESB, Nicolaus Silver, Gay Trip and Rag Trade. He was undoubtedly a smart buy.

In his first season as a four-year-old at Kinnersley near Worcester, he was sent to Chepstow for his first run over hurdles. Ridden by stable jockey Sam Morshead, he led briefly after the last but eventually went down by a short head and a head to Camino Crystal and Valeso. He won his next races, at Uttoxeter, Warwick and Doncaster, but was beaten by the decent Voice of Progress, owned by Lord Vestey and trained by the Duke, at Newbury on the last day of 1982.

It was only a brief interruption to his winning run. Instead of sending him to Cheltenham as a novice, Mercy sent him to Chepstow – she employed similar tactics with her Champion Hurdle-placed Celtic Chief – for the Panama Cigar Hurdle Final, a handsome prize the weekend before the Festival. He beat the Duke's Gambit very comfortably and then went to Liverpool for his final novice hurdle of the season, where he beat Connaught River five lengths carrying over 12st.

His next season began in the Bula Hurdle at Cheltenham in December 1983 when he finished third to Roger Fisher's very useful Amarach. Goldspun was a length second and Very Promising a further length and a half away in third. He was always going to be hard to place this season, indeed he was giving weight away all round in the Bula. Now being aimed towards the Champion Hurdle, he raced in the New Year's Day Hurdle at Windsor. He ran disappointingly and finished fifth behind Secret Ballot. Returning to handicaps in the Lanzarote Hurdle at Kempton he ran a better race and finished a close second to Janus, to whom he was conceding 12lb. Favourite for the Schweppes Gold Trophy he finished well down the field behind Ra Nova, but he was back on better form in the Kingwell Pattern Hurdle at Wincanton when third behind the dashing grey and rising star Desert Orchid.

50

Without a doubt he ran his best race of the 1983–4 season in the Champion Hurdle, finishing four and three-quarter lengths behind the great Irish mare Dawn Run and Cima. It was soon after a 5lb allowance had been brought in for mares, which gave Dawn Run an advantage. He had some very decent horses behind him that day, including Buck House, Fredcoteri, Amarach, For Auction, Desert Orchid, and Sula Bula, who became a jumping stallion. That afternoon, much to Mercy Rimell's fury, his then owner, Mr Mann, clinched a deal to sell Very Promising to John Maunders, an owner of trainer David Nicholson's. The horse never went back to Kinnersley and the opening chapter of Very Promising's career was over.

Very Promising's first run for the Duke was at the end of March at Liverpool, where he finished a ten-length second to Dawn Run. Peter Scudamore was in the saddle for the first time, replacing Sam Morshead. It was not a bad effort though. The Irish mare was at her best and Cima, who had split the pair at Cheltenham, was well down the field this time. At the same meeting a Mr R. Dunwoody had his first ride at Liverpool.

The following season, 1984–5, did not begin too badly when Very Promising was fourth to Ra Nova at Kempton in October. At Ascot he improved to finish second, albeit a well-beaten second, to Gaye Brief who, ironically, was trained by Mercy Rimell. He again filled the runner-up spot at Wincanton, beaten by Crimson Embers, the decent staying hurdler, over two-and-three-quarter miles.

The Duke was finding it hard to place Very Promising over hurdles. He wasn't quite good enough to win a Champion Hurdle over two miles and over longer trips he kept finding horses better than him at staying. To get out of trouble, the Duke had a mid-season change of plan, schooled Very Promising over fences, and sent him to Haydock in December for a two-and-a-half-mile novice chase. It was just the change he needed. At that time Haydock boasted the biggest fences outside of Aintree but Very Promising took to them instantly. He led from the last ditch at the end of back straight and came home ten lengths clear of the runner-up. After that, he never really looked back.

Next time out he was travelling very well over two miles at Newbury when he fell at the last ditch in a race won by Mr Moonraker. He was then second to Sula Bula at Ascot in February 1985. He returned to Newbury at the beginning of March for the Steel Plate And Sections Qualifier in which he absolutely bolted up by ten lengths from Townley Stone, an exceptional horse on his day. This was the first time I had ridden against him – on a horse belonging to Hugh O'Neill called First Quadrant, who was tailed off when I pulled him up turning into the straight.

On the strength of this Very Promising was made second favourite to win the 1985 Arkle Challenge Trophy at Cheltenham. The Irish challenger Buck House was favourite, his fellow countryman Boreen Prince was well fancied and there was a strong home team including Freight Forwarder, Townley Stone, Mr Moonraker, Destiny Bay, St William and Karenomore. I was riding Roadster for the late Colin Nash, a hunting farmer from Kingston Lisle, who had given me my early breaks in point-to-points. The Duke had not had a Cheltenham Festival-winner yet and Very Promising looked like breaking the hoodoo when he came to the last, with Boreen Prince and Buck House vying with him for the lead. He ran a great race but he found the two Irish horses just too good. Boreen Prince won it under Boots Madden, Tommy Carmody was two lengths back in second on Buck House and Very Promising was a further length and a half back in third. Roadster and myself were six lengths off him in fourth.

A few weeks later the Duke sent Very Promising to Ascot for the Golden Eagle Novice Chase where he again finished third, beaten this time by Townley Stone who'd been left clear in front at the second last when John Francome's mount I Haventalight fell. Graham McCourt always reckons that Townley Stone, when he was right, was one of the best horses he ever sat on. Boreen Prince, the hero of Cheltenham, was fourth in a reversal of the Arkle form.

52

The following season, 1985–6, his first out of novice company, began with a win in an Embassy Premier Chase qualifier at Chepstow. This was followed by the H. & T. Walker Chase over two and a half miles at Ascot, a race confined to novices and first-season handicappers where Very Promising convincingly beat Buck House, this time by eight lengths. He then went back to Ascot for the Embassy Premier Chase Final in January 1986. I rode Very Promising's joint-favourite Von Trappe in this race but he capsized seven out, as he often did. Scu made much of the running on Very Promising and the duel he had up the straight against Mr Moonraker made it one of the most exciting races of the season. Both the horses and Scu and Brendan Powell, their respective jockeys, gave their all. Mr Moonraker was beaten a short head. This season's first defeat came in the three-mile Charterhouse Chase back at Ascot in February where Very Promising made a bad mistake at the seventh. He never quite recovered from that error in company which comprised Cybrandian, Brunton Park, Door Latch, Castle Warden, Everett and Drumadowney. He finished seventh and last, and was found to have broken a blood vessel when pulled up at the end of the race.

His next run was his third visit to the Cheltenham Festival for the Queen Mother Champion Chase. The field included Badsworth Boy, who had won the three previous runnings of the race but had not had a race this season, his old adversary Buck House, and Bobsline, the Irish favourite. It was another vintage Champion Chase with Buck House taking it up at the third last. Again two Irish horses stood between Very Promising and an elusive Cheltenham victory. A mistake at the second

Top: In glorious isolation at Aintree. Unfortunately that year – 1988 – Rhyme 'n' Reason and two others finished in front of us.

Bottom: Negotiating the 'bogey' from the previous year. On the way to victory in 1986.

Top: Desert Orchid demonstrating his natural flamboyance when winning the Peterborough Chase at Huntingdon in 1991.

Bottom: All but in the bag. Landing over the last on the way to a record fourth King George VI Chase at Kempton in 1990.

Top: Charter Party proving our long-held belief that he had a Gold Cup in him, seen here winning in 1988. But for recurring lameness I think he'd have been a truly great horse.

Bottom: Always a good start to a season, to win its first big race. Very Promising cementing the new partnership of Nicholson and Dunwoody in 1986.

Above: A terrible worrier as a young horse, Remittance Man was often accompanied by a sheep. It seemed to do the trick! Here he is seen with Nobby – one of many woolly friends.

Left: With a spring in his step... Remittance Man and myself after schooling in Lambourn.

Top: Charter Party proving our long-held belief that he had a Gold Cup in him, seen here winning in 1988. But for recurring lameness I think he'd have been a truly great horse.

Bottom: Always a good start to a season, to win its first big race. Very Promising cementing the new partnership of Nicholson and Dunwoody in 1986.

Above: A terrible worrier as a young horse, Remittance Man was often accompanied by a sheep. It seemed to do the trick! Here he is seen with Nobby – one of many woolly friends.

Left: With a spring in his step... Remittance Man and myself after schooling in Lambourn.

Top: Charter Party proving our long-held belief that he had a Gold Cup in him, seen here winning in 1988. But for recurring lameness I think he'd have been a truly great horse.

Bottom: Always a good start to a season, to win its first big race. Very Promising cementing the new partnership of Nicholson and Dunwoody in 1986.

Above: Kribensis about to turn into the home straight in the 1988 Champion Hurdle – Cleeve Hill is in the background.

Right: Michael Stoute has led in winners of the Derby, the Breeders Cup, the Dubai World Cup and Japan Cup. Here he leads in his biggest ever National Hunt winner, Kribensis, after the 1988 Champion Hurdle.

Right: A job well done. Waterloo Boy, the Duke and connections cross the paddock en route to the most hallowed place in March: the winner's enclosure at Cheltenham.

Left: Highland Bud showing the way at Cheltenham.

Right: Auteuil, with the Eiffel Tower in the background. A more cosmopolitan backdrop than most British jump courses. Flatterer leaps off for the French Champion Hurdle in 1986.

Top: Morley Street just beginning to come back underneath me at Aintree in 1992.

Bottom: Flashing Steel points his toes, tracking Docklands Express during the 1994 Whitbread Gold Cup.

Top: Remittance Man was an exceptionally athletic jumper. This unusual shot captures
a rare mistake.

Bottom: It nevertheless demonstrates his strength. A lot of horses would not have recovered
from this handstand – it hardly mattered to him.

Above: A terrible worrier as a young horse, Remittance Man was often accompanied by a sheep. It seemed to do the trick! Here he is seen with Nobby – one of many woolly friends.

Left: With a spring in his step... Remittance Man and myself after schooling in Lambourn.

last by him and Bobsline handed the advantage to Buck House, and Very Promising, though he recovered and rallied up the hill, was beaten three lengths. Bobsline did not recover so well and was passed up the hill by Kathies Lad and Our Fun.

At Liverpool the horse lined up for the Whitbread Gold Label Chase over three miles and a furlong for his last race of the season. It was a small but select field of four, headed by the Gold Cup-winner and all-Ireland heroine Dawn Run, who was odds-on favourite. Wayward Lad, second to her at Cheltenham, was second favourite. Very Promising, attempting a pretty long trip for him, was 9–1, while Beau Ranger with Hywel Davies was a 40–1 outsider.

As so often happens at Liverpool, the Cheltenham form was worth little. The tracks are completely different and Cheltenham will have taken much out of a horse. The initial upset was when Dawn Run fell at the first. She had made one big mistake in the Gold Cup so it didn't come as a surprise, and it opened this race up. Beau Ranger and Hywel set a good gallop and found more when Wayward Lad joined the battle in the home straight. They kept finding a little bit more to beat him a length and a quarter. Very Promising ran like he had had a hard race at Cheltenham and didn't get home. He finished a weary and distant third.

The first time I rode Very Promising, in my new role as first jockey for the Duke, was on his reappearance at Sandown in November in 1987, the following season. There had been some fuss beforehand. Scu had left to join Fred Winter but was a friend of Paul Green, who now owned Very Promising. When I took the job I thought there might be a problem there. Very Promising was the one horse Scu wanted to keep the ride on. 'You're my jockey, you ride him,' said the Duke to me, and the matter was closed.

I hadn't schooled him that much but the first thing to strike me was his agility. He had a good method of jumping and undoubtedly knew more than me about it. He needed the Sandown race and blew up, but it was a hell of a run really when you look back on it. He was beaten four lengths and three lengths by Desert Orchid and The Argonaut. The weights? Very Promising 12st, Desert Orchid 10st 3lb, The Argonaut 10st.

My next ride on him was in the Mackeson Gold Cup at Cheltenham in November 1987. The first run had put him spot on but he was still having to carry 11st 13lb. It wasn't top weight because Fred Winter's Half Free, who had won the Mackeson the previous two years, had picked up a 5lb penalty for winning a recent race, which I remember Fred Winter being very unhappy about though I had no complaints. The two of us, with Scu on Half Free, had a titanic battle. Very Promising had a high cruising speed and though the Duke reckons that two and half miles was possibly his best trip I'm not sure. To have been upsides going to the last in Champion Chases suggests to me that he was at least as good at two miles with a good pace. I led at the third last and Scu stalked me round the bend going to the last. I was still inexperienced and I hit Very Promising several times, unnecessarily. But he battled for me, and we won. It was a thrill, my first big winner for the Duke, and made better by the fact that he had fought my corner over my riding Very Promising in the first place. I felt I owed it to him. (The celebrations didn't last long: the Duke rollocked me two races later when I put Long Engagement on the floor at the third last. It was his way of keeping my feet on the ground.)

54

In early December he went back to Cheltenham for the Glen International Gold Cup over the same trip but this time he gave me no sort of feel. He had 12st and he slipped and very nearly fell at the fourth last at the top of the hill. After that I looked after him. He still finished fourth but there were only six runners and we were a long way behind the winner Oregon Trail and Ronnie Beggan. He was such a genuine trier that he was probably still recovering from the Mackeson.

At the end of December he provided me with my first big winner in Ireland when the Duke sent him over to the Black and White Whisky Champion Chase over two and a half miles at Leopardstown. At the time Ireland had just had a huge increase in prize money for some of its top races and the Black and White was one of them. Worth £32,000, it was on a par with the King George VI Chase. We took over the lead four out and drew steadily away to beat Bobsline and Frank Berry by eight lengths. Royal Bond was third. It was quite a thrill in those days to be beating someone like Frank, who had long been a hero of mine.

The Duke got keen on these trips to Ireland then and sent him back to Leopardstown for the Vincent O'Brien (now Hennessy) Irish Gold Cup over three miles in mid-February. It was worth £50,000, a great deal of money in those days. The 1985 Gold Cup winner Forgive'N Forget was a warm favourite, Cybrandian was the other British runner, and Bobsline, Omerta, Daring Run and Royal Bond made up the majority of the home team. Very Promising ran a great race but he was no match for

Forgive'N Forget, who beat him eight lengths. We made a couple of uncharacteristic mistakes which didn't help our cause but we had all the others behind us.

It was now back to two miles for Very Promising's second Queen Mother Champion Chase in 1988 and his fourth successive visit to the Cheltenham Festival. The public get attached to the horses who pop up at the Festival year after year and you can understand why. It's not like Royal Ascot, where a horse is doing well to go three times during his career. Very Promising put up his best performance here at Cheltenham. There were eight runners, and it was a vintage Queen Mother Chase. Desert Orchid made the running and I dropped Very Promising in the middle of the field. I managed to get a run up the inner to challenge approaching the last. We pinged it and landed running but upsides Pearlyman. Scu on Pearlyman just battled us out of it up the hill and Very Promising was beaten a neck, with Dessie finishing three and a quarter lengths back in third. Townley Stone was twenty-five lengths back in fourth. It was a brilliant but extremely hard race. It was one of the best races I have ever ridden. I don't say that lightly – to say I rode one of my best races on a loser is something significant.

We turned the form round with Pearlyman at the start of the 1988–9 season at Exeter. We were getting 8lb from him in the Plymouth Gin Haldon Cup, always a popular starting point for some of the top two-milers. Both horses were having their first run of the season and I think Very Promising was probably a shade fitter. I made plenty of use of Very Promising that day and Pearlyman's cause was not helped by a bad mistake down the back. I was able to quicken clear of him away from the last to win the race. It was the same day that I was due to fly to America to ride Flatterer in the Breeders' Cup Chase and there was only one way I could get there in time. It was the first and only time I have ever flown Concorde and I have Very Promising and Flatterer's owners to thank for it.

In the 1988 Mackeson he was carrying 12st. He made a mistake four out and at the last ditch, and then faded out on me. He still finished fifth, although it was a long way behind Beau Ranger who beat Gee-A twelve lengths. He was in complete contrast to Viking Flagship, and was one of those horses who wouldn't run so well after he'd had a hard race and maybe the Plymouth Gin had taken more out of him than we thought. However, he was back in very good form in the Peterborough Chase next time out, beating Townley Stone eight lengths.

Very Promising went back to Leopardstown for another crack at the Black and White Whisky Champion Chase. Earlier that day I'd had a crashing fall on Paul Green's L'Ane Rouge and injured my neck. I took a race off but felt all right to ride Very Promising. He ran well but made a couple of mistakes – which he was increasingly doing – and finished third to Weather The Storm, a grey horse of Arthur Moore's, and Bobsline. The next day I went to Cheltenham and the first horse I rode smacked me in the face at the first fence. That really jiggered my neck and I was forced to take off the whole of January before I was allowed to ride again.

Very Promising didn't run again until mid-February, when he went to the Game Spirit Chase at Newbury, where Pearlyman was odds-on favourite. We were getting 8lb from him and coming to the last Very Promising, perhaps scenting victory, really sparked up and flew. He beat Pearlyman a very convincing seven lengths that day in bottomless ground despite a couple of mistakes. The question was, could he do the same at Cheltenham in the Queen Mother Champion Chase?

56

At Cheltenham he again ran a blinder but could only finish third this time. It was heavy old ground again but it didn't bother Pearlyman, this time partnered by John Edwards's new stable jockey Tom Morgan. Dessie and I battled it out for second and if I should ever have been strung up for hitting a horse it was on this day. It may have had something to do with frustration at having been beaten on Nick The Brief in the Sun Alliance Novice Hurdle earlier in the afternoon, and it may have been because Very Promising kept responding. None the less, it was a superb run, but we lost out to Dessie for the second spot by a length.

At only ten Very Promising saw his last run in the South Wales Mira Showers Silver Trophy at Cheltenham. Once he was beaten two out he tired very quickly. Beau Ranger won it from Chief Ironside, Bishops Yarn was third and we were fourth. After the race, Paul Green retired him, a commendable decision. He would have gone on winning but found it harder. It's nice for a horse like Very Promising, having had some really hard races, to have something less strenuous to do. A couple of mistakes had unsettled the horse, and he may have lost a bit of confidence with his jumping.

He went with The Duke from Condicote to Jackdaws's Castle. He lived until he was 25 and is buried at the yard. He was a cracking horse with a real bounce in him. On the gallops and on the racecourse he was a real competitor, he'd get stuck in. There were probably many horses with the same ability as Very Promising but he was gutsy and that was why he reached the heights that he did.

57

KRIBENSIS

5

THE BIGGEST THREE RACES FOR A JUMP JOCKEY TO WIN ARE THE GRAND NATIONAL, THE CHELTENHAM GOLD CUP AND THE CHAMPION HURDLE. Quite a few jockeys – such as John Francome, Jonjo O'Neill, Jimmy Frost, Mick Fitzgerald, Mark Dwyer, Norman Williamson and Tony McCoy – have been lucky enough to win two, but those who have won all three are few. Before Kribensis completed the set for me by winning the 1990 Champion Hurdle, the last person to win all three was Fred Winter, who won the National on Sundew and Kilmore, the Gold Cup on Saffron Tartan and Mandarin, and the Champion Hurdle on Clair Soleil, Fare Time and Eborneezer.

Kribensis was a great little racehorse. He was six when he won the Champion and now, almost white with age, he is still used as a hack at Sir Michael Stoute's yard in Newmarket, and has played a part in the training of horses like Singspiel, Pilsudski and Entrepreneur. If you watch Michael's horses working up the Limekilns early on a summer's morning, you'll more than likely see Kribensis in action, leading an awkward horse on to the gallop, off after a loose one or walking home with a bunch of horses that have just worked.

Kribensis showed what he was made of in March of his two-year-old career – or so one of Newmarket's great myths goes. A very colty individual, he had just cantered up Warren Hill with the rest of Michael's string. They had walked through a plantation at the top of the hill and come down to cross the Moulton Road on their way home. The string is usually well spread out, at least a length apart, to keep the horses, led by the colts, from kicking or biting each other. But at the road they bunched up to wait for a car to pass. Kribensis saw this as the main chance to demonstrate that, despite his age, he was more stallion than colt. He stood up on his hind legs and tried to mount the colt in front of him. He failed, but it was a close escape for the other horse's lad. He had, after all, just had his ears licked by Kribensis. When Michael Stoute asked the lad if he was all right he gave one of those immortal replies for which stable lads are famous. 'Don't worry, guv, I'm fine,' he said, 'but I don't think I'm a virgin any longer.'

It was one of the last sexual thoughts that Kribensis ever had. With some colts you put up with a certain amount of coltiness. You don't mind if they shout a bit at the fillies and it is not unknown for young colts to parade at the races with – I'm not quite sure how to say this – their tackle out. It is fairly drastic, however, if they are going to endanger lads by jumping on their stable companions. There are consequences to gelding a two-year-old: as soon as the vet's scissors go snip, it rules a horse out of the Derby, which is restricted to colts and fillies.

Kribensis was by a Derby winner, Henbit, out of a mare called Aquaria. He was bought, as a foal, at Tattersalls December sales for about 60,000 guineas by David Minton on behalf of Anthony Stroud for Sheikh Mohammed. The Sheikh enjoyed a spell of significant successes at Cheltenham at the end of the eighties and start of the nineties, including another Champion Hurdle with the James Fanshawe-trained Royal Gait. Among his other good hurdlers were Highland Bud, Thetford Forest and Duke of Monmouth, although not all of them ran in his own colours.

Kribensis was lightly raced throughout his career. He ran just ten times on the Flat in four seasons although he was more hurdler than Flat horse for the 1988 and 1989 seasons. As a two-year-old he had a couple of runs, the first at Yarmouth in August where he had a nice introduction, finishing sixth of twenty, before Michael sent him to Ayr a month later to win over a mile. At three he became a quite good although exposed middle-distance handicapper, winning his first two at Salisbury and Sandown. He was third in the King George V Handicap at Royal Ascot, sixth in the Extel Handicap at Glorious Goodwood and fifth in the Tote Festival Handicap at Ascot in September. A big offer to race in Australia was turned down by Anthony Stroud, who had it in mind for Kribensis to win the Triumph Hurdle. The horse had good hurdling appeal: he had won over a mile and a quarter on the Flat which is about the right trip for a two-mile hurdler. Michael Stoute also wanted to train a good hurdler – with winning the Champion Hurdle as his objective. The Duke was very good to me over this horse, though, and always made sure I was available to ride him.

The horse was Steve Smith Eccles's ride to start with. Steve was just about the only jump jockey based in Newmarket and he had a virtual monopoly on all National Hunt rides in the town – there weren't a huge number of them anyway. Kribensis's jumping was a bit scratchy to start with when he schooled on the Links at Newmarket, but he soon got the hang of things. Eccy rode him first time out over hurdles at Doncaster towards the end of January. He beat Eskimo Mite a neck and was not particularly impressive once he had got to the front approaching the last. I remember Michael had bought some new protective boots for the horse which were lined with sheepskin and looked furry. After the race John Francome, who was working for Channel Four, commented that the horse might be quite impressive when he got his jumping together and 'when Michael Stoute stops weight training with him', a reference to the boots. He never wore them again.

I got the ride then, quite why I'm not sure. I think the Duke, who often had Michael and Anthony Stroud to stay for Cheltenham, may have put me in for it. Eccy was still riding for Nicky Henderson at the time and they may have foreseen a clash with Surf Board, whom Nicky was also aiming at the Triumph. I always liked riding horses that Eccy had schooled because he taught them well. James Fanshawe, who had point-to-pointed and hunted a lot, was Michael's assistant and did a lot of the groundwork with Kribensis. I also have huge respect for Stoutey and he remains one of the best trainers I have ever ridden for. He is an exceptional judge of a horse's well-being and was always right with his predictions about how a horse would run.

I rode him for the first time at Huntingdon. We won nicely enough that day, and then went straight to the Triumph Hurdle. It is a horrible race to ride in (see Highland Bud in Chapter 7) but the horse made it easy for me. We took it up going to the last and he stayed on really well up the hill to beat Wahiba three lengths with Chatam and South Parade in third and fourth respectively. (It was the start of one of the best racing days of my life: I went on to win the Gold Cup later that afternoon with Charter Party.) Kribensis wasn't a big horse and was not the greatest jumper. He used to give the odd one too much height and wasn't the scopiest horse I've ever ridden but that might be a bit critical – you don't win Champion Hurdles, or

Triumph Hurdles for that matter, if you can't jump. The following month Michael ran Kribensis in the Group Three Gordon Richards Stakes at Sandown on Whitbread day. He finished last of five, ridden by Walter Swinburn, and it seemed, as is so often the case, that jumping hurdles had blunted his speed. Kribensis was turned out for the summer and brought back with a campaign aimed at winning the 1989 Champion Hurdle. His first run was in the Flavel Leisure Hurdle for four-year-olds at Newbury in October. He jumped impeccably this day and won very impressively by twelve lengths from Lyphento and South Parade. He went back there for the Gerry Feilden in November on Hennessy day. He got in a bit close to the second hurdle down the back and made a mistake but I got a lead to the last and then quickened him up to beat Calapaez by an easy five lengths. In the Top Rank Christmas Hurdle I was again able to ride a very straightforward race on him, where I took it up at the second last and he ran on really well, beating Floyd by a couple of lengths. I got some criticism for being too harsh on him with my stick.

Now unbeaten in six outings over hurdles, Kribensis not surprisingly went to Cheltenham a warm favourite for the Champion Hurdle despite the presence in the field of Celtic Shot and Celtic Chief, Floyd, Mole Board and Grey Salute. In the preceding race I won the Arkle on Waterloo Boy. In this race I rode Kribensis handy as usual but I don't think it was the greatest race I ever rode. Condor Pan kicked on at the top of the hill with Tommy Carmody. Kribensis jumped well and I was on the heels of the leaders. Hywel Davies was upsides me on Mole Board and I hit the front – briefly – turning in towards the last flight. I think perhaps I kicked a little too soon. I exposed myself to everyone who was queuing up behind me. Richard Guest, meanwhile, had ridden a very patient race on Beech Road and brought him wide up the straight with a very well-timed challenge to beat Celtic Chief (whom I had ridden the year before. I'd had the option of riding him but I stuck with Kribensis after Celtic Chief had run badly when he wasn't well at Sandown. It had been a difficult decision.). I eased Kribensis up once he had been passed and was out of the money. He finished seventh, beaten about eleven lengths.

Why did he get beaten? Well five-year-olds are at a big disadvantage in the Champion Hurdle – only two, Night Nurse and See You Then, have won it in the last thirty years. Over fences five-year-olds get a weight allowance but not over hurdles. They just aren't quite strong enough at that age to take on tougher, maturer more developed horses. The ground was also on

the dead side. A year on and he might have coped with it, but not then. Nevertheless it was a good season for the horse and he had a couple more runs on the Flat, without success, before being turned out at Dalham Hall Stud for the summer.

For the 1989–90 season he started off in the Fighting Fifth at Newcastle. Mark Dwyer rode him because I had to go to Newbury to ride Brown Windsor in the Hennessy (second to Ghofar). Kribensis beat Jinxy Jack and put up a good performance in doing so. He then went to the Christmas Hurdle where I had a great duel with Graham McCourt, who was riding Osric, a decent hurdler trained by Mick Ryan. We were hard at it from the last bend and for a while at the second last I thought Graham had me beat. By this stage in his career Graham had become as strong a finisher as there was. He went past me, I went past him, he came back at me and passed me, and we both pinged the last. Kribensis really battled for me that day. In all the races he'd won up until then he had been too superior to the opposition to have to struggle, and I had wondered what he'd do when faced with a fight. That day I knew he was gutsy as well as classy.

The previous year he had gone straight from Christmas Hurdle to Champion Hurdle, which may have put him at a disadvantage. This time Michael decided to tune him up with a run in the Kingwell Hurdle at Wincanton. He did it very well, jumped very big at the last, and beat Island Set a comfortable four lengths. It is always a good sign if a hurdler gives the last flight a lot of height. It shows they still have a lot left in the tank. Cruising Altitude was quite fancied for the Champion that year, yet at Wincanton we had him nine lengths behind us on level weights. See You Then, whom Nicky Henderson wanted for one more tilt at the Champion, fell at the second last when beaten.

I knew Kribensis was at his peak. He was a lot stronger than he had been a year before, he hadn't had a hard campaign and he was spot on after Wincanton. The ground was much faster than it had been the previous year. I also knew now that if it came to it – and it usually does in a Champion Hurdle – he would fight for me. Beech Road was favourite and his stable companion Morley Street was in the field along with horses such as Nomadic Way, Deep Sensation and the three times Champion Hurdle winner See You Then. Again Kribensis made it very straightforward for me. Nomadic Way wanted more of a test of stamina than two miles and Sudden Victory, also trained by Barry Hills, made it a blistering gallop for him. When Sudden Victory ran out of puff at the fifth, Peter Scudamore sent Nomadic

Way on. I was behind early and made steady progress on the inside following Scu. I was upsides at the last and, like he had at Wincanton, Kribensis almost ballooned it. When he did that I knew he had plenty left. He stayed on very strongly up the hill. Nomadic Way was three lengths away in second and Past Glories finished just behind him in third. Any winner at Cheltenham gives you a buzz but the Champion Hurdle is something special.

In the race Kribensis bruised a heel and he was given the summer off at Dalham Hall Stud. When they brought him back in August they discovered that he had a bleeding problem. One day he bled so badly through his nose after a piece of work that they feared he might bleed to death. He was given the whole season off and from there on his racing career was beset with ailments. He was sent to Sheikh Mohammed's Kildangan Stud in Ireland for a complete break but when he went back into training with Michael in June he still had a bleeding problem, albeit a controllable one. A vet specializing in testicular problems also had a look at him because Michael felt he wasn't letting himself go or striding out properly. The vet came to the conclusion that scar tissue around his gelding operation might be worrying him.

I went up to school him after Christmas at the start of 1992. I never particularly liked schooling round the Links at Newmarket because the hurdles were so far apart that the horses could get up tremendous speed between them. One day a former racehorse called No Bombs – whose ten minutes of fame came when he was disqualified from a race for eating a Mars Bar – wiped out over one of the hurdles and the poor lad who'd been riding him practically had to be dug out of the ground.

The long-awaited reappearance of Kribensis was at Haydock in February. He finished second to Bank View. Michael was training him with extreme care, not pushing him too hard. He ran well at Haydock but blew up on me in the closing stages. The important thing was that he hadn't burst a blood vessel. I thought he had every chance in the 1992 Champion Hurdle. It was won by Sheikh Mohammed's other runner Royal Gait. Kribensis hit the third hurdle hard and was never really travelling after that. He faded badly from the third last and finished last. Where my horse had hit the hurdle it was as if someone had taken a knife to his hind leg and sliced through to the bone. The skin sank to his ankle like a loose stocking. It was horrific, an extremely unlucky cut. It took until August to heal completely.

In August he went to Cliff Lines near Newmarket to be prepared to go back to Michael's yard just before a race. If they were satisfied with him after one run, they would have one final crack at the Champion Hurdle. Declan Murphy rode him in the Bula Hurdle where he finished fifth of six behind Halkopous, Granville Again and Morley Street. He then got well beaten by Mighty Mogul in the Christmas Hurdle, again ridden by Declan, and I rode him for the last time in the Kingwell at Wincanton. He was second, beaten five lengths by Valfinet, which wasn't bad. I thought he'd run a cracking race but he wasn't quite firing the way he used to. He was also a bit mulish at the start and reluctant to line up. I think he was trying to tell us that he'd done enough by now and that that cut had made him a little bit timid.

Declan rode him in the Champion because I was on Flown. Kribensis was never really dangerous this time and finished eleventh. He was honourably retired to the hunting field in Leicestershire where he was looked after by Joey and Emma Newton. One day he would be brilliant and the next he wouldn't go through a puddle. He particularly didn't like the mid-winter mud that you get out hunting. Eventually he was sent back to Michael's in Newmarket as a hack and he is still there today, thoroughly enjoying life. I know that Michael Stoute, despite winning most of the world's greatest races on the Flat at one time or another, still rates winning the 1990 Champion Hurdle as one of his greatest achievements. I know that the lads who were involved in the yard during Kribensis's years certainly regard that win as one of the trainer's high points. For my part, I am proud to have been associated with such a memorable victory.

65

WATERLOO BOY

ATERLOO BOY WAS A FAVOURITE HERO OF MINE. IF EVER A HORSE DESERVED A LONG AND HAPPY RETIREMENT, IT WAS HIM. He was not long into retirement and slipping into Very Promising's role as a lead horse at Jackdaw's Castle when, after David Nicholson's open day in 1996, he was found in his stable with a broken leg. Having jumped several thousand obstacles at home, and on the racecourse where he had won seventeen races, it was a sad end. There was no option but to put him down.

The start of his story is much happier. Late in 1984 David Nicholson had an order from Bicester-based owner Michael Deeley to buy two yearlings to go jumping eventually, total price not to exceed 10,000 guineas. The Duke passed on the order to Anthony Stroud, then a bloodstock agent shortly to become racing manager to Sheikh Mohammed's Darley Stud Management empire in Newmarket. The instruction was that Anthony did not buy anything by Green Shoon, a stallion the Duke did not like.

Anthony returned from the Ballsbridge Sales in November having filled the order which met most, but not all, of the requirements. He returned with Waterloo Boy, Another Coral, 2,000 guineas change and a chastisement. The Duke looked at Another Coral and asked, 'Why did you buy a Green Shoon when I told you not to?' He looked at Waterloo Boy. 'And why have you a Deep Run out of a sprinting mare?' But between them, they went on to win over £600,000 in prize money. 'The only other horse I have bought so cheaply which has been so successful was Pennekamp,' says Anthony. 'I bought him for $40,000 and he was worth about $8m when he retired.'

At the start it appeared that Another Coral would be the better of the pair. As it transpired, Waterloo Boy was consistently the better horse though Another Coral had his successes, most notably in the Mackeson and Tripleprint Gold Cups at Cheltenham. Besides leaving his name in the history books alongside most decent two-mile chases (with the exception of the Queen Mother Champion Chase), Waterloo Boy left his mark on steeplechasing via the handicapping system. The Duke has always, if he has the right material, been keen to pitch his novice chasers against handicappers first time out. When he did it with Long Engagement and Waterloo Boy, a chasing debutant was automatically awarded a rating 14lb lower than its hurdling rating. This was changed to 7lb, in large part due to the success of debutant chaser Waterloo Boy in a handicap chase at Worcester. What, perhaps, made Waterloo Boy so special was that although he was not the fastest thing on four legs he became a very quick crosser of an obstacle and many a time his jumping – particularly at the third last in his Arkle at Cheltenham – got him races he shouldn't have won. Not many horses have contested four consecutive two-mile Champion Chases and finished placed in three of them.

Laid-back at home, Waterloo Boy was a joy for the Duke to train and a joy for the lads to look after. One season he suffered a bit from corns but once they knew the corns might reappear they were able to control them. He was also hobdayed before the 1991–2 season. This operation to help keep a horse's airways clear is not always a success, but in Waterloo Boy's case it clearly helped him to continue racing at the highest level.

When the four-year-old Waterloo Boy went to Ludlow in 1987 for his first run in a National Hunt Flat race, he hadn't shown much at home. He was stocky, not tall but quite round and tubby. He didn't look the athletic horse he was. The Duke had another runner in the race which all the lads fancied: Duke's Whistle ridden by conditional jockey Dan Jones. Thinking Waterloo Boy was nothing special, the Duke put up Amanda McDowell, an amateur woman jockey, on him. Suddenly, about half a mile out, he picked up and flew. He just failed to catch the winner, Bullet Train, one of Jenny Pitman's bumper specials, by a fast-diminishing head.

As with many classy horses I've ridden, Waterloo Boy's hurdling career began at Chepstow in December 1987, but he got no further than the first flight where he blundered badly and unseated Jimmy Frost. I'd done a fair bit of schooling on him and he had jumped well in the Duke's old jumping paddock at Condicote – he'd jumped tree trunks and tiger traps, you name it. It was one of the best schooling grounds in the country. Jimmy had asked me what he was like and, of course, I'd told him Waterloo Boy was a brilliant jumper, so the unseating came as a bit of a surprise. After that, Waterloo Boy was thought not yet good enough to get the first-jockey treatment. At Towcester I rode another of the Duke's, a horse called Emrys which finished a place in front of Waterloo Boy in third. At Wincanton Waterloo Boy was second. My first ride on him in public came at Taunton at the end of January 1988 on heavy ground. He was my first ride back since a serious neck injury and I made most of the running until quite a good mare of David Elsworth's called Out Of Range passed me after the last and crossed me up the run-in. I objected to Colin Brown who was riding the winner for having taken my ground. My objection was overruled. At least Waterloo Boy was beginning to fulfil the promise shown at that first bumper.

His first and only win over hurdles came at Newbury where he made all. You have to be tough to make all the running on that track. He quickened up nicely three out to beat Grogan half a length. He gave me a good ride but I think I was pretty hard on him. Out Of Range, who'd beaten me the previous time, finished well behind us so you could see the progress Waterloo Boy was making. He ran a couple more times over hurdles without any great distinction but he'd had a busy season.

The Duke, as was his policy, found a pretty average handicap chase – at Worcester – to run his novice chaser in. Waterloo Boy got a stone less than he would have done in a handicap hurdle. I planned to give him a good school round and thought I could win the race at any time. I left it a bit late and only just made it. I'd have been in trouble if I hadn't won. Next time out he won a novices' handicap at Bangor under Jamie Osborne (I had to go to Sandown to ride Bigsun) but I was back on him for his third win out of three in a handicap chase at Towcester. He was still very well-handicapped and won comfortably.

In January 1989 he went to Cheltenham for the Steel Plate And Sections Young Chasers Novice Chase with just two opponents, Dictalino and Beech Road. The race proved a watershed in the career of Beech Road. I made the running on Waterloo Boy and he quickened up well going to the last where I heard Beech Road right on my heels. Beech Road was always quite flat over his fences, even though he won a couple of decent chases. I pinged the last and all I saw was Beech Road's head coming level with me. I put my head down and rode for my life up the hill. When I looked round I saw Beech Road lying motionless in a heap at the last. They put up the dreaded green

69

screens around him. But he was just badly winded and eventually got up. He returned to hurdles after that and went on to win that season's Champion Hurdle. That race proved to me that Waterloo Boy was gutsy if it got scrappy. Because of that he went on to have some very hard races.

He kept his unbeaten record as a novice by beating Positive at Kempton later that January, and suddenly, having beaten moderate handicappers of an advantageous handicap mark, he began to look like one of the smarter two-mile novices of the season.

His first defeat over fences came at the hands of Sabin Du Loir at Ascot in February. I was riding with Cheltenham in mind and didn't want to give him a hard race. When Peter Scudamore set off at a blazing gallop on Sabin Du Loir I didn't chase him. I never got to him on the quick ground and he beat me twenty lengths. I was criticized for the way I rode Waterloo Boy that day, but Sabin Du Loir was spot on and I couldn't have beaten him whatever I'd done.

So we went to Cheltenham for the Arkle. Sabin Du Loir's slaughter of Waterloo Boy was fresh in people's minds but racing in the Arkle is a completely different experience. Sabin Du Loir was the 5–4 favourite while we were pretty much unconsidered at 20–1. I thought I'd finish close and that he would run on well but I wasn't in any way confident. How could I be with twenty lengths to make up on Sabin Du Loir? The ground was a bit softer though, and Waterloo Boy didn't mind any ground. This time I took on Sabin Du Loir from the outset. I was always handy, led here and there, and Waterloo Boy was putting in some huge leaps. It was a duel with Sabin Du Loir. Scu led me into the straight and I thought we were going to get beaten but Waterloo Boy fought and battled all the way up the hill to beat Southern Minstrel, who had run on strongly from behind, by half a length, with Sabin Du Loir rallying again to finish a length away in third. It was a great result and capped a wonderful first season's chasing for Waterloo Boy. He'd defied everyone's predictions by becoming the top novice two-miler.

At the start of the 1989–90 season he was beaten first time out at Worcester, obviously in need of the race. Then Jamie Osborne rode him again at Chepstow in December because I was riding Desert Orchid at Sandown the same day. This time he beat the former Champion Hurdler Celtic Shot, although it must be said that Celtic Shot was never quite as good over fences as he was over hurdles. For his third run he went to Ireland. The Duke was keen to win the Black And White Whisky Champion

Chase at Leopardstown, a race he'd won with Very Promising a few years earlier. We all travelled over on the horse flight. The little horse hated flying; as soon as we went to take off, he started cowering. The only person on that flight who hated flying more than Waterloo Boy was the Duke himself.

It proved to be an eventful day. I was not in the best of moods when I managed to get Waterloo Boy beat although, in fairness, I think it was a good effort to go down by less than a length to Maid of Money. There's a rail at Leopardstown which runs from the last fence until about 50 yards before the line. When Waterloo Boy, an intelligent horse, came to the end of the rail I think he thought the race was over and Maid of Money managed to get her head in front close to the line. I also felt that, though he had won over two and a half miles before, he didn't really get the trip in Ireland.

In the race after the Black and White I picked up a four-day ban from the stewards for 'stopping' a horse of Mick O'Toole's called Fourth of July. Mick had said go out there and enjoy yourself, intimating that I wasn't to have too hard a race. So I went out minding my own business and still a bit aggrieved that Waterloo Boy had been beaten. The worst thing if you are not – how shall I say this? – at your busiest, is when the rest of the field go off flat out. I was still a bit inexperienced at the time, and suddenly I found the whole field coming back to me, most of them out on their feet. Fourth Of July saw this too, picked up the bridle and started to run. In the end I was beaten only three lengths. From the last it was certainly not one of R. Dunwoody's strongest finishes but I had taken the opinion that I would rather be beaten three lengths than an even more embarrassing half or three-quarters. Misjudgements had been made, and I rightly had to pay the penalty.

At the end of January Waterloo Boy ran very flatly in the Arlington Premier Series Chase final over two and a half miles at Cheltenham. He didn't jump well and again I felt that two and a half miles was beyond the limit of his stamina. Since the journey and hard race in Ireland may have taken their toll, the Duke gave him a rest from racing, then freshened him up and brought him back for the Queen Mother Champion Chase at Cheltenham.

The Champion Chase of 1990 was one of the best races I have ever ridden in. Barnbrook Again, who had won the race the previous year under the then retired Simon Sherwood, was ridden by my great friend and rival from our Tim Forster days, Hywel Davies. He was the 11–10 favourite, and the rest of the field included Sabin Du Loir, Pearlyman, another previous winner, Feroda and Impertain from Ireland, the popular Panto Prince from the West Country and the idiosyncratic front-runner Private Views.

The race was run at a very fast gallop. Barnbrook Again was held up by Hywel and I sat in the middle with Waterloo Boy. Sabin Du Loir, who was never quite the horse at Cheltenham that he was anywhere else, took over from Private Views after the fourth and by the third last it was developing into a three-horse race. Sabin Du Loir was just about in front with Barnbrook Again and Waterloo Boy breathing down his neck. Even at such a strong pace both horses picked up off the bend and winged the last, galloping all the way to the line. It was nip and tuck all the way but Barnbrook Again proved just the stronger and beat us half a length with Sabin Du Loir in third. You can tell when you've ridden in a good race, and though he was beaten, it had been Waterloo Boy's greatest. Barnbrook Again was a brilliant horse on his day. In any other year a performance like that would have won Waterloo Boy the race.

It didn't end there, however. Hywel had drifted right-handed across me slightly up the run-in and there was a lengthy stewards' inquiry. I think on the Flat he'd have lost it. Waterloo Boy hadn't been intimidated or hampered but it had taken us off a true line. It didn't look that bad but I made the point that I thought it had cost me at least the distance that I was beaten (half a length). I tried to tell the truth – with a little elaboration! The inquiry went on for quite a while when Hywel, who could talk for Wales, got into full flow. Outside the Queen Mother was waiting to present the prize. In the end they said the placings remained unaltered – Barnbrook Again was the best horse on the day.

72

Later in the afternoon the racecourse must have had a few calls from BBC viewers who weren't happy with our use of the sticks. We went back into the stewards' room at the end of the day and were each given two-day bans, although the stewards hadn't seemed too bothered about it earlier. I wanted to appeal. The Duke was backing me but Michael Caulfield, secretary of the Jockeys Association, said I could only appeal if Hywel did as well. It seems that someone told Hywel that if a different set of stewards (the Disciplinary Committee) had a look at the film they might take the race off him. I think this was highly unlikely but he refused to appeal so I couldn't either.

It brought the whole whip debate to a bit of a head. I felt that my actions had done Waterloo Boy no harm. I was hitting him in rhythm and not too hard, and he was responding, as was Barnbrook Again. Both horses quickened up all the way up the hill. We weren't flogging tired horses: one ill-advised slap with the whip on a tired horse only does damage.

After a race like that you're both disappointed and exhilarated. Hywel and I both thought we'd ridden the race of our lives in one of the great chases of my generation. First we were punished for the whip and then John Hislop wrote a letter to the trade press criticizing us both, me for not making more of a meal of Hywel's coming across me, and Hywel for carrying his stick in the wrong hand.

Waterloo Boy ran once more that season, in the Captain Morgan Aintree Handicap Chase. He had a lot of weight, like so many horses who go to Aintree after Cheltenham, and could not improve on that performance. He finished a good fourth. Then, as he did every summer, he and Another Coral went home to Deeley's Farm near Bicester for his summer break.

During the 1990–91 season, which began with Waterloo Boy unseating Jamie Osborne in the Plymouth Gin, I felt he was being hindered by his wind problem. The Duke gave Jamie a bit of a reprimand for that performance and from then on wouldn't let me off Waterloo Boy to ride Desert Orchid when they clashed. At Haydock in the soft he was just beaten by Katabatic – giving 24lb to the winner. It wasn't until the Castleford Chase at Wetherby after Christmas that Waterloo Boy won again, this time reversing the form with Young Snugfit who'd beaten him in the Tingle Creek.

73

His next run was in his second Champion Chase. He was evens favourite and I thought we had a great chance. It didn't look a vintage Queen Mother Chase and, though he was improving, he still had a great deal in hand over Katabatic – or so we thought – on the Haydock run. But Waterloo Boy made a couple of mistakes, and Katabatic came to take it up and win in great style. I have no real excuses in the way the race was run and was, naturally, delighted for Simon McNeill, whose biggest winner this was.

This was the first race in which Waterloo Boy had made a real noise with his breathing all the way round. This is usually to do with partial paralysis of the working parts of the windpipe. After finishing in the frame at Aintree (third to Blazing Walker), he went to the South Wales Mira Showers Chase at Cheltenham in April. There were four runners, Pegwell Bay, Norton's Coin, myself and an outsider called Aston Express. No one wanted to make the running and we crawled. The Duke's instructions were simple. Whatever I did I was not to make the running and I was to be the last to make a challenge. It was over two and a half miles and we knew Waterloo

Boy had this wind problem now so we were looking for one short, sharp sprint with the idea that he would beat the others for foot. It was the closest I've come to a slow bicycle race on horses until we turned in. Then we went flat out. In countless races I've never travelled so fast up the hill at Cheltenham. We didn't have time even to pull our sticks through before we were at the line. Graham McCourt just threw the reins at Norton's Coin (whose wind could also be a problem) and he beat me a head. Though the race was run twenty seconds over standard, everyone, including Graham and myself who both wore huge grins, was buzzing about the finish afterwards. It lit up that Cheltenham meeting, which often has an end-of-season feel about it.

It was after that that Waterloo Boy was hobdayed, and then turned out for his summer holidays. The only proof of the success of the operation is when you run the horse the following season. He needed his first race of the 1991–2 season at Exeter, but at Sandown in the Tingle Creek proved that it had been an unqualified success when he beat Young Snugfit three-quarters of a length in a tremendous duel up the Sandown hill. He was still making a bit of a noise but he battled really well. The Castleford at Wetherby was becoming a standing order and after that he went for the Victor Chandler Handicap Chase at Ascot. We had 11st 1olb, and Young Snugfit 11st 2lb, and I think this was one of Waterloo Boy's best handicap performances. Young Snugfit made the running and I joined him at the last. Waterloo Boy went away from him really well to beat him two lengths. The rest were out of sight. He then won the Game Spirit on the same day that I won the Arlington Final on Remittance Man. The Duke, who could see a clash coming up in the Queen Mother Chase, said there and then that I would ride Waterloo Boy in it.

The Queen Mother Chase was billed as a two-horse race (see Chapter 10, Remittance Man): Man versus Boy. I knew the only way to beat Remittance Man was to get him into a drawn-out slog but he got to me easily at the last and trying to beat him probably cost Waterloo Boy second place. His wind didn't sound great that day either and Katabatic passed us up the hill for second. Nevertheless he had now finished placed in three Champion Chases, a highly creditable record.

The 1992–3 season saw him start off with a victory in the Plymouth Gin Haldon Chase. Then in the Tingle Creek he beat Deep Sensation, who was getting two and a half stone off him. We made most of the running that day and I was hard pressed from the Pond fence but he battled on gamely to

win by two and a half lengths. He didn't win the Castleford this year but finished second in it to Katabatic, who was still very useful on his day. We beat him next time out in the Game Spirit, before going back to Cheltenham for his fourth and last Champion Chase. It was won by Deep Sensation – which shows what a good performance Waterloo Boy had put up in the Tingle Creek – but he ran no sort of race in the Champion Chase even though he'd been second favourite. He ran flat and finished tailed off. He had broken a blood vessel which accounted for the disappointment. He did the same in the Mumm Melling Chase at Aintree in which I had to pull him up, and he was roughed off for the season. It was disappointing. It looked like a signal that Waterloo Boy, an old friend to everyone, was running out of miles on the clock. Some horses get over breaking blood vessels, others never do.

The following season I was with Martin Pipe and Adrian Maguire took over on Waterloo Boy. He pulled up first time out, showed more positive signs in the Tingle Creek when third to Sybillin and Deep Sensation, but disappointed again in the Victor Chandler, that season run at Warwick, which I won on Viking Flagship. Adrian was out of action when he went to Cheltenham for the last time at the end of January, so I was on board for the Lobb Partnership Hall of Fame Chase. We knew he wasn't as good as he used to be, that he could bleed and had wind problems, so I settled him in behind early. It was the same day that I rode four winners, including my 1,000th on Flakey Dove. He travelled well this day and led at the third last, battling gamely to beat Richville by a head. We had 12st, he had 10st 2lb. Though the company wasn't as good as it had been in the past, it was vintage, battling Waterloo Boy.

His last race was in the Racing in Wessex Chase at Wincanton on 10 February 1994. Aged eleven, he was just not the force of old. He was still having to give weight away all round, and he ran well into the straight but had no response when Garrison Savannah and Ryde Again, who were both old warriors themselves by then, came past him. The Duke and Michael Deeley sensibly decided to lower the curtain on a great career. One of the most popular horses of his generation, and a great mate of mine, was retired. Sadly, 18 months into his retirement, he broke his leg in his box and was put down.

HIGHLAND BUD AND
FLATTERER

D URING MY CAREER I HAD THE PLEASURE OF RIDING SOME OF THE
BEST HURDLERS OF THEIR GENERATION IN AMERICA. It came
about through Marigold Coke, who was secretary to Captain Tim
Forster for most of the time that he trained at Letcombe Bassett. She
spent a month of her annual summer holidays visiting friends in and
around Maryland in America and when Jonathan Sheppard, one of the
leading jumping trainers out there, wanted someone who could do
10st 2lb – his regular jockey Jerry Fishback could not do the weight – on
Flatterer in the French Champion Hurdle at Auteuil in June 1986, it was
Marigold who put me in for the ride. It was the start of a good friendship
with Jonathan and, over the years, I had some great trips to America to
ride for him.

In America hurdlers are known, strangely enough, as 'steeplechasers',
and Flatterer was one of American jumping's true greats. He was on a par
with Neji, a horse of similar ability in the sixties. He is still the only horse
ever to have been voted Champion Steeplechaser in America four years in
succession, he won the Colonial Cup (until the short-lived Breeders' Cup
Chase series the biggest chase in America) four times, and his weight-
carrying record for winning a stakes race (12st 8lb) still stands. 'I felt like a
butcher putting the weight cloth on him that day,' recalls Jonathan. At the
point of his retirement he was the leading prize-money winner. He won
everything worth winning on his own side of the Atlantic and his two forays
into Europe resulted in him finishing second in both the British and the
French Champion Hurdles. It was in 1987 that Jonathan brought him over to

Cheltenham for the Champion Hurdle and he came to the British racing public's attention when he narrowly failed to prevent See You Then winning his third title in a row.

He was an amazing horse. Jonathan had bred and trained not only his dam, Horizontal, but his sire, Mo Bay. As is so often the case, the marriage of the two horses was more accident than planned. Jonathan had been asked to help find half a dozen cheapish mares to send to Malaysia. The deal fell through but at the time he and Bill Pape were starting a low-budget breeding programme in which they planned to buy some broodmares and race the offspring. Believing that Horizontal, one of the mares originally destined for Malaysia, looked quite good value, Jonathan purchased her for his and Bill's own small collection of mares.

He had trained Mo Bay with great success for George Strawbridge and when the horse was retired to stud Jonathan was given two lifetime breeding rights to the stallion. He sent Horizontal to him and the result of this fortuitous marriage was the bay Flatterer, born in 1979. He didn't run aged two but won at Keystone on his third outing as a three-year-old. In twenty-eight runs on the Flat – later in his career they were used as prep races for big jump races – he won eight and was placed a further eight times at places ranging from Saratoga to Aqueduct and Belmont Park.

Early in his jumping career he was a little flighty and headstrong. He carried his head quite high and after John Francome rode him in a Colonial Cup prep race he requested that Jonathan put a neck strap on Flatterer for the big race – which they duly won. John felt he could give him his head over an obstacle a bit more if he could just put a finger in the neck strap. Later in his career, certainly by the time I came to ride him, he was quite a gentleman to ride.

Tim Thomson Jones also won a couple of races on him, including a $100,000 chase, but I got the call-up for the French Champion Hurdle after I'd won the National on West Tip in 1986. It was a year before he came over for Cheltenham. I'd been to France to ride Solar Cloud at Auteuil for the Duke a week before so I wasn't a total stranger to the place and I went to stay with Flatterer's connections in Chantilly. In America the ground is usually firm or even faster which was the going preferred by Flatterer – he would happily have raced up a road! When we walked the course our hearts sank because as usual they had produced a very well-watered course! In America they call it soft if a horse makes a print on the ground. At Auteuil the horses were up to the fetlocks. Not only was the ground soggy but it was grassless and worn out on the inside. The first thing Bill Pape said was: 'I've brought this horse all the way from America, now I'm going home.' Jonathan was a lot keener to run but he was also worried about the ground.

Flatterer was a lovely horse to sit on. He would have made a top-class British steeplechaser. There were seven runners in the race, which is run over three miles and a furlong. Most interest centred around Dawn Run, that year's Gold Cup heroine. Gaye Brief, who had won the Champion Hurdle in 1983 and finished second to See You Then in that year's Champion Hurdle, was also in the race as well as a couple of local horses, Le Rheusois and Gacko, who went on to win a Breeders' Cup Chase the following year.

The first disaster of the day befell Peter Scudamore on Gaye Brief. In France, as they do in most of Europe, you jump a practice hurdle on the way to the start and Scu got buried at it by Gaye Brief. He was covered from top to bottom in sand; Gaye Brief had it in his ears and didn't look very happy. Eventually we got started and at the first past the huge grandstands, at the start of the second circuit, Scu got buried again. Down the back I was travelling well despite the ground. I heard a crash close behind me and when I had a look across I could see Dawn Run falling but it did not look too horrific. Flatterer, however, was running a blinder and was upsides at the last but the ground just got the better of him in the run to the line and he finished a very creditable second, beaten five lengths, to Le Rheusois who came up the favoured stands rail. Gacko was two lengths away in third. He was keen enough so that you knew he was there on the end of the reins but not so strong that he was burning himself out. I thought it was a great performance, considering it was over three miles. He came back to finish second in our Champion Hurdle the following year over two miles – he must have been extremely versatile. Unlike the French and British horses, he was also on the wrong end of a transatlantic journey.

The tragedy of the race was Dawn Run. In her fall she broke her neck. She was a real racing heroine in Ireland and in Britain, the only horse to have won a Champion Hurdle and Gold Cup; owned by a slightly eccentric old lady called Charmian Hill, who used to ride the mare herself in bumpers, and trained by Paddy Mullins. Her fall hadn't looked bad from my vantage point and I was shocked by the news when we came in. I was sure she'd have got up and completed the course loose. As that was sinking in,

Flatterer began to get very dehydrated after his efforts – it had been a very hot day – and the vet had to be called out to stabilize him.

The following year, 1987, Flatterer came over for the Champion Hurdle in which Jerry Fishback, who partnered him through most of his career, rode him. He was beaten a length and a half by Steve Smith Eccles and See You Then. Flatterer was catching the winner all the way up the hill from the last but he had lost his place mid-race and I think if they could have planned the race again they would have ridden Flatterer closer to the pace. As it was if he had really pinged the last – instead of popping it – he might have caught See You Then, whose stride was shortening near the line. It was, nevertheless, a hell of a performance to have come from America and Jonathan was quite rightly proud of the horse. He beat Barnbrook Again a length. I was fifth on Stepaside Lord for the Duke.

I rode Flatterer once more in his last race: the Breeders' Cup Chase at Fair Hill. He'd won his fourth Colonial Cup and the Iroquois the season before but by then he was nine and his connections were worried about running him in the Breeders' Cup Chase because of his legs. I had been riding at Exeter the day before and the only way to get to Fair Hill in time was to fly Concorde to New York and take the owner's private jet down. In the race Flatterer was travelling really well down the back when he broke down badly. He was a brave old sod and didn't want to pull up so I steered him on to the inside of the track round the obstacles. He still didn't want to stop racing even when I got to the far end of the back straight. As I had taken a bit of a shortcut I met the field as they were going into the bend and cannoned into about three of them. We were in the home straight before I finally managed to stop him! A horse who has broken down badly has to be pretty courageous to want to go on racing like that and I know John Francome rated him as one of the best he ever rode.

80

Flatterer was retired to a place near Jonathan's yard in Unionville where he competed at intermediate level at dressage. Obviously a horse who has spent most of his life racing is never going to make it to the top in an event as technical as dressage but he enjoyed himself and was rarely out of the ribbons in local low-key dressage competitions.

The other very good horse which I rode for Jonathan was Highland Bud. He was bred in Kentucky, America, by Northern Baby out of a mare called Fleur d'Or. As a foal he was bought by Sheikh Mohammed and his advisers for $125,000 and sent to be trained by John Oxx in Ireland. There he was placed in both outings as a two-year-old before, the following year, he won his first three races, including the Ulster Derby at Down Royal when sheep on the neighbouring farm escaped on to the course and delayed the start of the race. He was also third in the Ulster St Leger.

It was about this time that Sheikh Mohammed, following on from Kribensis's success in the Champion Hurdle, was keeping one or two half decent Flat horses in training as hurdlers – Champion Hurdler Royal Gait was another. I think in Highland Bud's case it was probably so that he could prove himself a decent juvenile hurdler and then be sold on at the end of the season – which is exactly what happened.

He came over to the Duke's in the autumn of his three-year-old career in 1988 and immediately started to school well. He took his reputation with him to Newbury for his first run over hurdles on 30 December that year and won very comfortably by ten lengths. He followed that with another comfortable win at Cheltenham a month later and didn't run again until we went to the Triumph Hurdle at the Cheltenham Festival. Enemy Action and Nomadic Way were favourites and we were rated 8–1. It was the day Desert Orchid won the Gold Cup and they had to pump water off the course; it was desperate going. The Triumph is the first race on Gold Cup day and is not a nice race to ride in. There were twenty-seven runners: a lot of horses, especially when they are juveniles, most of whom are used to running on the Flat and run around a hurdle when they see it blocking their path. When I won the race on Paddy's Return in 1996, it was one of those days when I felt like retiring on the spot. Four fell at the first, two at the second. It's a cavalry charge. Everyone goes a great gallop. There is always traffic going up the hill while those that are cooked start coming back and those at the rear start to improve. You end up jumping into the heels of the horse in front.

81

Despite the ground Highland Bud, who was a little horse at only 15hh 3in, gave me a great ride. He travelled well, splashing through the water lying on the track like he'd been doing it all his life. Turning in towards the last we galloped through a huge puddle which wiped out my vision – my goggles became useless. Don Valentino and Mark Pitman led away from the last but Ikdam and Nigel Coleman and me and Highland Bud, my vision somewhat restored, went past them. In that ground the 66–1 shot Ikdam just outstayed us but it was a brave performance.

In the Glenlivet Hurdle at Liverpool, Highland Bud found Vayrua, whom he had beaten at Cheltenham, five lengths too good and in the Guinness Trophy Champion Hurdle at Punchestown he found Royal Derbi, whom he had also beaten at Cheltenham, too good along with Lunalee, ridden by Anne-Marie Crowley (now Mrs Aidan O'Brien).

When he went to Doncaster sales he was going to be attractive to an American buyer. His sire Northern Baby was a very successful sire of British and American jumpers, he was an athletic horse and a good mover and, essentially for the fast tracks of America, he was very sound. Paul Webber, who knew Jonathan and some potential owners, a couple called Jesse and Margaret Henley, got them interested and Jonathan came over the night before the sale. He was eventually knocked down to him for 105,000 guineas. He just about paid for himself in his first season.

I was asked to ride him in his first Breeders' Cup Chase at Fair Hill in October 1989. It followed a disastrous day I had had at Ascot earlier in the week when I had two rides for Arthur Stephenson. The first, Sir Jest, was an old character and was left in front when Scu and Huntworth ran on to the hurdle track at the last. Instead of just popping it, Sir Jest refused, almost firing me over the fence. The second was Slieve Felim, a really decent horse, who fell at a fence down the hill and was killed. Then I had another ride called Red Procession which fell at the last. I was behind at the time but determined to complete and I got concussed in the process. I came to sitting in the sauna, not knowing why on earth I was not riding in another race. Simon McNeill gave me a lift home and I watched the video of the BBC racing – of me talking to the course doctor. I had no clue that I'd ever spoken to him! By rights I should have been signed off for a week and missed the Breeders' Cup but I must have been on auto-pilot when I spoke to the doctor. I took the Thursday off, broke a three-mile chase record at Newbury on the Friday on Royal Cedar and flew by helicopter from there to Heathrow.

Fair Hill, New Jersey is just like a very tight point-to-point course with a massive crowd on Breeders' Cup day. The race, worth $125,000 in 1989, has now been disbanded. In the race before, the winner had been disqualified for interference that had occurred as they left the start. In this race Ronnie Beggan was riding a horse called Polar Pleasure. As we were going down the back I was travelling really well and Ronnie, on my inner, was trying to edge out from behind the leaders. Of course, with $125,000 at stake, I was not going to move out. When he tried to ease around them I bumped him back in so that he stayed all dressed up with nowhere to go. Bud then quickened with me around the final bend, pinged the last and won by ten lengths. It was a very good performance but remembering the

outcome of the previous race I said to Ronnie, who was second, as we pulled up, 'Look after me, Ronnie.' The reply was slightly incoherent. Next thing after we'd weighed in I heard that he had objected. In terms of prize money this race was bigger than the National. So we got up to the stewards in the stands where they asked us questions and made us give our accounts. They didn't show us the film although they clearly looked at it. In England you do see the film and can see what damage you've done. I told them I'd kept a straight line, Ronnie told them I hadn't. Then we were told to go down and wait. When you're waiting on $125,000, five minutes can seem like a lifetime; I must have sweated more than I do in a race. In England it would not have even crossed a jockey's mind to object, let alone the stewards to inquire, because it was so minor and so far out. I was extremely worried though and even today the thought of disqualification can leave a very numb feeling. Eventually they said that they were happy for the result to stand but I was worried for days afterwards because someone had told me there might be an appeal. Ironically the appeal would have come from Bill Pape, Flatterer's owner who owned Polar Pleasure, and as Jonathan trained both the first and the second he didn't mind what the stewards did.

I then went back out to ride Bud in the Colonial Cup at Camden, South Carolina. These are slightly bigger than the usual American fences, a type of hedge/fence which horses brush through. Camden is a very open track with a few loops and for that race you go round an inner one then the outer one. Highland Bud gave me a terrific ride that day. He jumped immaculately, and won in a hack canter. Not many a horse has won a Colonial Cup so easily. Coming back from the Colonial Cup was almost as exciting as the race: we had to rush to make our connections to enable us to get home to ride the following Monday. This meant changing in the car after the race (no shower) and then getting straight on an internal flight to connect at Atlanta. Not too pleasant for anyone sitting near us.

In 1990 I rode Moonstruck in the Breeders' Cup and he finished third to Morley Street. In 1991 I rode Cheering News, who also finished third. The next time I rode Highland Bud was in the 1992 Breeders' Cup Chase at Belmont Park: he won that too. That was a good trip, with Jamie Osborne riding Young Pokey, and Charlie Swan on Cock Cockburn. We won it pretty easily – by three lengths from the American horse Mistico. In a race the previous day I was 'scrubbed out' – disqualified – on Ninja, an ex-David Nicholson horse, after someone, attempting an inside run, made slight

contact with a wooden wing, breaking a couple of the jockey's toes. I didn't know about the disqualification until I read it in the paper the next day.

Had he stayed in Britain, Highland Bud would have been good enough to be placed in a Champion Hurdle. He strengthened up a lot in America and was one of the most consistent chasers of his time out there. Without the various training setbacks he endured, he wouldn't have been far behind Flatterer. When Jonathan retired Highland Bud he kept him at his yard for a couple of years. His owners, Jesse and Margaret, had both passed away during his racing career and one of Margaret's nephews rang up out of the blue one day to find out what the horse was doing. He ran a show-jumping yard in Nashville, Tennessee and wondered if Highland Bud might make a show-jumper. He never made the grade as a show-jumper, probably because of his old legs, but he remains happily retired there near Nashville.

84

MORLEY STREET

ONE OF THE BEST-LOOKING HORSES I EVER RODE WAS MORLEY STREET. HE HAD THREE PRINCIPAL JOCKEYS DURING HIS HURDLING CAREER: JIMMY FROST, WHO WON THE 1991 CHAMPION HURDLE ON HIM; ME, WHO HAD A COUPLE OF GOOD WINS WITH HIM; AND GRAHAM BRADLEY, WHO RODE HIM IN THE MEMORABLE 1993 MARTELL AINTREE HURDLE. He was a lovely tempered horse with a great deal of ability. He had tremendous acceleration and as he got older his habit for pulling up once he had hit the front became more exaggerated. He became one of the most exciting horses to watch in a finish.

Morley Street used to spend his summers turned out with Jeffrey Peate in Frant, Sussex. He now does the occasional parade before the Champion Hurdle and at local Plumpton Racecourse.

Apart from one short spell towards the very end of his career when he was sent, incognito, to Charlie Brooks, Morley Street spent nearly all his racing career in the very capable hands of Toby Balding, first at Weyhill, then at Whitcombe Manor and then back at Weyhill again. He was bred in Ireland by Marshall Parkhill and bought as a yearling by Captain Charles Radclyffe at a place called Lew, near Witney in Oxfordshire. Pretty much retired now, he used to buy stores, break them in and then turn them away before selling them as three- or four-year-olds. He's had some very good horses through his hands in the past and he was also well known for getting bad jumpers to jump, some time before Swedish eventing coach Yogi Breisner became the jumping guru for Lambourn trainers. Captain Radclyffe only ever bought three horses from Marshall

Parkhill: this fellow, Corbiere and Mole Board. Not a bad trio. By the prolific Irish jumping stallion Deep Run and out of a mare called High Board, Morley Street was also a full brother to Granville Again, another Champion Hurdler.

When Toby went to see him at Lew he took Richard Guest along with him to ride the horse. After Guesty had got off he told Toby that this was the most naturally athletic horse he'd ever sat on. And so a deal was struck and Morley Street was bought on behalf of Michael Jackson. From the day that he arrived at Weyhill, a yard from which Toby had sent out National winners Highland Wedding and Little Polveir, Morley Street knew he was special and that he ruled the roost. He was as good on the gallops as he was on the racecourse, unlike some horses who save the best for the racecourse.

Morley Street was primarily a hurdler. He also proved in seven outings on the Flat that he was, even at the age of eight, a Group-class stayer. He was second in a thrilling Doncaster Cup, he beat a previous season's St Leger winner (Michelozzo) in a conditions race at Goodwood, he ran in the Ascot Gold Cup without disgracing himself, and was fourth in a Northumberland Plate. Because Morley Street was really a firm-ground specialist, Toby used to get him ready for races such as the Breeders' Cup Chase by running him on the Flat.

I said he was primarily a hurdler but he was twice voted Steeplechaser of the Year in America: after winning the 1990 Breeders' Cup Chase at Belmont Park and then after winning the following year's race at Fair Hill. Mind you, the obstacles jumped out there are more like our hurdles than our fences. Of his five runs over fences in Britain he only ever won one: the Fred Rimell Novice Chase at Worcester, in November 1990. His second run over fences here was at Ascot against Remittance Man. Not only did he have a marked preference for left-handed tracks but he was trying to give the future two-mile champion chaser 3lb. He finished second. The next time he ran over fences, in the Feltham Novice Chase at Kempton on Boxing Day, he broke a blood vessel. It was a problem he had to cope with throughout his career. After that he was switched back to hurdles except for several years later when, at the age of ten, he ran in the Mackeson and Tripleprint Gold Cups at Cheltenham – without success.

Although a lovely, strapping, well-put-together horse, Morley Street clearly had his internal problems. Toby had to train him through most of his career knowing that he was liable to break blood vessels internally and rarely show it in the form of a bloody nose. The leg problems he had were patchable and, until his stint in Lambourn, never caused him to miss a season. Without the blood-vessel problem how good would he have been? When he was at Whitcombe Manor Toby had daily access to a vet, Brian Eagles, and so could train him, albeit reluctantly, on Lasix – more or less a last resort after trying everything else. A side effect of this treatment is that it works like a diuretic and on a warm morning Morley Street would lose up to 15kg. Horses are not allowed to race on Lasix in the UK. The best hope was to try to get enough work into Morley Street at home – so that he was racing fit – without bursting him.

Morley Street's racing career began at the end of the 1987–8 season with a couple of bumpers. He won his first at Sandown in a hack canter at 16–1 under Tony Charlton but in a bumper final at Liverpool he hit the front too soon and, on soft ground, was caught close home by a decent horse of Jenny Pitman's called Black Moccasin. The following season he started off in a bumper again at Sandown which he won easily again.

As Tony was a claiming conditional jockey he was replaced by Jimmy Frost for Morley Street's hurdling debut at Sandown in December 1988. Jimmy is a great West Country horseman and was riding quite a lot at the time for Toby, indeed later that season he won the Grand National for him on Little Polveir. He won his first three races, including the Ramsbury Hurdle at Newbury. His first and only defeat that season came in the Sun Alliance Hurdle at Cheltenham when he finished fourth to Sayfar's Lad. He wasn't beaten far and it looked like he might not have quite got the stiff two and a half miles in the soft ground but he won over the same distance and at the much sharper Liverpool to round off a successful novice season.

89

I kept an eye on him as a novice and had ridden against him a few times but never had the opportunity to gauge just how good he was. I got the chance in the Mercury Communications Hurdle at Cheltenham the following season – it was part of the Sport of Kings Challenge series which provided a huge financial bonus for any horse who could win races both sides of the Atlantic. I rode Deep Sensation who was no slouch but Morley Street virtually left me standing. I was impressed. I was still worried about him in Kribensis's Champion Hurdle in 1990 because I knew he would appreciate the fairly fast ground. Luckily for me, he wasn't finding the form he was to get the following year and he finished fifth, beaten about twelve lengths. However, he was devastating in the Sandeman Aintree Hurdle that year. It was a perfect firm ground for him and he slaughtered a reasonable field of hurdlers by fifteen lengths. Once Jimmy said go at the last the response was electric.

The following season, after winning his prep race at Goodwood, he went to America for his first Breeders' Cup Chase: 1990 at Belmont Park. I was riding Moonstruck for Jonathan Sheppard. Again Morley Street was an impressive winner, coming home by eleven lengths. Having won a chase in America it was a now-or-never case of chasing in Britain because he would have to run in handicaps the following season. Though that first one at Worcester was impressive – he didn't beat much – his next was at Ascot against Remittance Man. He jumped way out to the left at each fence and I beat him by eight lengths. I think Toby reckons that he would have made a very good chaser had he perhaps started earlier in his career but he had by then become very used to hurdles and the art of hurdling, which is so different from chasing.

After the blood-vessel problem at Kempton he was given a break and, much like Beech Road who tried chasing before going back to hurdles, Morley Street was switched back to hurdles for his next run: the Berkshire Hurdle at Newbury at the beginning of March 1991. Though he won by only two lengths it was an extremely comfortable two lengths as Jimmy, with the memory of a broken blood vessel fresh in his mind, did not want to let him down drastically.

He went to the 1991 Champion Hurdle as favourite. I rode Nomadic Way and, knowing he was one of those horses who wanted further, was very handy all the way but Jimmy came past me with a double handful at the second last. My only hope was that he had got to the front too soon, but when I just about got to him again after the last, he quickened away again to win by a length and a half. It was due reward for the horse who was clearly the best hurdler in the country at the time. Toby says, modestly, that he was lucky ever to win a Champion Hurdle with Morley Street because he was not a March horse. He much preferred the faster ground of Liverpool but it had been an open winter and the ground at Cheltenham that day had been pretty good.

He finished the season with another smooth success in the Sandeman Aintree Hurdle in which he beat Nomadic Way and me, this time by six lengths. It was his third consecutive win at the meeting and his second of four in that race.

The following season I again had no answers to him in the Breeders' Cup Chase. I was on Cheering News and finished about twenty-five lengths behind him in third. He jumped hurdles well but he was best at those brush hedges in America which are halfway between hurdles and fences. He loved jumping them, and it used to take your breath away to watch him. Back in England he won the Ascot Hurdle but was beaten into second by Chirkpar in the Irish Champion Hurdle on the good-to-soft at Leopardstown. He then finished sixth, only beaten about seven lengths, to Royal Gait in the 1992 Champion Hurdle.

For some reason his owner Michael Jackson blamed Jimmy for that defeat and after Cheltenham they approached me to ride the horse in the Aintree Hurdle. When it came out in the press there was a huge fuss and I think everyone felt indignant on Jimmy's behalf. Of course I commiserated with him, as he is a good friend, but if I'd turned it down someone else would have been asked.

I had schooled him over some small hurdles and ridden him in a piece of work at Whitcombe. He had worked nicely without being over-impressive with some dual-purpose horses on the all-weather track. Then came the Sandeman Aintree Hurdle at Liverpool, and the pressure was on. It was very much his race, his track and the going was in his favour. He was 4–5 favourite in a field that didn't have half the class of the Champion Hurdle. He felt scopey to ride and a little on the forehand which was probably why he never really took to jumping fences. Over his hurdles he was economical and quick.

Tony Mullins was riding Minorette's Girl in the race and Richard Guest was riding Toby's second string Forest Sun, also owned by Michael Jackson. We set off and by the second hurdle Minorette's Girl was beginning to open up quite a lead. Halfway through I had a minor panic hoping that Guesty would not let Minorette's Girl go because I knew she was a big danger. So, halfway down the back, I went to go after her worried that she wasn't going to come back to us. Guesty was shouting, 'Take your time, take your time.' And he was dead right. Minorette's Girl hit the last down the back quite hard and I got to her as we turned into the Mildmay Course's long straight. She kept going but from the second last I was running away. It's an amazing feeling at that stage of a race to feel like your horse has just joined in, especially in a valuable race like that. Going to the last I said to Morley Street, 'OK, have it your way,' and I let him go.

Immediately he went two or three lengths clear and pinged the last. But when we got opposite The Chair with about a furlong to run he started to tie up with me. I was grinding to halt, all out on Morley Street, and Tony, giving it everything (which earned him a four-day whip ban), was coming at me again on Minorette's Girl. Morley Street took a deep breath on me by The Chair and when he heard the mare coming again he just dug a bit deeper. Whether he thought he'd done enough or had broken a blood vessel internally it is difficult to say, but it was a hairy moment and Jimmy very nearly had the last laugh. Eventually, desperately, we won by half a length. Although the race is always overshadowed by the National, the press would have loved it if I'd been beaten that day. It was one of the high points of that meeting for me. I was in bits at the end of it after six fallers – including Brown Windsor at Becher's in the National – and four winners.

Morley Street's acceleration was fantastic and in a sprint he'd have always beaten Kribensis. I would go as far as to say that Morley Street on his day, on fast ground, was as good a hurdler as I have ever sat on.

My first ride on him the following season, 1993–4, was in the Coral Elite Hurdle at Cheltenham on a Sunday in November. It was the first experimental Sunday jump meeting and there was no betting. His brother Granville Again, trained by Martin Pipe, looked the main danger of the three other runners. It was a real cat-and-mouse tactical race. Tyrone Bridge, who wanted further, made the running but we virtually ignored him as neither Granville Again, Oh So Risky nor I wanted to hit the front too soon in case it became a sprint. I was half a length down on Granville Again at the last, took it up shortly afterwards and ran on to beat him a length. He did it really well that day.

This was the first autumn that Morley Street hadn't been to America for two years. His next run was in the Ascot Hurdle over two and a half miles. I got quite a lot of stick this time but I was riding a horse that did not want to hit the front too soon. I switched him off and he made his usual progress on the bridle but not running away this time, and I was just a length behind Muse at the last. Of course we pinged it and made up more than a length while Muse walked through the hurdle leaving me ahead too far out. Halfway up the run-in he stopped to a walk again and I was going up and down on the spot, treading water. The way he stopped when he hit the front that day led me to think that there must have been something wrong. Muse won the race.

I also received criticism the next time I rode him: in the Bula Hurdle at Cheltenham. It was expected to be, again, between the two brothers Granville Again and Morley Street but Halkopous and Adrian Maguire won very easily. Scu and I were blamed for letting Halkopous go and being too aware of each other rather than the eventual winner but it was holding ground that day and Halkopous loved it. He beat Scu ten lengths and me a further six. Morley Street took a couple of blows on me that day and I had got after him turning down the hill to the second last.

The fifth and last time I rode him was in the Agfa Hurdle at Sandown in February 1994. He never travelled at all. That was the race that Mole Board won aged eleven. I dropped Morley Street in but he was off the bridle early on and he stopped very quickly. I virtually pulled him up to walk up the run-in. He was found to be dehydrated afterwards and he blew hard as if something was amiss.

Consequently I got off Morley Street in the Champion Hurdle in preference to Nicky Henderson's Flown who was favourite. I never got back on him again – which was understandable. The race was kept in the family. Granville Again won under Scu. Flown finished eighth and Morley Street, ridden by Graham Bradley, finished twelfth.

At Aintree my choice came home to roost. Brad's performance on Morley Street was voted one of the best of the season – though he still earned a roasting from Toby for getting there too soon. The 1993 Aintree Hurdle – his fourth – was Morley Street's last and, maybe because of the ride he was given, his most famous win. That is to take nothing away from Jimmy Frost who had won so many races on him, including the Champion Hurdle in his younger days. I rode Flown and set out to make all on the fast ground. I quickened it up turning into the straight and thought I might have stolen it going to the last. At this point a chestnut head ranged alongside my boot on the bridle, running away. We jumped the last and I went for everything. Brad still hadn't moved and Morley Street's head was being restrained in behind my boot. He was so close to me that I could have taken his bridle off without a problem. I was doing everything to keep Flown going, all the while knowing it was completely in vain. Brad was so busy leaving his challenge late and taking a pull that he hadn't noticed Scu on the Champion Hurdler Granville Again coming wide at him. The crowd were roaring meanwhile, marvelling at Brad's coolness. Eventually, it can only have been fifty yards from the line, Brad pushed Morley Street out to win by a length and a half. One of the coolest rides of all time, although Toby reckoned he should have sat a bit further off me rather than on my shoulder.

Unfortunately for Morley Street it was downhill from there. You don't get

many great hurdlers beyond the age of nine. It's a young man's game. Guesty got his chance to ride him in public for the first time back over fences in the Mackeson but finished well down the field. Jimmy Frost was called up for the Tripleprint Gold Cup when Morley Street started getting naughty at the start but failed to get a tune out of him. Brad was reunited with him for the 1994 Champion Hurdle in which he pulled up.

He was retired a couple of times, sent to Charlie Brooks, and eventually came back to Toby's as an eleven-year-old for one last go. He had been working well at home, as he did throughout his career, and when he got tired in the Coopers and Lybrand Hurdle at Ascot Brad looked after him and he came home a distant third. His last run was in the Long Walk Hurdle over three miles and a furlong, also at Ascot. It was the first time he had been ridden by Tony McCoy – an outgoing champion seeing in a future champion. He didn't get the trip and was retired for the final time. He owed his connections nothing and I was delighted to be given the opportunity to ride him – he and Kribensis were the best hurdlers I ever sat on. Looking back, probably the best view I ever had of him was when his big, old head was tucked in behind my right boot at Aintree. If you're going to be beaten it is best to be beaten by a horse with style and Morley Street had an abundance of it.

94

FLORIDA PEARL AND
DORAN'S PRIDE

TOWARDS THE END OF MY CAREER I RODE INCREASINGLY IN IRELAND. MAKING MYSELF MORE AVAILABLE THERE PRESENTED OPPORTUNITIES WHICH, HAD I STAYED IN ENGLAND, MIGHT NOT HAVE COME MY WAY. One of those opportunities was to ride the once-raced Irish hope for the Cheltenham Bumper, Florida Pearl. In Ireland, bumpers had always been fierce betting contests. They had also been restricted to amateurs which meant a nucleus of riders, well known to punters, with vast experience in these races.

I had won that first running of the Cheltenham Bumper with the extremely promising Montelado for Pat Flynn. In 1996 Willie Mullins had trained and ridden the winner with Wither Or Which and, at that stage, all but one of the five Bumpers run at the Festival had been won by the Irish. In the competition between the Irish and British at the Festival, the Bumper was becoming something of a 'gimme' for the away team

Willie had the Bumper mapped out for Florida Pearl for sometime. A good pal of mine, James Nash, had ridden him to win his first Bumper at Leopardstown on Boxing Day where he beat the well regarded Promalee by five lengths. James had said afterwards that he thought Florida Pearl was 'a right horse.'

Between then and Cheltenham, Willie was content just to keep the horse ticking over without a run. He had just turned five and was a big horse who did not need over-racing at this stage of his career. I first became acquainted with him in a gallop at Leopardstown. He gave me a good feel but didn't over-impress.

The Wednesday of the 1997 Cheltenham Festival had got off to a good start for me when Hanakham – a class horse, had his career not been beset by injury – won the Royal & Sun Alliance Chase. The Bumper was the last race, and with no obstacles and often a few flat jockeys riding there, had a fun feel yet was still rough, as Richard Hughes and Kieren Fallon would testify.

In the paddock, Florida Pearl towered over the flat-bred types and it was hard to imagine that he would have a better turn of foot than them. Our plan was to be handy with him to keep out of trouble. In the event I found myself hitting the front halfway down the hill, a bit sooner than I wanted but, having got there, I thought there was no point hanging around, so I kicked. We had the race pretty much sewn up as we turned for home. We beat Arctic Camper, of David Nicholson's, by a good five lengths. After Montelado (who won by 12 lengths) it remains the second-longest winning margin for the Bumper, which goes to show how competitive it is. Apart from Florida Pearl, the best horse to emerge from that year's race was French Holly, otherwise it was not a vintage running.

98

The following season, Florida Pearl was to go straight chasing thereby missing out on a season's hurdling. It made sense, he looked a chaser through and through and Willie was already regarding him as a future Gold Cup horse. He was to bring him back at the Leopardstown Christmas Festival. Before then, I rode him in a schooling session at Galway. He already had a reputation as a good jumper but on this occasion he took a while to warm up. At the first he virtually head-butted the fence but recovered and I ended up somewhere nearer his tail than his neck. If a horse can make a mistake like that and still stand up, in a perverse way it gives you confidence that it won't want to lie down every time it makes an error. By the time we had completed the session he was jumping nicely.

He went to Leopardstown for the Farming Independent Beginners' Chase even favourite to beat a field of sixteen others. In heavy ground he duly obliged, coming away to beat Delphi Lodge 20 lengths despite the race being over barely more than two miles. Having won that well he was odds on next time when we took on Boss Doyle, who had the difficult task of trying to give us 7lbs, in the Dr P.J.Moriarty Memorial Novice Chase, again at Leopardstown, in February. We jumped the last upsides and I had to be reasonably vigorous to win by a length. It cemented his reputation as one of the leading Irish novices and he was now off to the 1998 Cheltenham Festival as one of the Irish bankers of the meeting.

The Royal & Sun Alliance Chase is the 'Gold Cup for novices' but the inexperience of the horses meant that avoiding fallers was a problem. The opposition, though novices, looked like good jumpers and rather than keep out of trouble by making all the running I thought I'd take the risk of dropping him in behind for a while, thereby expending less energy. Half way down the back for the last time I was regretting my decision. I'd nearly been brought down three times, by Ottawa in front of the stands and by Fiddling The Facts who made mistakes and nearly fell in front of me twice. I pulled out wide and began to make my way unhindered towards the sharp end. We hit the front at about the same spot as we had done a year before in the Bumper and began to go away. He jumped very well for a horse having only his third run over fences and, though he only beat Escartefigue a length and a half, it was comfortable enough. Though the pressure of riding an Irish banker at the Festival is greater than riding a no-hoper, so is the joy and, of course, the reception after winning.

That was it for that season and Willie resisted the temptation of taking him to Punchestown for their festival in April. He never missed a season and, apart from the 02/03 season he never failed to win a Grade One chase. The general idea was that the horse was well above average so, rather than take him to every cock-fight in the county, he'd prepare him for two or three big races.

The next season didn't begin until Christmas – Florida Pearl sometimes returned from summer grass with a problem in a hind leg for some reason – when he went for the Ericsson Chase at Leopardstown. I had the choice of him and Doran's Pride but with two Festival wins behind him and youth on his side I opted for Florida Pearl. Paul Carberry was asked to ride Doran's Pride.

We weren't going that well on the soft ground and when we came to the last ditch I needed a big one. I asked but Florida Pearl said no and ended up putting his feet in the ditch. On reflection, it had been a very big question to ask! Doran's Pride, ironically, went on to beat Boss Doyle a distance and the Florida Pearl bubble was slightly burst. He'd not only lost his unbeaten record, he had fallen, too.

That was put behind him the following February when he won what was to be the first of four Irish Hennessys at Leopardstown. This first was a rematch with Escartefigue and the main thing I remember about this race was that I'd damaged my neck and it was affecting my arm (the injury was eventually to bring about my retirement). I was having to ride virtually one-armed. The injury, which had first affected me the previous May, recurred in January but I'd made up my mind. As it wasn't going to get better, I'd try the next best option which was riding through the pain. In fact it wasn't that painful, I just couldn't lift or use my whip in the right hand. He beat Escartefigue easily enough and he would go to Cheltenham a worthy favourite for the Gold Cup.

For some reason I felt that the 1999 Gold Cup would be my last. The arm still wasn't working but in the end expectation exceeded result. Three out in the race, I was travelling well with every chance of winning myself a second Gold Cup, but Florida Pearl couldn't get home. It set a pattern for him in the Gold Cup. My immediate thought was that he didn't quite stay — I always thought his best trip was even short of 3 miles and the extended distance at Cheltenham just did him. He finished 18 lengths behind See More Business in third and he was also not one hundred per cent after the race, finishing slightly tied up.

That year he ran at Punchestown but finished 14 lengths behind Imperial Call in the Heineken Gold Cup. With my career cut short the following season, it was the last time I rode Florida Pearl, one of the most popular horses of his era in Ireland. Paul Carberry, Richard Johnson, Barry Geraghty and Adrian Maguire all won on him, while Ruby Walsh was second on him on a couple of occasions. He was always given a mighty reception in Ireland and his greatest hour outside of Cheltenham was winning the King George VI Chase for Adrian in 2002 when he beat the subsequent three times Gold Cup winner Best Mate.

100

Florida Pearl never did win that elusive Gold Cup but Irish racing fans would forgive him that. His last run was his fourth win in the Irish Hennessy in 2004. He is now happily retired at Willie Mullins' yard where he is ridden out most days and he also does a spot of hunter trialling with Willie's son Patrick.

In thirty-three outings for his owner, Violet and Archie O'Leary, Florida Pearl won sixteen times and the thick end of £900,000 in prize-money. In contrast, one of the other great Irish horses I rode, Doran's Pride, ran sixty-two times, winning twenty-seven and almost £650,000 in prize-money. When I opted to ride the younger Florida Pearl in the Ericsson Chase in 1998, it marked my last ride on Doran's Pride.

Doran's Pride had become the ride of popular, up-and-coming young Irish jockey Shane Broderick and the pair became a formidable combination. He had already beaten the likes of Imperial Call, Sound Man and Idiot's Venture over hurdles in Ireland but came to our attention in Britain when falling almost upsides another Irish hero, Danoli, at the last hurdle in the Royal & Sun Alliance Hurdle of 1994. The following year I'd been on Cyborgo in the Stayers Hurdle. I thought my horse was pretty good but he had no answers for Doran's Pride who beat us five lengths and really put Shane on the map.

At Cheltenham, trainer Michael Hourigan took the bold decision to run Doran's Pride in the Gold Cup instead of the Royal & Sun Alliance Chase, on the basis that he had fallen at Thurles and would be better off with better jumpers in the Gold Cup than being tripped up by a bunch of novices the day before. He ran a hell of a race for a novice, finishing nine-and-a-half lengths third to Mr Mulligan and AP McCoy.

His next run was in the Power Gold Cup at Fairyhouse over Easter and it was to prove one of the most emotional wins of my career. Shane had taken a horrific fall earlier at the meeting and it was already clear that if he pulled through, which was touch and go at the time, he would be paralysed from the neck down. Paralysis or serious head injury are the two worst enemies of the jump jockey and you go about your daily business without giving either a second thought. It really brings it home when a colleague gets paralysed or killed riding.

Doran's Pride was very nearly withdrawn out of respect to Shane but it was finally agreed he would not have wanted that and I was given the ride. Kay Hourigan led us out in tears and when Doran's Pride won, beating Jeffell by 5 lengths, everyone was crying. It was the most emotional winner I ever rode.

101

Unlike Florida Pearl, he ran once a month or more in the winter and often took in a flat race or two in the summer. He won his first three with me the next season, beating Lord Singapore 6 lengths giving him 2st in the Kerry National at Listowel to start with. He then beat Imperial Call and Jeffell again. He ran flatly at Naas and seemed to lose his confidence jumping but he returned to winning ways in a poor renewal of the Irish Hennessy which he won well. It was enough to send him off as 9-4 favourite for that year's Gold Cup. It was one his greatest races. He was beaten no more than 2 lengths by Cool Dawn and Strong Promise after a terrific battle.

I still think he was unlucky. His confidence was still not sky-high and at the third last, when I needed a big one, he put down on me, missed it and, though never looking like falling, it cost me a length and momentum. He then stayed on all the way to the line. Of all the Gold Cups I was beaten in, that was the one I felt was the unluckiest. Who knows whether he would have beaten Cool Dawn without the mistake.

At Aintree next time he was over the top. I rode him three more times. At Gowran at the start of next season he jumped well when beating Hill Society. At Clonmel he beat Merry People a distance but it was a bad race and he kept slipping into his fences. The more careful he tried to be the more he slipped. Then, of course, I opted for Florida Pearl. There was no fall out and under new rider Paul Carberry he won the Ericsson while I was sprawling about on the deck.

Eventually he became the ride of Michael's son Paul but by that stage he found winning at the highest level hard work. He was rarely out of the money, however, and won three flat races as well. He was clobbered in handicaps but age had just taken the edge off him in the big chases.

He returned to Cheltenham for the Christies Foxhunters in 2003 aged 14. Sadly he was killed in a fall in front of the stands. It was a heart-breaking end to a once great horse.

102

Man could make between fifteen and twenty lengths with good, fast, accurate jumping.

It is hard to measure one Cheltenham Festival winner against another: it is difficult to equate a Champion Hurdle win with two-mile chasers, for example – they are all sweet. I won the Arkle three times: on Remittance Man, Waterloo Boy and Ventana Canyon. But, certainly from a jumping point of view, this one was the best. The Arkle was the second race of the meeting and it was confidence-boosting to get one under the belt so early in the week. Remittance Man had done his stuff for the season though and went into a well-earned summer break back at Chetwode with his owners.

His purple patch continued at the start of the following season. He went back to Newbury for the Hennessy meeting in November. I had a crunching fall from Le Piccolage in the previous race and there was nothing like the prospect of a round of jumping from Remittance Man to make me feel better. It was another two-horse race: a fact Nicky would later come to rue in the King George VI Chase. Jamie Osborne rode the other, Golden Celtic, for Henrietta Knight. Remittance Man, as expected, popped round. By the time we had jumped the tenth Jamie was out of speaking (or shouting, for that matter) contact and it turned into nothing more than a schooling round.

A further complication to the David Nicholson–Nicky Henderson tug-of-war, which at that time was still working all right, was a one-off deal that I ride Desert Orchid. Nicky still believed Remittance Man would get three miles at Kempton, an easy track, and he was keen to try it out in the King George VI Chase. I had the choice between the two: the young pretender, or Dessie who had won the race four times and given me some great moments.

I'd had the choice of ride ever since the Arkle when Nicky had declared his intention to run in the King George VI, a race which was also to be Dessie's target. The papers got mileage out of debating which horse I'd ride. It was one of the hardest decisions in my riding career. Do you stay loyal to Dessie, the nation's favourite horse who by then, aged twelve, was getting on a bit, or do you ride the most exciting, up-and-coming horse in the country but about whom there are stamina doubts? I'd been associated with each horse as long as the other – I first rode both of them in November 1989. After agonizing, I decided to stay loyal to Dessie. I'd asked Nicky whether, if I chose Dessie, I would be able to get back on Remittance Man and he had told me the ride was mine, which went some way to helping me make my mind up. I knew that my heart was over-ruling my head but there are times – they are getting fewer and fewer in racing – when you have to stay

REMITTANCE MAN

SCHOOLING MORNINGS CAN BE EXHAUSTING, EXCITING AND EVENTFUL AFFAIRS, ESPECIALLY IN THE AUTUMN WHEN YOU START TO FIND OUT HOW YOUR NOVICE CHASERS ARE GOING TO TAKE TO FENCES AFTER A COUPLE OF SEASONS OF HURDLING.

A warm, autumn morning up on the Mandown schooling ground above Lambourn in Berkshire, enough moisture in the ground to make it safe for the horses to take off and land without injury, the whole season ahead of you. Anticipation and trepidation in equal measure: expecting one horse that jumped hurdles well to be a 'natural', expecting his stablemate who flattened every hurdle he ever jumped to bury you before breakfast. The former falls and you can't even persuade the latter to make a mistake.

Horses are going in all directions: Oliver Sherwood's, Mark Pitman's and Charlie Mann's horses all converged on the schooling ground. Their horses not far off a run but the ground, until now, too firm to school upon. Suddenly, a drop of rain, and they're all there with a dozen horses each to give them practice in the art of jumping. Some will never completely master it in race conditions. Others, you feel, could do it with their eyes closed.

It was October 1990 when we took Remittance Man up to Mandown. Nicky Henderson was still training at Windsor House in Lambourn, rather than Seven Barrows where he is now. Until then the only remarkable point about Remittance Man's career was his inability to win over hurdles. Although one of the leading novice hurdlers of the previous two seasons, he had a habit of finding one horse too good. He had been an agile hurdler but not the most robust of horses and a bit of a worrier in his stable. The morning we took him up to Mandown to jump fences for the first time, I'd thought he might just be a bit too light to be a really good chaser. I was wrong. He was electric and from the first fence we jumped I knew he would be exceptional.

Schooling is a gradual process. When you start off a National Hunt horse it is probably over small logs on the ground, then slightly larger logs and then some 'baby' hurdles which you might even have laid on the floor to start with. If you get going well over the logs you might even call things to a halt: the horse has gained some confidence, has not been rushed and has enjoyed it. The next time, maybe a week later, you'll start over the logs again and move on to the 'baby' hurdles. Eventually, shortly before the horse is ready to run, he'll be going at a racing pace over full-sized hurdles.

With jumpers the system is similar. They're accustomed to leaving the ground over hurdles although it is possible to uproot one without falling. In Lambourn you start the novice chasers over 'baby' fences which might not be much higher than a full-sized hurdle but obviously stiffer and thicker and a different shape.

On Mandown there are about six lines of three fences, all varying slightly in size, and on a normal morning there will be one line of three small fences open and another line of three full-sized fences open. The rest of the ground is saved and the head gallop man will rotate the fences through the winter to avoid excessive poaching.

It is common practice to get a novice to jump the 'babies' three or four times competently before moving on to the full-sized fences. Remittance Man was instant. He had always been an athletic horse and he was always going to be a better chaser than hurdler. When you have schooled more horses than had hot dinners few of these sessions, unless someone has had a fall, stand out. I won't easily forget Remittance Man's first morning over fences. He was so good over the 'babies' that we sent him straight up over the big fences. Again he was mustard, a complete natural. You could have run him without any further practice. It really stands out in my mind. In this game you're always looking for perfection and with Remittance Man that morning I thought we had found it.

Nicky had bought Remittance Man at the Derby sales in Ireland as an unbroken three-year-old for IR£25,000. Another trainer, Josh Gifford, had also been keen on the horse. At that time it was a sort of mid-market price, a few of the top ones were making £50,000. He was by Prince Regent, an unlucky loser of the 1969 Derby when his French jockey came from way off the pace to go down by two lengths to Blakeney. He reversed the form when they met in the Irish Derby. Remittance Man's dam was Mittens, a well-related mare who had raced at two for Ian Balding. She was also the dam of the useful Irish hurdler Treble Bob.

The sales are held in June during the week before the Irish Derby. When you buy a horse at auction he has to pass a veterinary inspection and wind (breathing) test. If he passes that you also have seven days to reject him if he either box walks, crib bites or wind sucks. The first usually indicates a mental problem while the other two are bad habits which can result in anything wooden being chewed.

The three-year-old Remittance Man was a box walker. Occasionally when a horse frets or worries he walks round and round his box. In the mornings you can see a track he's made through his bed and because a box walker is exercising while most of the other horses are sleeping it is often hard to keep the weight on him. Nicky was on the verge of sending him back.

While he was at Windsor House, Nicky used a yard belonging to Barry Hills called Bourne House as his overflow yard. Part of it was fairly old and it contained some old coaching stalls, much narrower than your average stable. Here the young Remittance Man was attached to a metal ball through a slot in the wall by a chain. Thus he could lie down, get up, drink and eat but if he wanted to go walkabout the slack on the chain was taken up and he was prevented from doing so. It sounds a bit severe but it was for his own good and health. One day the yard was being filmed for the BBC and on the programme Nicky mentioned that Remittance Man was attached to a 'ball and chain', which he was – though not quite in the fashion that prisoners are. The BBC received two dozen letters of complaint from people who thought it cruel!

107

Remittance Man remained a bad doer and a worrier for much of his career. He often resembled two planks put together and it was his athleticism that kept him going. Some horses – like some humans – find life stressful and Remittance Man, though you wouldn't have guessed it if you saw him winning the Arkle Trophy or the Queen Mother Champion Chase at Cheltenham, had a troubled mind. Even in retirement the prospect of hunting and a field of horses was too exciting for him, and the prospect of riding him in such conditions was a challenge for his owner's daughter Belinda Cubbitt.

With such horses it is common practice to keep another animal, like a goat or a sheep, with them. Desmond Morris, the animal-watcher, says that some horses cannot cope with the isolation of being in a box on their own.

Many stables are designed with bars between boxes so the horses can see and touch their neighbours but, for some, this is not enough. Obviously keeping two valuable horses together in the same box would create problems. With shoes on they could do a lot of damage to each other if they had an argument. The solution with Remittance Man was a sheep.

There have been three sheep in Remittance Man's life: Allan Lamb, Ridley Lamb and Nobby. The idea was that a lamb be procured from Nicky's father's farm, fed on oats, bran mashes and best racehorse hay for a winter, and then be returned with someone's dining-room table the eventual destination. This was the reward for poor old Allan Lamb and Ridley Lamb's season of companionship. Nobby was heading the same way and had been returned to his farm to rejoin the flock. When Remittance Man was turned out during the summer with other horses, he did not miss his ovine companion.

When he returned for the start of a new season, a fourth sheep-friend was introduced. It was not a marriage made in heaven. Remittance Man detested his new partner. He bit and kicked him, all but defleeced him and threw him out of the stable. The call went up to find Nobby – the horse's career at the top depended on it. But how do you find one sheep in a flock of six hundred? Remarkably, if you put a horse in a field of six hundred sheep, 599 will go to the far end and the one who likes horses will go to the horse. Thus was Nobby found and this time purchased by Tim Collins, who owned Remittance Man, for the princely sum of one Scottish sovereign. It was a cheap price to pay for a happy horse.

Remittance Man's career as a racehorse began positively at Cheltenham in April 1988 when he won a National Hunt Flat race known as a bumper (on hindsight a bad one – I don't think the other twenty-four runners subsequently put together half a dozen wins between them). Unless it was on the schooling ground he was never impressive at home and his starting price of 12–1 reflected this. Ridden by one of Nicky's conditional jockeys, John Smith, and carrying the famous colours of Lord Bicester, he scrambled home by a neck from Rowlandson Diamond. (Tim Collins had inherited the colours through his late wife, a granddaughter of Lord Bicester, who had owned such famous chasers as Finnure, Roimond and Silver Fame.)

It is normal for a potential chaser like Remittance Man, then aged four, to have a quiet season with just the one run in a bumper at the end. National Hunt-bred horses aren't ready mentally or physically for a great deal more. He was first broken in by Caroline Gordon near Wantage and although he had been a worrier there he was able to jump from the start. He would then have returned to Windsor House and started going out with the string and gradually learning the ropes without doing too much fast work – too much of that too early and you can blow a horse's mind. So it would have been gently, gently for that first season. In recent seasons the firm dry ground in the spring has meant that many trainers have got their young horses ready but have not been able to run them. They will try, however, to get one or two runs in bumpers as an important part of the education process.

The following season Remittance Man was sent hurdling. His debut was at Huntingdon in December 1988. Ridden by Jamie Osborne he finished third to Espy over two miles. He showed none of the devastating cruising speed that he was later to show over fences and he ran as if he wanted further. On Boxing Day he went to Newton Abbot where he finished a twelve-length second to Sayfar's Lad, who went on to win the Sun Alliance Novices' Hurdle at Cheltenham that season. At Towcester in January he was again second, this time beaten a neck by Duke De Vendome. He went back to the Northamptonshire course in March for a maiden hurdle and again found one too good in Martin Pipe's Dan Marino. Again he was beaten only the length of his neck. In April he went back to Cheltenham for the same meeting that he had won a year previously. This time, because he had been running on a bit one-paced at the end of his races, Nicky stepped him up to two and a half miles. The result was largely the same: third, beaten five and half lengths, by Knighton Lad. This was a novice handicap hurdle and consistent performance meant he carried second top-weight of 11st 12lb and gave over a stone to the first two.

After a summer off with his owner Tim Collins at Chetwode near Bicester he returned to Nicky. The Collins family – the increasingly rare traditional type of owner – used to do a month's roadwork with Remittance Man before sending him back to Nicky's. Nicky then sent him to Ascot for another two-and-a-half-mile hurdle. During the summer of 1989 I had come to an agreement with David Nicholson whereby I would ride for Nicky Henderson as well. It was always going to be a tricky arrangement because, at some stage, they were both going to want me to ride for them in the same big race. At Ascot I was on Remittance Man for the first time.

My first impressions were of an agile little horse, not the most robust, but one who jumped hurdles well. He ran a good race but frustratingly found one too good again, this time in Josh Gifford's Tom Troubadour. Remittance Man was beginning to look like the best hurdler in the country not to have won a race.

At long last Remittance Man got his head in front: at Cheltenham that December. On firm ground and over two and a half miles he had a ding-dong battle with Regal Ambition (who also went on to win at the Festival) and beat the odds-on favourite by a short head. Peter Scudamore had led on Regal Ambition and when I'd joined him in front between the last two I quite expected him to surge away from us as Martin's horses often did. He tried that all right but Remittance Man matched him all the way. There was relief all round that Remittance Man had finally broken his duck.

That Boxing Day he went to Huntingdon and reverted to filling the runner-up's spot. John White rode him that day as I had to go to Kempton for the King George. To be fair I think the ground was probably a bit soft for him; as a chaser he was never quite the same horse on tacky ground. Jamie Osborne rode him again at Doncaster at the end of January 1990 and once more he was second, this time to Jenny Pitman's Black Moccasin. The ground at Doncaster is often firmer than it is anywhere else: if it is soft at Wetherby up the road it is still often quite good at Doncaster. When Remittance Man went back to Doncaster in February he recorded his second win, this time ridden by Paul Harley who was claiming 7lb.

As he had always seemed to be running on at the end of his races, Nicky stepped him up in trip again, this time to three miles, at Newbury in early March for the Philip Cornes Saddle of Gold Final. On good ground he was comprehensively beaten by the evens favourite, the talented Miinnehoma. In typical Martin Pipe fashion Miinnehoma made all the running under Scu (Peter Scudamore) and John White, Remittance Man's jockey, was always having to chase the winner. He looked like he might have a chance coming to the second last but his stamina must have been reaching its limits and he was eventually beaten twelve lengths. He was still a difficult horse to assess for his perfect trip. He ran like a horse who just wasn't fast enough rather than one who wasn't getting home. In reality it was probably his class (as yet only latent) that was getting him home over these longer trips. As he was to prove as a champion chaser, a stiff two miles at Cheltenham was his ideal.

Nicky fairly sensibly bypassed Cheltenham's novice hurdles – they can take so much out of a young horse if you're not careful – and headed instead for Aintree where he was to run in the Mumm Prize Novice Hurdle. I had to ride Olinstar for David Nicholson and John White again teamed up with Remittance Man for the two-and-a-half-mile novice hurdle. Guess where he finished? Second, beaten a length and a half, to Jenny Pitman's Vazon Bay.

REMITTANCE MAN

After his annual summer break and the memorable schooling session when we saw the light in Remittance Man, Nicky sent him to Leicester for his first run over fences. It was as a novice that Remittance Man's jumping stood out. By the time they get to running in the Queen Mother Champion Chase most horses are fairly outstanding in the jumping department – they wouldn't be there otherwise. However, with a novice, even the best, there is a certain amount of guesswork involved. Take for example the good novice Mulligan running in 1997 for David Nicholson when Adrian Maguire was injured. He went to Cheltenham with better write-ups than Entrepreneur was to have before that season's Derby but he fell and subsequently lost confidence because of it.

For Remittance Man there was never any guesswork involved. From the start he would measure his fences. He could get in close or stand off – it was all the same to him. He had unbelievable spring and was extremely clever with it. A lot of it is coordination: he knew where his feet were in relation to a fence and the messages got through from his head. You may think that's obvious but I can assure you that some horses jump fences as though their heads were connected to another horse's feet. It was a long time before he ever made a mistake. For all facets of jumping – scope, spring, accuracy, consistent fluency, agility and speed – he is the best I have ridden.

The Leicester race was a bad one and with his hurdling form he was made the odds-on favourite. There were only seven runners and the other six were pretty moderate. It was an ideal introduction. He cantered round and clearly loved jumping fences, which come so much quicker than hurdles. I took it up at the second last and he never came off the bridle. It was confirmation of our schooling morning on Mandown. Jumping fences had transformed our useful hurdler into a potential champion chaser. That run at Leicester was on Monday, 19 November 1990. He could hardly have had more exercise had he stayed at home and so Nicky did what he describes as a very un-Hendersonish thing and ran him again that Saturday, five days later, at Newbury.

The result was the same. Newbury's fences can be daunting to a novice but not to Remittance Man. The aptly named Hopeful Chase has been won by some good horses in the past and he added to the roll of honour. It was a three-horse race over two and a half miles. One of the opposition broke down after jumping the fourth and the other was tailed off from about the same point. From Remittance Man's point of view it was just another schooling session. I was slightly worried. One likes a bit of company for a novice round somewhere like Newbury, especially at those big ditches and with a big Hennessy crowd around, and it is easy enough for a horse out on his own for so long to be distracted, lose concentration for a split second and make a stupid or needless mistake. He wasn't distracted and won on a tight rein.

Impressive though he'd been, at this stage he had not encountered any serious oppposition. His first challenge was to take on the former Champion hurdler Morley Street at Ascot the Saturday before Christmas. Morley Street was odds-on to beat us but I felt Ascot might undo his jumping. It was expected to be a slaughter with Morley Street first and the rest nowhere, and it was – only they got the wrong horse. Ascot is a difficult track for inexperienced or unconfident jumpers and though Morley Street had done everything right at home and won a Breeders' Cup Chase over lesser obstacles than those at Ascot, I was riding a horse who jumped better than nearly every handicapper in the country in a novice chase. Nicky had already described him as a cross between a pussycat and a gazelle. The downhill fences away from the stands catch out novices who get a bit keen and on the forehand. The last ditch can often be a problem too. Morley Street jumped left all the way which cost him a lot of ground. I let Remittance Man bowl along in front, the plan being to get a length or two out of Morley Street at each fence. It worked to perfection. He was always chasing us and Jimmy Frost was having to get after him after each fence to make up the ground he'd lost by jumping away to the left on the right-handed course. We beat him eight lengths. Now people were beginning to sit up and take notice of Remittance Man and, for us, we were beginning to think he was a good horse, certainly Cheltenham material. He won that race in a decent time and you can judge a horse's ability well on its race times.

112

With some horses, and he was one, every time you get on them you think, 'Hey, I'm seeing a good stride today.' You meet every fence spot on. Those horses definitely help you. You ride some horses and they gallop at a fence as if it isn't there, not in any way trying to vary their stride. Remittance Man gets more 'jumped well' or 'jumped very well' comments in my rides book than any other horse I rode.

His next outing was in the Wayward Lad Novice Chase at Kempton on Boxing Day. I had just won the 1990 King George VI Chase on Desert Orchid, and Sparkling Flame had also won the Feltham Novice Chase for Nicky. By now, though, people with half-decent novice chasers were beginning to seek alternative engagements when we were due to run. This day there were only three runners, us, Calapaez and Amrullah. Amrullah went on to become almost as famous a loser as Remittance Man did a winner. He ran many times and never won although he often picked up a half-decent prize in three-horse contests like this. We won it by twelve lengths from Calapaez but the race was memorable for only one thing: Remittance Man's first mistake. It was quite a bad one but I blame myself. I eased him down going to the last and he just galloped into it. The ground was also quite tacky which he didn't like and he was getting a bit tired in it.

In February 1991 he went back to Kempton for the Galloway Braes Novice Chase on Racing Post Chase day which he won by thirty lengths. He wasn't favourite but the two ahead of him in the betting fell: Trefelyn Cone at the first and File Concord at the second last (although we had him beaten at the time). He'd made the running in most of his chases so far and the plan here was to get him used to being in behind a few others. He would, we thought, be hard pushed to dominate in the Arkle at Cheltenham, for which this was his final prep race, like he had in all his other races. We didn't take up the running until the twelfth but it made no difference to him: he still won in a common canter.

It was now to Cheltenham for the Arkle Trophy. He was evens favourite. I knew he had a very good chance but I'd ridden long enough at Cheltenham to know that you can go there with a favourite or short-priced mount and it can count for nothing. You don't go out for a race there thinking you already have it in the bag.

The Arkle went to plan. There were fourteen runners, including Uncle Ernie, Redundant Pal, My Young Man and Last O'The Bunch. I dropped him in and got a lead to the third last (the first down the hill) where I joined Last O'The Bunch and Uncle Ernie in a line. Last O'The Bunch was probably feeling the pressure when he clipped the top of that fence, leaving Uncle Ernie as my main danger. I looked round and could see Mark Dwyer tracking me going to the second last. Over the second last I kicked as soon as I landed to make sure I had the rail round the last bend and so that I could steal a length. He winged the last – it was sensational, Nicky says one of the best photographs he has of any of his horses is of Remittance Man jumping the last to win the Arkle – and that just about sealed it. He tied up a little up the hill but he had already won the race and he eventually beat Uncle Ernie by six lengths. Redundant Pal was the same distance back in third.

In a fast two-mile chase such as the Arkle a horse like Remittance

Man could make between fifteen and twenty lengths with good, fast, accurate jumping.

It is hard to measure one Cheltenham Festival winner against another: it is difficult to equate a Champion Hurdle win with two-mile chasers, for example – they are all sweet. I won the Arkle three times: on Remittance Man, Waterloo Boy and Ventana Canyon. But, certainly from a jumping point of view, this one was the best. The Arkle was the second race of the meeting and it was confidence-boosting to get one under the belt so early in the week. Remittance Man had done his stuff for the season though and went into a well-earned summer break back at Chetwode with his owners.

His purple patch continued at the start of the following season. He went back to Newbury for the Hennessy meeting in November. I had a crunching fall from Le Piccolage in the previous race and there was nothing like the prospect of a round of jumping from Remittance Man to make me feel better. It was another two-horse race: a fact Nicky would later come to rue in the King George VI Chase. Jamie Osborne rode the other, Golden Celtic, for Henrietta Knight. Remittance Man, as expected, popped round. By the time we had jumped the tenth Jamie was out of speaking (or shouting, for that matter) contact and it turned into nothing more than a schooling round.

A further complication to the David Nicholson–Nicky Henderson tug-of-war, which at that time was still working all right, was a one-off deal that I ride Desert Orchid. Nicky still believed Remittance Man would get three miles at Kempton, an easy track, and he was keen to try it out in the King George VI Chase. I had the choice between the two: the young pretender, or Dessie who had won the race four times and given me some great moments.

I'd had the choice of ride ever since the Arkle when Nicky had declared his intention to run in the King George VI, a race which was also to be Dessie's target. The papers got mileage out of debating which horse I'd ride. It was one of the hardest decisions in my riding career. Do you stay loyal to Dessie, the nation's favourite horse who by then, aged twelve, was getting on a bit, or do you ride the most exciting, up-and-coming horse in the country but about whom there are stamina doubts? I'd been associated with each horse as long as the other – I first rode both of them in November 1989. After agonizing, I decided to stay loyal to Dessie. I'd asked Nicky whether, if I chose Dessie, I would be able to get back on Remittance Man and he had told me the ride was mine, which went some way to helping me make my mind up. I knew that my heart was over-ruling my head but there are times – they are getting fewer and fewer in racing – when you have to stay loyal. Jamie Osborne was to ride him. I remember ringing him just before Christmas when I had made the decision and playing 'Under Pressure' by Queen down the phone to wind him up.

Throughout the race I kept watching Remittance Man and wondering how he would do. I led for a while on Dessie but by the fourteenth fence we were the ones under pressure. Jamie came cantering past me. Turning into the straight it looked impossible for him and Remittance Man to get beat. Desert Orchid fell at the third last, adding insult to my misery as I assumed Remittance Man would hack up. He hit a wall at the second last, however, and was passed by The Fellow and Docklands Express. He had run a very good race. Nicky still isn't sure whether it was the distance that he failed to get in that company (he was beaten by a subsequent Gold Cup winner) or the fact that he hadn't had a hard enough race at Newbury and was short of a gallop. He was a difficult horse to train: he didn't take much work at home to get fit and if you'd worked him too hard he would have gone to nothing but getting the balance right was clearly not easy. As it is we will never know.

After that we were reunited in the Arlington Premier Series Chase Final over two and a half miles at Newbury in February 1992. It was back to normal again. He won as he liked, beating Captain Dibble twenty lengths – although he hadn't shown quite the same sparkle that he had before Christmas. Later that afternoon I rode Waterloo Boy to an impressive win in the Game Spirit Chase. As I pulled up David Nicholson came to greet me. 'You will ride Waterloo Boy in the Champion Chase, won't you?' It was asked as a question but I knew it was an order. That was it, end of subject. Waterloo Boy was still rated 11lb higher than Remittance Man so it might have been a difficult decision to make anyway – it took that pressure from me – although my agreement with both trainers was that if such a choice ever arose in a big race it was up to me to decide who I should ride. If I hadn't have ridden Waterloo Boy, then I feared the Duke would have gone to war.

The Queen Mother Champion Chase was billed as a two-horse race between Waterloo Boy and Remittance Man – all the headlines read: 'Man versus Boy'. But they forgot the previous winner, Katabatic, and Simon McNeill. It was a great race, a vintage Queen Mother Chase – involving three horses – and even David Nicholson described it as magic although he doesn't particularly enjoy being beaten. Scu made the running on Star's Delight but slowed the pace down in front which suited me more than Remittance Man, who we knew wanted a test of stamina over two miles. Coming down the hill Jamie was off the bridle and I think I was going the better. We went virtually flat out from the top of the hill. Turning into the straight it was always going to be an exciting race with all three horses relishing the challenge ahead, none of them giving an inch. Rarely have you seen three horses try so hard.

Our only chance in that race, I thought, was to get Remittance Man into a long drawn-out fight like he'd had in the King George, it was the only chink I could see in his armour. A good battle was Waterloo Boy's forte. I put the gun to his head at the second last but saw another head appear beside me going to the last. I knew then that Waterloo Boy and I were beaten. Remittance Man landed marginally in front at the last, and Katabatic made a mistake there. Waterloo Boy was outstayed up the hill. Katabatic went down by a length and I was a further three and a half lengths away in third. It was breathtaking stuff. Each horse had given its all, and Remittance Man was a remarkable winner. It was the Festival at which Jamie Osborne rode five winners and three of them were horses that I could have ridden, had circumstances been different. He was picking up my cast-offs and winning on them. It is something we'd joke about now but if you're at all competitive it is hard to take at the time.

The philosophical approach to this is to accept that you can't ride everything. I had to go out and ride Mr Gossip for Nicky in the next and you have to go out there and say well done. A retainer from a trainer, such as the one I had with the Duke, is as much compensation for the winners you miss riding for other people as it is a payment for riding your trainer's horses. In a way I was fortunate riding for two such good yards and until then there had not been many serious clashes. The Queen Mother Champion Chase remained something of a bogey for me though. I was placed in it nine times but never won it.

Unbeaten but for the King George VI Chase, Remittance Man's purple patch continued with a facile victory in the Mumm Melling Chase at Aintree in April where he beat Edberg and Pat's Jester. The only other runner, Uncle Ernie, had fallen at the first. I was back on him and it was a good run but he felt a bit flat after Cheltenham and the ground was also on the soft side. It was the meeting at which I had six falls in three days. I was a walking wreck at the end of the meeting and the Jockey Club medical adviser, Dr Rodney O'Donnell, insisted I take the following Monday off even though he couldn't find anything physically wrong with me.

The 1992–3 season began as the last had ended – on a winning note at Wincanton. The Desert Orchid South Western Pattern Chase over two miles

Above: Rushing Wild showing his scope in the Irish National at Fairyhouse. A big talent, sadly short-lived.

Right: Spare rides don't come much better. Rushing Wild leading the field in the 1993 Gold Cup.

Right: Miinnehoma lands
awkwardly over
Beecher's second time in
the 1994 Grand National.

Left: Picking himself up.
Most horses have an
instinct of self-
preservation.

Right: As if nothing had
happened. You can see
that this potentially
catastrophic mistake has
hardly cost him ground.

Top: A cold Saturday in January 1994. Warmed up by Flakey Dove, marking one thousand winners in my career.

Bottom: Getting to know you. My first ride on Alderbrook at Kempton prior to the Champion Hurdle in 1996.

(Inset) Even in a photograph you can see the excitement and pent-up energy in a horse before a race. Sound Man at Cheltenham 1996.

Sound Man winging the open ditch – Ascot 1995.

Right: Hard as nails. As a young horse, Viking Flagship loved nothing better than a good scrap. Here winning the Victor Chandler Chase at Warwick in 1994.

Below: Still battling, this time up the hill at Cheltenham. Third in the Queen Mother Champion Chase, 1997.

Left: Showing horses a fence is a ritual for jockeys. Experienced horses like Viking Flagship don't pay much attention! They know what it's all about.

Top: A few furlongs earlier, One Man had looked like winning the 1996 Gold Cup. Here, he has scrambled – just – over the last. The Irish were already celebrating Imperial Call's win.

Bottom: Kempton 1996. One Man's second King George – and my fourth. Upsides is Strong Promise.

and five furlongs was a good starter for Remittance Man. He did make a mistake at the third last, which was rare for him – a lapse in concentration of mine or his – and he also blew up, which was to be expected. He beat King's Fountain, the only horse ever to have fallen twice in the same Gold Cup (once with a jockey and once without!). Norton's Coin, a former Gold Cup winner but now suffering from wind problems, was a long way back in fourth.

With a nagging belief that Remittance Man might have blown up rather than failed to get the trip in the previous season's King George VI Chase, Nicky decided he'd have another run before Boxing Day and sent him to Huntingdon for the two-and-a-half-mile Peterborough Chase, a race which often attracts some of the previous season's leading two-milers.

He was odds-on favourite, with just three other runners and Uncle Ernie the only one to beat. Emsee-H and Adrian Maguire set off at a blistering pace on tacky old ground. Remittance Man's jumping was 100 per cent on this day and it needed to be. I took it up at the third last but on the ground couldn't shake off Uncle Ernie who was being given a patient ride by Mark Dwyer. We were upsides and I was all out on Remittance Man when Uncle Ernie capsized at the last. It would have been very close and I couldn't say whether we would have won or been second had he stood up but if you thought I was lucky then I wouldn't disagree with you. But in terms of Remittance Man's wellbeing it was something of a Pyrrhic victory. He never had given me a great feel on the soft and I felt he wasn't quite right. Nicky wasn't happy either and when he returned home he was found to have what is called a touch of a leg (tendon strain). He must have pulled it around in the mud. However minor the strain, usually evident in a slight swelling, bow of the tendon or on a veterinary scan, the injury is serious. A touch of a leg is a bit like a little bit pregnant – there are no such halfway things. Nicky decided to rest him until the following season.

117

His return in the Emblem Chase at Kempton in late February 1994 was eagerly awaited by the racing public. Remittance Men don't grow on trees and racegoers love the sport's four-legged stars. It was a smashing race. He hadn't run for fifteen months and was expected to need the race. He and Deep Sensation were carrying level weights but Wonder Man, getting half a stone, was favourite. I was now riding for Martin Pipe and Mick Fitzgerald had taken over at Nicky's but as I knew the horse so well I was asked to ride him again.

He ran a hell of a race, one of his best. Deep Sensation was a funny character but Declan Murphy knew him better than anyone. They led with

Wonder Man and Adrian Maguire. I sat in behind them and Space Fair tracked me. It all happened at the ninth when Wonder Man made a mistake, came under pressure and surrendered his lead. I joined Declan in front at the third last. Remittance Man, enjoying his return to the racecourse, was travelling really well and toyed with Deep Sensation, running on from the last to win by three and a half lengths. He had, it seemed, lost nothing for his fifteen months off. His jumping was impeccable as usual and his engine had not seized up. We were all delighted.

It wouldn't be the first time that a horse had returned from a long lay-off and run up to his old form. Why they do it I don't know. However, they often don't run so well in their second race back. Remittance Man's second race back was in the Queen Mother Champion Chase, the race he had won two years previously. The punters had taken him to their hearts again – in his absence they had only grown fonder – and he was favourite ahead of Nicky's other runner Travado, and Viking Flagship, Sybillin and Deep Sensation. I had drastically got myself banned and was enjoying myself skiing – to have watched it live would have driven me mad – and Mick Fitzgerald was to have his first public ride on Remittance Man.

118

It turned out to be one of the races of the meeting, a line of five going to the third last. Remittance Man fell there, the only fall of his career. The form book says he still had every chance and that is how it will be perceived in racing history, but I had my doubts. He was in the front line but he wasn't travelling like he used to in the old days. Mick had had to ask him for a long one at the third last just to keep in the front line and hold a decent position at a crucial point. He asked him a big question but it was not impossible. I have no doubts that two years earlier he would have responded, but now, probably feeling his legs as he galloped downhill, he tried to put in another, short stride. At that speed you have no chance and he took a heavy fall. I don't think anyone ever wrote anything critical of Mick but they were all talking about it when I returned from holiday. I felt that the criticism was unfair – he'd definitely have come up for him before his injury. Up ahead, as Mick picked himself up and Remittance Man galloped on loose, Adrian was throwing everything at Viking Flagship. He was flying at the time and he just got home a length ahead of Travado – some consolation for Nicky – and Deep Sensation.

I rode Remittance Man once more that season, in the Mumm Melling Chase at Aintree. The fall had knocked the confidence out of him and it was very soft ground which he didn't like. He nearly fell with me a couple of times, was collared at the eleventh fence and finished tired and tailed off. The race was won by Katabatic. The day after that Miinnehoma won the Grand National. Remittance Man's leg problem recurred and he had the whole of the following season off.

But what do you do with a ten-year-old who gets too lit up to go hunting and yet has ten years of active retirement ahead of him? You can't just turn a horse like that out in a field and let him get bored. So they gave it one more try. He always ran well fresh and, aged eleven, he had one run at Sandown in December 1995, twenty months later. It was his seventeenth chase and only the fourth that he'd not won. Victory went to the American horse Lonesome Glory. Remittance Man had looked a picture before the race and had felt in great shape at home. He led them along to the end of the Railway fences and then tired going to the Pond Fence, three out. The spark had gone. Tim Collins and Nicky decided that he should be retired and I was glad to have ridden him in his last race.

What defines a great horse is a matter of personal opinion. I think he was a great horse, his record speaks for itself, and he was the most exceptional jumper I have ever ridden. With all manner of viruses attacking yards and with leg problems so common it is virtually impossible for a jumper to remain unbeaten for any length of time these days. You wouldn't think a light horse like Remittance Man would have suffered leg problems – it just goes to show the pressure a horse's tendons are under in a race. Without that Achilles heel he might have been one of the best two-milers we had ever seen.

It is believed that Remittance Man had a heart attack while hacking home from his first day hunting and, sadly, died on the spot.

119

RUSHING WILD

FOR SEVENTEEN YEARS I WAS DEVOTED TO NATIONAL HUNT RACING. The struggle for unattainable perfection in the sport gave me the greatest highs of my life, some indescribable thrills and a leg-up into my hobby – motor racing – but it also brought about some extreme lows and some difficult emotional times.

Jump jockeys put up with the scars of race riding, mental and physical, because we are addicted to the speed, the element of danger involved in jumping a fence at 35 m.p.h., and that eternal search for the perfect horse, the next Arkle or Desert Orchid. The worst thing about National Hunt racing is that accidents do happen and a number of potential stars over the years have injured themselves, sometimes beyond repair, before realizing their potential. The worst is when a horse you think might be the tops injures itself fatally. In one split second all that potential is cruelly taken away from owner, trainer, lad and jockey.

The loss of the talented Rushing Wild when leading the 1993 Irish National at Fairyhouse was a loss not just to his connections but to British racing. He wasn't the first and won't be the last to have suffered injury before reaching his peak. How good he might have been we will never know. Having ridden him twice, once in the Gold Cup, only his seventh run under Rules and in which he finished two lengths second to Jodami, and the other time in that fateful Irish National, I believe he was a Gold Cup winner of the future.

Rushing Wild was discovered by leading West Country point-to-point trainer Richard Barber who was asked to go and look at a horse in a Sussex field not far from where Josh Gifford trained. Richard liked what he saw and bought, for about 6,000 guineas, the four-year-old for a point-to-point owner of his called John Keighley.

That first winter with Richard Barber, Rushing Wild was given time to mature and was sent hunting with his local pack, the Cattistock. There is no better schooling ground for a young horse (or jockey) than the hunting field. A four- going on five-year-old would learn to jump all sorts of obstacles, jump out of boggy bits of ground where he would have to be sure of his footing, watch where he was putting his feet when cantering across plough and learn to equip himself among a large field of horses. The hunting ban has left a huge gap in the education of the young steeplechaser. A young horse must learn so much more on a morning with hounds than he would learn having a hack round the roads and a canter up an all-weather gallop.

122

Rushing Wild was by all accounts a superb hunter and I can well believe it having ridden him in the Gold Cup. Justin Farthing, who rode him in all his point-to-points, says he had the best season's hunting on a point-to-pointer ever and, because the horse was not highly regarded at the time, he was hunted hard. He took to it immediately. Once when jumping a line of hedges with one of Richard's jockeys on board one of the leathers attached to the saddle snapped. Instead of pulling the horse up – which nine out of ten people would do on nine out of ten horses – the lad kicked his other foot out of its iron, gave Rushing Wild a kick in the ribs and aimed at the remaining hedges, such was his confidence in the horse's jumping ability. He was a very brave horse.

After another summer out at grass the five-year-old Rushing Wild was sent hunting again with the idea, this time, of qualifying him as a point-to-pointer by attending on a set number of days. At home he progressed to working with the other pointers and hunter-chasers in the yard and earned the nickname Turtle because he was only marginally faster – or so it seemed on the gallops – than a tortoise and at times could only just get to the end of the all-weather gallop. He was not considered much good. A big horse only just beginning to fill out his frame, he was sent to a point-to-point for a run but was left in the horsebox after Richard and his owner, John, had walked the course and decided it was too firm for such a big horse who was still developing.

Patience, in such circumstances, is a virtue. Rushing Wild was roughed off and didn't run that season because the ground continued to dry up. It

may have been the making of the horse. After another summer at grass –
he was a very good doer at grass – the process was repeated, hunting with
the Cattistock until Christmas. It is a good job John wasn't looking for
instant results as a good Flat horse could have run fifteen times and had a
couple of seasons at stud by the time it had reached the same age. As a six-
year-old, the horse was prepared for his first point-to-point, which was due
to be at Nedge in late February. He still wasn't impressing at home but he
jumped pretty well in the schooling field and had three seasons hunting
behind him.

Many professionals knock point-to-points. I used to enjoy riding in them,
particularly for the late Colin Nash and his family when I first arrived at
Captain Forster's. They serve several purposes, not least of which is as a
further schooling ground for young National Hunt horses. In Ireland it is
even more the case. In many instances an impressive maiden winner
instantly commands a good price from a British trainer. They also allow
people to enjoy a hobby at an amateur level.

Having looked back through a lot of memory-jogging form for this book
I found it remarkable how ordinary-looking form can turn out, with the
benefit of hindsight, to be very good form. For example, a race run not too
long ago at Larkhill was won by Hanakham, winner of the 1997 Sun Alliance
Chase, who beat Harwell Lad, winner of the same season's, Whitbread Gold
Cup. Rushing Wild's first race, an adjacent hunts maiden at Nedge, was
much the same. Ridden by Justin, whose weight eventually got the better
of him before he retired to full-time farming, Rushing Wild finished a five-
length second to Double Silk. It is amazing that probably the best two
hunter-chasers, both of them subsequent winners of the Cheltenham
Christies Foxhunters, should begin their careers in the same Division of the
Mendip Farmers' maiden.

It wasn't long before Rushing Wild got on the score sheet with a win at
the Beaufort Point-to-point at Didmarton near Badminton. For a big horse
he showed a good turn of foot from the last. He progressed through the
ranks, winning a restricted open at Badbury Rings and an open at Toller
Gate Down. At Kingweston in a lowly hunt members race he blotted his
copybook for the one and only time when he appeared to run out,
unseating Justin in the process. However, Justin has always blamed himself
for that. He had kicked on in the lead and the horse had been getting a bit
bored in front. He rectified that back at Badbury with his fourth and final
win of the season on his sixth and last run. Occasionally Tim Mitchell or

another local rider would come to him at the second last thinking they could overhaul Rushing Wild but Justin always liked to give him a breather. He would then say, 'See you back in the weighing room.' With that he would change gear and the race would be over.

The following season he was immediately impressive winning at Bishop's Court and again at Didmarton, where he had won his first race the previous year. It was about this time that Richard and John had to make a decision. The end of February/beginning of March is lateish in the National Hunt year, particularly if the ground dries up quickly. If they sent Rushing Wild hunter-chasing he might win a couple but would automatically be a handicapper the following season if he were to run under Rules. Much better, they reasoned, to stick to point-to-points that time before having the whole year to send him novice chasing the following season. They were prepared to make one exception though, and to run him in the Christies Foxhunters Challenge at Cheltenham. They figured he could win an ordinary hunter-chase without too much difficulty, but if he was beaten they could send him back to the point-to-point field until the end of the season. If he won it, well the prize was very good and they would happily forfeit the following season as a novice. By this time Rushing Wild was, very occasionally, putting in a stunning piece of work at home. Not every time, just every now and again.

On 12 March 1992 the stage was set. Cool Ground had just won the Gold Cup under a terrific ride from Adrian Maguire and in the weighing room the professionals sat down to watch the amateurs have their 'Gold Cup'. There was a bit of a word for Rushing Wild among the West Country amateurs but the small mare Dun Gay Lass from the north was a warm favourite ahead of the impeccably bred Wall Game, who belonged to bloodstock agent James Delahooke. When the American-bred horse had grown too much too soon ever to be a Flat horse he was rescued for hunter-chasing. Raise An Argument had been a good horse but was thirteen now and Rushing Wild, considering he had won six out of eight, was a generous 9–1. I also remember the race because Knox's Corner was Noel Chance's first runner at Cheltenham and by 1997 he had sent out Mr Mulligan to win the Gold Cup itself. Noel, who was still in Ireland then, said he always knew his horse wouldn't win after he had walked the course with his jockey. When they got to the first big fence down the back the amateur turned to Noel and said, 'Jay-sus, that's big.' It instilled little confidence in the trainer.

Rushing Wild was a strong galloper though and was near the front all the way. At the eighteenth Justin let him stride on. He soon had the rest of the field in trouble and despite clouting the second last – bearing in mind it was only his first run under Rules and Cheltenham's fences would be twice the size of some point-to-point obstacles – he strode away with the race, winning by twenty-five lengths in a time that was eight seconds slower than the Gold Cup. Considering he was not even racing out in front it was an impressive time and Justin, who said afterwards that he had never ridden a horse so 'spot on', reckons he would have made a race of it with Cool Ground had he been in the Gold Cup itself. As it was, Ardesee was the distant second. Rushing Wild's high cruising speed and ability to quicken off it caught my attention. He had relentlessly galloped his rivals into the ground and the only worry Justin had was lining him up at the start. He did have an ability, probably mental immaturity, to get a little bit uptight at times but he was perfectly behaved once he knew what Justin wanted him to do. After the race he spent a quiet week on the road – most likely thinking about what had happened. It must be quite a shock for a horse to go from a local point-to-point to the spectacle of Cheltenham with its roaring crowd of 55,000 without any gradual preparation.

As night follows day, so the Foxhunter winner at Cheltenham normally goes on to try to complete the double with victory at Aintree in the Martell Fox Hunters Chase. Now that was quite a tall order – Rushing Wild having a crack at Aintree on only his second outing under Rules. With twenty-nine runners it was more like a mini-Grand National. He and Justin were 9–4 to complete the double. Marcus led them along as far as the Canal Turn on the front-running and mightily keen No Escort until the horse – not Marcus! – broke a blood vessel. Rushing Wild jumped well on the whole, blundered at the Canal but was still in third with a chance when he fell at the third last, leaving Paul Murphy and Gee-A to come with a late run and catch Raise An Argument. It was the first time Justin had been really happy in the race: he had survived a couple of previous mistakes, one of which was at the Chair and was cruising in behind the leaders. Justin is confident he would have won had the horse stood up.

His last run of that season was disappointing. Expected to follow up that Aintree fall with a comprehensive victory in the Marlborough Bookshop Hunters Chase at Chepstow, he made heavy weather of beating Fiddler's Pike, who was admittedly a good staying chaser on his day, as his fifth in Miinnehoma's National proved. Instead of beating him half the track he hung right-handed and only just got his act together to lead near the finish.

It slightly took the gloss off his productive season but the horse was, it turned out, well over the top by then. Nevertheless, John knew that he was in possession of a good horse.

Just how good a horse he wanted to find out and to that end sent him to Martin Pipe the following season where he would have the benefit of top-class facilities. When Richard delivered him, straight from grass, he had put on so much condition that Martin asked if they had been in a chocolate factory for the summer! At the time Peter Scudamore was still riding and was first jockey to Martin. However, as he was at Kempton on Boxing Day for Rushing Wild's first run for his new yard, the ride at Wincanton fell to Jonothan Lower, who remained second jockey at the yard until he was forced to stop riding for eighteen months when discovered to be diabetic. Martin had not quite managed to work all the chocolate off him and, rarely for one of his charges, the horse looked a little backward for this first outing. It didn't matter. Though Rushing Wild was top-weight, he was a big horse and could carry it and he was taking on a bunch of Wincanton old regulars. He and Jonothan were left in the lead at the seventh but were already well clear when he made his only mistake at the fourth last. He won by an impressive twelve lengths from the favourite Fit For Firing.

Next time out he went for the Anthony Mildmay/Peter Cazalet Memorial Chase at Sandown at the end of the first week of January 1993. In the field was the previous year's Gold Cup winner Cool Ground – already the winner of this race – Nick The Brief, 1991 Grand National Winner Seagram, Kildimo, Ghofar, Brown Windsor and Sibton Abbey. That was quite a collection of handicap chasers, with a Gold Cup, Whitbread, National and two Hennessys under their belts. This time Scu took over and despite the horse's usual single mistake (this time at the eighteenth), on a favourable weight of 10st 1lb Rushing Wild annihilated the opposition and came home easily by twenty-five lengths from Cool Ground. Even allowing for a pound a length, it still made Rushing Wild equal to the Gold Cup winner. I was dumped at the sixth from a horse of David Nicholson's, a particular favourite called Duntree, and watched the closing stages on my feet. It was an impressive run, and had people speculating early about his chances in the Gold Cup.

The Agfa Diamond Chase at Sandown was, so the script had it, just a stepping stone to Gold Cup glory. He had gone up in the ratings from 127 on Boxing Day to 152. He was now carrying 12st and 2–1 on. Only two

126

others were prepared to take him on, the Luke Harvey-ridden Country Member and Captain Dibble. Country Member beat him six lengths. He appeared to be done for toe from the last and Scu was criticized for not having gone fast enough but I don't think Rushing Wild can have been right that day, and the winner did go on to run very well at Cheltenham that season. I was watching on a monitor in the changing room. It was very disappointing at the time, almost as if the bubble had burst.

His next race was the 1993 Gold Cup, to be surrounded by the controversy of my 'jocking off' Jonothan Lower. Martin had asked me three weeks before the race if I would ride Rushing Wild but I was committed to ride Another Coral for the Duke. Scu had already plumped for Chatam, who had won the Hennessy sixteen months earlier, after experiencing Rushing Wild's disappointing run at Sandown. On the morning of the race it was announced that Another Coral had been withdrawn with an injury to his tendon and I asked my agent, Robert Kington, to ring up Martin and see if the door was still open. It was.

He looked fantastic in the paddock. He was a lean, sleek racing machine. In the race we jumped off near the front. Run For Free hit a downhill fence early on. Cherrykino fell heavily at the seventh, another potentially very useful horse fatally injured. Rushing Wild jumped right over the first few fences as I had been warned. After Run For Free dropped out of the picture it left us and Sibton Abbey up at the front. Once we had jumped the fence at the top of the hill where the landing side just runs away from horses who make a mistake, I asked Rushing Wild to go on for the last time. It was a long way from home, but I knew he was a galloper. Going to the second last I thought I would win – until the large brown head of Jodami, and, worse still, Mark Dwyer sitting pretty motionless, drew alongside. I drove him into the last and got, as I had throughout, a terrific response, but so did Mark on Jodami. I hoped we might out-battle Jodami up the hill but he just had that bit of acceleration to put two lengths between us. It was a very good performance. Royal Athlete was third, seven lengths away, The Fellow fourth, Sibton Abbey fifth and Docklands Express sixth. Afterwards I was convinced that Rushing Wild would be a winner the next year. Even taking into consideration Charter Party's win for me three years earlier, it was one of the best rides I have ever had in the Gold Cup.

His last run of the season was to be in the Jameson Irish Grand National at Fairyhouse, a traditional Easter Monday fixture. He had top weight of

12st and was second favourite behind Zeta's Lad, who had been travelling well in the void Grand National before he pulled up after a circuit. I remember John Upson, Zeta's Lad's trainer, had said something disparaging about Irish point-to-points in the aftermath of the Grand National and there was a worry – unfounded – that he might get lynched, or worse, when he arrived. From the outset I wasn't particularly happy with Rushing Wild. He had not been willing to line up, which may have been a sign of his being over the top, but he didn't give a good feel in the race either. If you're leading a race like the Irish National you can't pull up if you're not getting a good feel even when a horse is jumping very well, which he was. It was perhaps to be like Aintree the previous year when he eventually came on to the bridle for Justin, but as we turned away right-handed round the bend at Ballyhack I felt him change legs and heard a crack. Rushing Wild immediately lost his action behind. I knew instantly that it was serious and pulled him up. He was desperately lame behind with a fractured pelvis. Quite a few horses suffer hairline fractures of the pelvis and survive, but this was a serious fracture which had clearly moved. You get hardened to these occasions. I hate it for the lads – after all, they are the people who become so attached to the horses. The first time it happens is very distressing and I never liked hanging around or having to hold a horse to be put down. There was nothing worse than walking back to the stands with an empty bridle.

128

Rushing Wild was put down very quickly and thankfully endured little pain. He was eight years old at the time, and I'm convinced he would have been a much improved horse the following season. I include him here because, although his career was tragically short-lived, he was one of the greatest chasers I have ever ridden.

MIINNEHOMA

T HE UNDOUBTED HIGHLIGHTS OF MY TWO YEARS AS FIRST JOCKEY TO MARTIN PIPE WERE, OF COURSE, WINNING TWO CHAMPION- SHIPS AND MIINNEHOMA'S WIN AT THE END OF THE FIRST OF THOSE SEASONS IN THE 1994 MARTELL GRAND NATIONAL. It was my second win in the race and only Brian Fletcher, who partnered Red Alligator and Red Rum (twice), had won the race more than twice – although Carl Llewellyn and Ruby Walsh have also won two since I did, and are still riding.

That first season with Martin, 1993–4, had got off to a slow start for both of us. I was under pressure from the press, some of whom were predicting a split before the end of the season, I was going through a bad time at home, and I wasn't enjoying my racing. Martin had had only twenty-five winners by the end of November because of some coughing in the yard but people were intimating that he was missing Peter Scudamore.

Then in February I got banned for putting Adrian Maguire, my title rival, out through a wing at Nottingham, forcing me to miss my first Cheltenham Festival attached to the yard. With Adrian doing so well for David Nicholson there were moments when I had twinges of regret at having left the Duke, but 9 April 1994 was the day when all that was forgotten.

Miinnehoma was, of course, owned by the outrageous comedian Freddie Starr. He had bought the horse on the recommendation of Newark trainer Owen Brennan, whose son Martin was a good friend and colleague of mine in the weighing room for years. Owen used to train a horse for Freddie called Kouros, who won ten races for them. Unfortunately Kouros broke his neck in a fall at Bangor one day. Freddie said he would pay a fair price for a replacement and Owen kept an eye out for the right sort of horse.

At Doncaster's spring sale Owen saw a couple of horses that might have done the job before he bumped into a friend, Pat Doyle, who was looking after some Irish horses there. He said he had the right horse but that it was a sod to ride. It could buck with the best of them but if you could find someone who could sit on the horse, who had been a nightmare to break in, then he had ability. This was Miinnehoma, who had been bought as an unbroken three-year-old at the Derby sale two summers before for 5,800 guineas. His owner had just finished reading the biography of Paul Getty and named the horse after the place where he first struck oil in Texas. 'Miinnehoma' had clearly been a lucky name.

He was bred in Wexford by Patrick Day. His sire was a local stallion called Kambalda, who had won the Ascot Stakes and is also the sire of Barton Bank. His dam, Mrs Cains, had an undistinguished career on the racecourse, pulling up in her only race, a bumper. You wouldn't have bought the horse on his breeding, that was for sure. However, his two runs in Irish point-to-points had suggested that the awkward horse did have some ability. Gauging Irish point-to-points is difficult. Some horses arrive with huge reputations from the Irish point-to-point field but prove an expensive disappointment here. It is sometimes difficult to know exactly what they have beaten. Miinnehoma had won his first one ridden by Nicky Dee, the only person who could ride him. At his second point-to-point, Nicky had broken his collarbone earlier in the afternoon and another jockey had ridden him and been beaten – just.

132

Owen had a look at the horse though and liked him, 'though he had a funny old eye on him'. When he got home he rang up Freddie Starr in Windsor and said he had found the right horse. Freddie asked what it would fetch. 'Maybe 25,000 guineas, maybe thirty, maybe thirty-five,' replied Owen. 'Well,' said Freddie, 'you can go up to 50,000 guineas for it.'

The night before the sale, Freddie rang at 11.00 when Owen was in bed. He wanted to come with him to the sale the next morning and would be arriving shortly. Could Owen meet him in Newark and give him a lead home? The next morning they went to Doncaster. During the course of the day Freddie had got involved talking to a few people and when Miinnehoma came into the ring the comedian was nowhere to be seen. This worried Owen who, nevertheless, began bidding for the gelding. 'I'm sure he never saw the horse until he came in the ring,' recalls Owen, who handed over the bidding to Freddie. He was knocked down to him for 35,000 guineas. On the advice of Pat Doyle, Owen turned Miinnehoma out for the rest of the summer.

When he came in he indeed proved to be a swine to ride. Though he was a gentleman in his box he was lethal when anyone rode him. He dropped everyone left, right and centre. Then, to cap it all, later that autumn he caught salmonella poisoning and rapidly went downhill. There was nothing Owen could do but lay him off for a while and bring him back into exercise in January. He was soon going quite well for Martin Brennan but then Martin broke a collarbone at Nottingham one day. Owen wasn't worried about Martin's health, he was worried about his own – he was going to have to ride 'the sod' out the following morning! Trainer and horse got on well though, much better than Owen, a former jump jockey, thought they would. He made him work round Doncaster and used to take him off on his own down to a water meadow near Newark. The one thing you couldn't do with the horse was give anyone a leg up on him. You had to jump on at the walk.

The day came for his first bumper on 28 March 1989 at Uttoxeter. Jamie Railton had the ride but was dropped twice before he got to the start, once in the paddock and once on the course. Eventually Owen managed to run down to the last fence with the horse and get Jamie going on his way to the start with one hand in the neck strap and the other holding on to a plait. After his antics in the paddock he was 33–1 and Owen invested a fiver. The race went like clockwork and he hacked up by five lengths from Hey Cottage who had already won a bumper. Next time out he went to Doncaster for the Doncaster Bloodstock Sales Supreme National Hunt Flat race. He made virtually all the running but was beaten a head on the line by a horse called Judge's Fancy who had come up the other side of the track. They were twenty lengths in front of the third.

His third and last run in a bumper was at Market Rasen where he finished a good third on the firm. Owen turned him out for the summer in the belief that he had a right horse on his hands. The anticipation was short lived. Freddie rang up one evening and told Owen that he had sold the horse. 'I hope it's not true,' said Owen, and when he asked to whom Freddie refused to say. He added that a box would be arriving at 7.00 on Sunday morning. When it arrived Owen asked the driver where he was taking the horse. The driver was not allowed to say. 'I know bloody well that he's going to Martin Pipe's,' said

Owen. 'Do one thing for me though, tell the head lad he's a sod when you first get on him. If he doesn't know that someone will get killed on him.'

And with that Miinnehoma left Owen Brennan. 'The best horse I've had here on the gallops,' he reflects. 'I was heartbroken when he went. He was a sod and you never felt safe on him but I loved him all the same.'

The first time I began to notice Miinnehoma was on his second outing over hurdles for Martin. He had already won his first race by a couple of lengths at Fontwell, and I rode a horse of the Duke's called Tug of Gold against him at Haydock. He made all the running, typical of one of Martin's horses, and when the rest of us looked like we might get to him at the second last he just picked up and went again. The next time he ran I rode Gatterstown against him at Newbury and again he did the same thing to beat Sunninghill Celtic by a length and a half. This was a horse trained by David Elsworth who I knew was pretty good. That was a Philip Corne's qualifier and he went back to Newbury for the final, in which he beat Remittance Man by an astonishing twelve lengths. He was beginning to look special but he was put in his place by Dwadme on fast ground in the White Satin Hurdle at Liverpool, in which he finished fourth. That was the year Mr Frisk won the National and the first time the ground had been firm for the race since the War, so you can imagine how fast it was.

134

At the end of that season and during the start of the next he was bothered with a niggling back problem which has since been linked to the fractured pelvis he was discovered to have later in his career. It was almost twenty-one months before he was seen out on a racecourse again – at Newton Abbot for a three-and-a-quarter-mile novice chase. Sent off 6–5 favourite despite his long absence, Miinnehoma made much of the running to beat my ride, Calabrese, trained by Nicky Henderson, a couple of lengths. I cut out some of the running on the last circuit but effectively ended up only in giving Scu a nice lead to the last where he passed me. His second chase was at Chepstow where I rode another of Nicky's, called Mutare. He was a very good horse, a fair bit better than Calabrese, and on his day he had the potential to become one of the best I have ever ridden. He was owned by Michael Buckley who had a dreadful run of bad luck with some expensive horses, including Mutare who had increasing problems and eventually started breaking blood vessels. In the end he collapsed and died at Ascot one day. I think Michael lost three good horses like him at Ascot in the space of two seasons.

I thought the Chepstow race was a really good novice chase. Mutare was in cracking form and I couldn't see him getting beat but, though we had every chance at the last where we were upsides, Miinnehoma ran on strongly to beat us three and a half lengths. That really made me sit up and take notice of Miinnehoma. And the form of the race went on to work out well. Danny Harrold, a horse of Jenny Pitman's who was a good novice but never really went on to fulfil his potential, was twenty-five lengths back in third.

Miinnehoma and Mutare met again in that season's Sun Alliance Chase at Cheltenham. It turned out to be one of the hottest Sun Alliances there has ever been. Mutare and I made much of the running and had been passed by Miinnehoma but we were still just on the heels of the leaders when he put down on me at the second last and fell. I don't think we would have won anyway. This left Miinnehoma in front with Bradbury Star breathing down his collar. It was a great finish with Scu all out on Miinnehoma to beat Bradbury Star half a length. Scu was at his very strongest, and needed to be because it looked like Bradbury Star would beat him at the last. Ten lengths behind them were future Scottish National winners Run For Free in third and Captain Dibble in fifth. Future Grand National winner Rough Quest was fourth. General Idea, who went on to win a Galway Plate, was further down the field. One hell of a supporting cast.

135

The 1992–3 season began in the Rehearsal Chase at Chepstow, a prep race for the Welsh National but a graveyard for favourites and former Gold Cup winners such as Jodami and Master Oats who used it to launch their title defences. Miinnehoma was odds-on but never really got a look in. His stable companion Run For Free made all the running for Mark Perrett who got on so well with him. Miinnehoma was not an easy ride, and seemed to get quite tired. He finished second to his stable companion and beat another from Martin's yard, Bonanza Boy. A one-two-three for the Pipe stable.

He was second in the SGB at Ascot to Captain Dibble, making a few uncharacteristic mistakes, and third in the Welsh National where Martin had the first four home, headed by Run For Free and Riverside Boy. Bonanza Boy was fourth. His fourth and last run of that season was in the Timeform Hall of Fame Chase at Cheltenham which Sibton Abbey, a late spare ride for Steve Smith-Eccles, won. Miinnehoma ran no sort of race and was tailed off when Mark Perrett finally pulled him up. Though he had been placed three times in good company you'd expect a Sun Alliance winner of Miinnehoma's calibre at least to have got his head in front somewhere during his first season as a handicapper. However, when he got home the root of the problem was exposed: the cracked pelvis. It is a reasonably common modern racing injury – it probably was in the old days too but it was too hard to detect. Now with modern veterinary equipment you can X-ray a horse's pelvis. The injury is not necessarily fatal, but it required days and weeks of treatment in the hands of Mary Bromiley, the famous horse physiotherapist, at her old home in Baydon, near Lambourn.

My first ride on Miinnehoma was at Newbury fourteen months later on 5 March. Horses like Miinnehoma who have had two lengthy spells off the course don't often make a worthwhile comeback. One long lay-off and they might make a bit of a comeback but very few do after two. I don't know why it is. Maybe they are wary of the pain that may strike, or maybe the lungs, out of work for so long, don't function quite so well. The other thing horses tend to do after long rests is run one good race – perhaps showing extra enthusiasm for a job that they've missed – before sliding back into the also-rans. On the plus side, though, Miinnehoma didn't have that many miles on the clock and though his back was dodgy his legs were fine. He wasn't a big horse to sit on. There was very little in the way of neck in front of you. I'd schooled him over three of Martin's small schooling fences and he had jumped them well but that didn't give me much idea of how he would handle Newbury and, quite frankly, I wasn't much looking forward to the ride. There were five runners besides Miinnehoma: Chris Maude on Guiburn's Nephew, who usually made the running, Forest Sun who was past his best, Smartie Express and Mr Entertainer, two good handicap chasers.

Though he hadn't won since the Sun Alliance, Miinnehoma was still top weight with 12st. I jumped off and rode an ordinary race letting Chris make the running. Miinnehoma was entered for the National and this trip, we thought, was much too short – getting him round in one piece was the plan although I knew Martin would have him fit. Guiburn's Nephew led to the third last where I took it up. He had jumped well and I enjoyed the spin but coming to the last he started looking around and began to idle. When Forest Sun came to me he picked up and went away to win by a couple of lengths but it gave me a crucial insight into the temperament of the horse. Though he had made all the running in his hurdles and in some of his chases it appeared that he needed to be held up much longer than

I had done at Newbury. That was to be very important when it came to tactics at Aintree later that season. Even Martin was surprised by the Newbury win though. 'He needs a lot further than two-and-a-half miles,' he said afterwards.

For that season's Gold Cup I was banned so Adrian Maguire rode him (ironically because he was leading the championship and, three weeks later, turned out to be our biggest danger in the National). He ran a great race for three miles but tailed off over the last quarter mile to finish a respectable seventh to The Fellow. It wasn't a particularly fast-run Gold Cup – it was only four seconds faster than the Foxhunters on the same card – and they were all bunched up coming round the last bend, which wouldn't have suited him. He was beaten less than twenty lengths and Adrian said he'd had a good ride off him. I cast an eye over the video when I got back. I didn't enjoy watching Cheltenham, particularly when I hadn't been there.

The 1993 Grand National had been declared void after two false starts – the starting tape had got wrapped around my neck on the second start – and while it had not been a disaster for the popularity of the race, which has a great, colourful history, it was important that the 1994 Grand National got off to a good start if nothing else. The new start had been tried and tested the previous autumn and there seemed to be no problems. It was, however, the British weather that looked like causing serious problems. It rained and rained. The ground was bottomless and there was talk on Friday night of the race being cancelled. It was certainly the softest it had ever been at Aintree during my career.

Martin had four runners in the race. Riverside Boy didn't mind the soft but he was a quirky character and was running for the first time in blinkers. Mark Richards rode him. Run For Free had always been Mark Perrett's ride and Paco's Boy didn't really have much chance. I didn't really fancy my own chances. Aintree's fences seem a foot higher when you jump them out of heavy ground and I didn't think Miinnehoma was quite big enough to handle them. If I got round, I thought, I'd have an each-way chance, but I knew only a handful would complete in those conditions.

Increased security surrounded the race. Part of the problem the previous year, apart from the failure of a system that relied on flag-waving to stop the false starters, was the presence of animal-rights demonstrators. This time a security fence had been erected and was dotted with police. Beforehand all the jockeys were herded into one of Aintree's two changing rooms for a lecture from the stewards. This is traditional. Someone like the late Dick Saunders, who probably did exactly what he told you not to when he rode in the race, got up on a table and told you not to go too fast down to the first fence. That always amuses me, mainly because I know it goes in one ear and out the other without snagging on anything in the way of brain matter in between. This time they also held up one of the new 'advance flagmen's' flags. To be one step ahead of any demonstrators they had a coloured chequered flag and we were told it was the only flag we should recognize – in case demonstrators invaded the course with red flags.

There is always a great deal of camaraderie before a National. Jockeys who don't really know each other, or don't even like each other, wish each other well and tell each other that the main thing is to come back safe and sound. A few have one last drag on a cigarette, much like you'd imagine a condemned man would before facing the firing squad, you have a last polish of your many pairs of goggles to make sure they're not fogged up, and then it's out past the cameras to your date, one hopes, with a benevolent destiny.

All the interviews are done with, forty jockeys who have all talked up their chances go out to the paddock, thirty-nine of them to see just how misplaced their optimism had been. My stomach always tingled at this stage with the prospect of riding in the world's greatest race, the prospect of attacking those thirty fences, of a pretty reasonable rider's record in the race to be upheld. My return to the weighing room was, I thought, more likely to be in an ambulance or vet's car than on a horse escorted to the winner's enclosure by two policemen. In that ground I'd have been in the majority. Martin didn't give me any orders. I just said to him that I didn't want to hit the front too soon.

In the National it is important to know beforehand which horses to track and which to avoid. There was the Gold Cup winner The Fellow, Moorcroft Boy, and Master Oats who both loved that ground and was in cracking form. Double Silk had won the Aintree Foxhunters the previous year, Romany King had been second before and Young Hustler was a good staying chaser but, like Miinnehoma, not the largest.

We set off to a roar from the crowd. The pace was sensible on account of the softness of the ground rather than the stewards' briefing, and it took Miinnehoma only a couple of fences to acclimatize to the course and start travelling well and enjoying himself. We'd lost three at the first, Henry Mann, Elfast and Fourth of July. Elfast was ridden by Graham McCourt who was paying homage, yet again, to his favourite landing side. Ushers Island made a bad mistake at the first big ditch, the third, and lost Tony Dobbin, and at the next Romany King, who was hating the ground, turned over on the inside. We lost three more at Becher's, all Irish horses, and Gay Ruffian at the seventh, the smallest fence on the course.

I saw Double Silk take a crashing fall at the thirteenth – the second last on the following circuit and one of the fences that was earning a reputation as a modern-day Aintree bogey. He had been almost running away in front. Behind me at the same fence Master Oats came down. By the time we jumped The Chair we'd lost seventeen of the thirty-six starters and many of those still going didn't look like they were going to get much further. The attrition rate on the ground was even higher than we'd though it would be, but luckily the softer ground meant a softer landing and fewer injuries. I pulled wide to ensure daylight at The Chair.

Passing the stands Jamie Osborne on Garrison Savannah and I had a bit of a chat. We were both travelling well and having a good ride. Mark Richards was up with us on Riverside Boy. I was handy, which I knew you would have to be on that ground, and I didn't really see that many others. 'How are you going?' I asked him. 'Great,' he replied. 'The old horse is loving it.' Martin must have been quietly pleased as we passed the stands with three of his four runners all handy and with a chance. The quirky Riverside Boy was just about in front but with blinkers on the first time hung very wide round the stable bend. Some might describe that as good sense. When he did rejoin us he was very wide and, wearing the blinkers, couldn't see the others so he refused at the next.

We went down towards the first fence for the second time, the seventeenth, and bang, a loose horse hit Jamie broadside and took him out. He could so easily have taken me out instead. God knows which horse it was but it also hampered Mark Perrett on Run For Free who ended up in the mêlée on the deck.

Suddenly Martin, who moments earlier had three out of four with a chance, had just one left on its feet. That's the Grand National for you. This left us nearly in front, just where I didn't want to be, and going to the big ditch, the nineteenth. I was screaming and shouting to Miinnehoma, urging him to get over it. He was half-inclined to stop. It wouldn't be the first time a horse, left in front, has had a good look at a fence. I know that Marcus believes Mr Frisk, through surprise back in 1990, thought briefly about refusing at the twenty-third, the smallest on the course, after Uncle Merlin had fallen at the previous fence. Miinnehoma got over it and was luckily joined on the landing side by The Fellow, Just So and Ebony Jane. It was proof of what a sensible pace we were going that Just So, not known for his foot, could lay up so close to the pace.

I was happy with the way things were going to Becher's. We weren't in front like I had been nearly ten years earlier on West Tip when he'd fallen. Miinnehoma jumped the fence well. He'd really got the hang of Aintree by now, but he went a stride and seemed to leave his front leg underneath him, a combination of the ground, slipping a bit and the drop causing him to stumble. I felt him on his knees and thought we had blown our chances. Any other horse would have turned over but from somewhere he found an extra leg. It was very quick and he was almost immediately back on his feet and galloping towards the twenty-third. It had me worried for a while. I didn't pick him up – you can see from the photographs that the reins are in loops – he did it all himself. I just sat there, hoping. And I suppose one of the key reasons for my remaining in the saddle was that he kept straight. It is when they skew sideways that it presents a problem.

We were soon back on an even keel and I was beginning to think that if I could just get him to pop away at his fences we might have a chance here. I knew there weren't many of us left standing, and then I heard The Fellow crash into the Canal Turn. He must have done his best to break it judging by the noise and crack of splitting wood it made. I was repeating to myself: concentrate, concentrate, get a lead, get a lead.

Then Adrian Maguire and Moorcroft Boy arrived upsides Miinnehoma. He was the one person I'd completely forgotten about. He'd quietly crept into the race and all of a sudden he arrived on the scene running away. Down at the Canal Turn he hadn't been going that well according to Adrian, but he'd come back right on to the bridle. I thought it was all over. Moorcroft Boy should get the trip well and there was a doubt in my own mind about Miinnehoma getting it in the ground. It became a game of cat and mouse. I wanted a good lead off Adrian and he was conscious of me doing this. He tried to keep me hemmed in at the back of the loose Young Hustler, behind whom I just had to pop the last fence. Suddenly I went from running away to off the bridle in a matter of strides. Adrian had jumped the last and quickened up. Damn, I thought, I've definitely played the wrong card here. I should have gone with him. I pulled my stick through and gave Miinnehoma a slap. As soon as I did that he picked up and came back on the bridle, running away. At the same time Moorcroft Boy started tying up.

It was Adrian's final effort and fifty yards from the last it was as though he had fallen in a hole. I didn't want to play all my cards and be exposed so I sat and sat and sat and took a pull. I know it's a dangerous thing to do at the end of four and a half miles in the mud but I also know that going too soon would be equally dangerous. I was between a rock and a hard place. Wait until the Elbow I told myself.

There were cones and fence attendants with bright jackets on the inside at the Elbow which, now that I'd asked him to go, Miinnehoma started looking at and, simultaneously, a head appeared on my right-hand side at my boot. It was like all my nightmares coming at once – to finish so close and yet so far in the Grand National. I didn't know which horse's head it was but I thought it was going to take the National off me. I went to pull the whip through and missed with my right hand so picked it up and used it in my left. It was panic-stations. As soon as I gave him a couple of cracks he went away again. He won by a length and a quarter from Just So and Simon Burrough. Talk about confused emotions. I thought I'd won and lost that race a dozen times over the last mile, half a dozen times since the last fence.

It had long been one of my ambitions to win the National a second time. The first time you win it you get swept along on a tide of emotion. So much packed into a couple of hours afterwards that you only remember certain, isolated things and the rest is a blur. This time I could sit back and enjoy it at my leisure. For that reason I rate it above West Tip's National when I was so young that I hardly managed to take it in at all.

I was escorted by a couple of burly policemen to weigh in. John Buckingham, my valet, took my saddle and I went back out for an interview with Martin and Des Lynam. Martin was on the phone to Freddie Starr who was appearing in one of his shows that night so couldn't be there. When Martin passed the phone I thought there was a dog barking on the other end of it. And I was meant to be having a conversation with my owner! We had a late night afterwards, celebrating, but the overriding feeling for a jockey after winning a National is one of complete and utter tiredness, you're just drained.

On Sunday I went to Martin's yard at Nicholashayne near Wellington in the West Country where everyone was going mad, mainly led by Freddie Starr. You'd think he was in the middle of saying something important and he'd come out with a joke. I don't think the racing press knew quite how to take him and I'm very sure I didn't! Miinnehoma, I must say, did not look like he'd slogged round four and a half miles in the heavy the previous day.

We had a late night in the local that evening that led into the next day, then I was to do morning TV in London. The first few days after a National are a whirlwind of activity before it settles down again with racing at Ascot the following Wednesday. Quite rightly that was the last race for Miinnehoma for that season. As if proof were needed of how bad a ride he could be, Miinnehoma showed his true colours when being photographed by Mel Fordham for a promotional calendar. He was a nightmare to sit on, very fresh, and he whipped round and bucked, making a complete mess of Martin's beautifully manicured lawn!

The following season he was to have a light campaign aimed at the National again. In the soft he won first time out at Haydock, beating General Pershing and Katabatic over two and a half miles again. He felt as good as ever although I'm not sure the other two were on song that day. He then ran a terrific third in Master Oats's Gold Cup. It was very soft ground again. I knew he had a good each-way chance but I had to be quite hard on him for much of the second circuit. But for a twelve-year-old he ran a hell of a race. So going to the 1995 National I thought we had an even better chance than we'd had the previous year.

Between Cheltenham and Aintree the ground dried up very quickly. There were big discussions about whether they would run Master Oats in the National although they eventually gave him the go-ahead. This time, however, Miinnehoma made a mistake at the first and after that he was never happy. I'm sure he hurt himself: he banged a fence hard when he wasn't really warmed up and that would not have done his pelvis the world of good. Like Last Suspect, horses sometimes give their all in a National which they win and then – and you can't blame them – don't really want to do it again. Even though he'd appeared fresh the Sunday following the previous year's race it had obviously taken the stuffing out of him. And remember we're talking about an intelligent horse here. I was tailed off from Becher's first time and pulled up before the twenty-first. I remember going round with Graham McCourt on Gold Cap, keeping each other company. We were jumping the last on the first circuit when the leaders were jumping The Chair but there is something about the race – I suppose Foinavon lurks at the back of your mind – which means you don't pull up until things are beyond the futile. When I saw Desert Lord and Nuaffe fall, who were also behind, it reminded me that it would be a shame to put Miinnehoma on the floor for reasons of personal vanity and I pulled him up to a halt. Way ahead of us Royal Athlete and Jason Titley were leading the field into the history books. I was disappointed not to be with them.

I suppose in an ideal world Miinnehoma would have been retired there and then. But he was a wild, mad character. I don't think he'd have been suited like so many old Aintree horses to retirement to the hunting field or, for that matter, to a grass field. But at the end of that season I parted company with Martin so it was not an issue for me.

He ran for another season but showed nothing. He'd done his bit and showed no sort of form in four runs the last of which was, sadly for a National winner, a long-distance novice hurdle at Newton Abbot at the age of thirteen.

As for comparisons with West Tip, he did not have quite the scope of my 1986 National winner. But they were two of the most intelligent horses I have ever ridden. People go through the form until they are boss-eyed before a National but they don't seem to take intelligence into their calculations. If you could conduct an equine IQ test on all the runners I bet the winner would be among the top ten per cent almost every time.

143

FLAKEY DOVE

OLD MACDONALD HAD A FARM, AND ON THAT FARM HE HAD CATTLE, SHEEP, CHICKENS, DUCKS, A GOAT AND SEVERAL GENERATIONS OF THE SAME FAMILY OF NATIONAL HUNT THOROUGHBREDS DISTINGUISHED BY THEIR CONSISTENT SUCCESS AND THE WORD 'DOVE' IN THEIR NAME. The farm was near Leominster and it was owned by Tom Price whose sons Richard and Ernie farmed and trained horses. His mares shared the pasture with the cows and his gallop was in a field alongside the Leominster bypass when it wasn't under water. When it was, the sheep field on the hill above the farm buildings made a good alternative.

When Flakey Dove stormed up the hill at Cheltenham in 1994 to win the Champion Hurdle, a dream of a spare ride for Mark Dwyer, it was the happy conclusion of a rags-to-riches story that had started in the fifties when farmer Tom Price paid £25 for a mare called Cottage Lass.

That triumph partly explains the difference between the breeding industries of the Flat and the National Hunt, the conglomerate against the cottage industry, the six-figure stallion fees against three- and four-figure fees. In Ireland, potential Gold Cup winners can be bred virtually in back gardens and, in Britain, a trip down the road to the local stallion, which Tom Price took with Cottage Lass all those years ago, can ultimately result in a Champion Hurdle winner.

The line's foundation mare Cottage Lass was by the top-class jumping sire of his time, Cottage, but was out of an unknown mare. A trip to local stallion All Red produced the mare Red Dove whose exploits on the racecourse made her something of an equine heroine. She ran ninety-three times and won sixteen hurdle races, including the last of them when she was retired from racing aged twelve. She was good up to two and a half miles and franked all her offspring with family traits of toughness, honesty and, in most cases, ability.

One of her offspring was Shadey Dove, the dam of Flakey Dove, who ran until the age of ten. Shadey Dove's second foal was Flakey Dove who, though I was unable to ride her when she won the Champion Hurdle, provided me with a notable landmark when winning the Cleeve Hurdle in her Champion Hurdle season. It was my one thousandth winner in Britain.

Flakey Dove was instantly successful for Richard Price when, as a four-year-old in January 1990, she won a bumper race at Ludlow, ridden by the now successful point-to-point trainer Damien Duggan whose brother was the talented but wild Jimmy Duggan. Jimmy rode for Fred Winter for a number of years. It wasn't a bad race looking back at it. She beat Silent Chant a head and had Mudahim, the 1997 Racing Post Chase and Irish Grand National winner, also making his debut, two and a half lengths away in third. She led from just over halfway and showed just how game she was in the closing stages.

She was second in her next two bumpers, beaten once by Pameva, partnered by the 3lb-claimer Norman Williamson, and the following time by Little Sail at Hereford before being put away for the summer.

It was in her first hurdle, a mares-only novice hurdle at Worcester in late February 1991, that I first noticed her. I was riding A Day Late for Nicky Henderson and I remember her at the start. She was being ridden by Ronnie Beggan, looked a bit backward, had a long mane and a tail down to her feathery heels. We all thought sarcastically, 'Ronnie's in for a good ride here.' Indeed he was – she buried him fairly promptly at the second flight.

Damien got the call-up again after that and she ran a solid race, probably still in need of it, when she was a fourteen-length third to Springaleak, Oliver Sherwood's good mare at Warwick. I was riding Shamana for David Nicholson and I noticed she ran a good race, and noted the performance. In the weighing room John Buckingham, our valet, who had ridden against Red Dove and followed the family ever since (as had many National Hunt enthusiasts of his generation), was already raving about the next 'Dove'.

Until the 1993–4 season when she won the Champion Hurdle, Flakey

Dove's season was usually cramped into ten weeks during the spring. In fact her appearances on the racecourse usually began when the daffodils started flowering in late February and continued until they stopped in April. She was a bit like the first cuckoo: when you saw her running, you'd know it was spring.

Her third quick run in 1991 was at Uttoxeter when she was ridden by Bruce Dowling. Bruce had been a student at the Royal Agricultural College, Cirencester but, having missed so many lectures riding out, decided to jack it in to become a professional jockey. He seemed inextricably linked to controversy during his career – he once had a barging match with Peter Scudamore going to the cross-hurdle at Newbury and both were stood down for a few weeks. We knew Bruce as the 'doctor'. His father was a racecourse doctor and good old Bruce had a mate who had been stood down with an injury and was not allowed to ride until he had been passed by a doctor. To save any messing about, Bruce forged his father's signature for him but they were found out; from that day onwards Bruce became known as Doctor Dowling. He, like the others before him, tried to make the most of Flakey Dove's stamina by leading, but in the heavy ground that day she was passed three out and finished a distant fourth.

That put her right for the following weekend, however, when in her fourth run in three weeks she won the Hoechst Panacur Mares Novice Hurdle Final at Newbury. This time she was ridden by Dai Tegg. For the first time she was held up, made steady progress to land in front at the second last. Dai only had to push her out and she beat Church Leap an impressive twelve lengths. I was third on David Gandolfo's Gray's Ellergy. She absolutely hacked up and it was the first indication of what was to come.

Her fifth and last run that season was possibly a bit disappointing after her previous success although she had run pretty often in a short space of time. Ridden by Damien again she finished twenty-one lengths behind Sweet N'Twenty in third and was then turned out at Eaton Hall Farm for the summer.

It was again towards the end of February before she appeared out in her third season, her first as a handicap hurdler. This was at Warwick where she continued her unbeaten association with Dai. Still very well-handicapped despite her runaway success in the mares' final she beat myself and Dara Doone a very easy three lengths with Dusty Miller who went on to win the County Hurdle at Cheltenham that season back in third. We were giving her 1st and 20lb respectively.

Ten days later Dara Doone and I reversed the form with Flakey Dove in the Ladbroke Racing Handicap Hurdle at Haydock. She was 6lb out of the handicap and only getting 4lb from Dara Doone instead of 10lb. We beat her two and a half lengths. However, being 10lb better off with her this time I was determined to have the beating of her. She nevertheless ran a good race.

A week later she went to Doncaster and again bolted up with Dai beating Hypnotist two and a half lengths over two miles. Having already won on the soft she proved here that the ground was not a worry – it was good to firm. A week later she was a twelve-length second at Mariner's Mirror at Chepstow – this time partnered by Martin Jones.

By this stage she was fairly charging up the handicap and, reunited with Dai, won the Kestrel Hurdle at Ascot, beating a useful bunch of handicap hurdlers, three of whom had won last time out. It was a good solid performance but within a week she was in her horsebox again and thriving on it, this time heading for Liverpool where she was due to run in the Cordon Bleu Handicap Hurdle over two miles. It was the first race on the day in which Party Politics galloped to victory in the 1992 Grand National. I was riding Viking Flagship who had just finished fourth in the County Hurdle and went there with great expectations.

148

It turned out to be Dai's biggest win on her. Down the paint all the way she was brave at her hurdles, throwing herself at them in a bid to keep up with the fast pace I was setting. Off the bridle all the way she came on it going to the last and ran on to beat Cheerful Times three-quarters of a length with Viking Flagship three lengths back in third. The picture of us jumping the last upsides was used by Aintree for promotion the following season. In many ways that race was Flakey Dove all over. Really she was a two-and-a-half-miler but two miles in a truly run race with top-class company suited her just as well.

The last big hurdle of the season used to be the Swinton at Haydock and now rated 127 having started the season on 96 she again tried her heart out to finish five lengths third to the Irish-trained runner Bitofabanter. Castle Secret was second and I finished fifth on Ninepins.

Her first run of the 1992–3 season was in February again when, carrying 12st, she was beaten three-quarters of a length by Albertito, carrying 9st 12lb, in a two-mile handicap hurdle at Stratford. Her next run, eight days later, was in the Tote Gold Trophy at Newbury, one of the toughest handicap hurdles of the whole season and one of the highlights of

February's racing. The race was won by King Credo, given an inspired ride by Adrian Maguire, who beat Native Mission five lengths with Bitofabanter third. Flakey Dove finished a good fifth and if anything looked just a little one-paced over this trip. Her next run was the following week in the minor Champion Hurdle trial at Warwick, the Regency Hurdle, in which she beat Lift And Load pretty comfortably.

The following time (nine days later), Lift And Load got his revenge and beat her in the Berkshire Hurdle at Newbury. She ran a brave race but I particularly remember it for the performance of my mount Royal Derbi who ran really moderately and finished twenty lengths fourth. He then went and ran out of his skin to finish a length second to Granville Again in the Smurfit Champion Hurdle at Cheltenham.

The 1993 Champion Hurdle had its human drama. At 2.00 the afternoon before the race Richard Price received a telephone call. Dai Tegg, who was now Flakey Dove's regular jockey, had been taken seriously ill with a brain haemorrhage. He had not had a bad fall, just a headache that had got worse, and his life was in the hands of brain specialists. It cast a dark shadow over the 1993 Cheltenham Festival.

149

Carl Llewellyn was booked to ride Flakey Dove at the last minute. Coming out into the paddock he expressed the slightly ambiguous sentiment that he would rather not have been there. By that he meant that he would much rather that Dai Tegg had not been so ill. Richard Price took it to mean that he didn't want to ride the mare. As it was, Carl did as he was told, dropped her out and she ran on really well to finish seventh. I rode Flown and she finished one place in front of me. It was a good run and had Carl had her nearer the front he feels he might have finished a lot closer. It was, though, his first and last ride on Flakey Dove. The good news throughout the meeting were daily more optimistic reports about Dai's health. All the jockeys signed a huge get-well card for him.

At the end of March she went to Ascot for the Kestrel Hurdle again and though she ran well she found a stone and a half too much to give to Doc's Coat. At Uttoxeter at the beginning of May she beat me and Beech Road a length. Jamie Osborne rode her this time and I led to the last. I was not happy with myself because I let him up the inner. Her last run was in the Swinton when she finished tailed off with Damien back in the saddle claiming 7lb.

The following season Richard Price got her up considerably earlier than he had done before and she was ready to run by the end of October.

Brendan Powell rode her and her convincingly beaten fourth over an extended three miles at Wetherby behind Deb's Ball gave no indication of what was to come.

She was being campaigned for the staying hurdles and the Champion Hurdle at this stage was an open race, but not so open that Flakey Dove came into calculations – yet. Granville Again didn't look up to retaining his title, indeed he hadn't won since. Morley Street, his brother, was getting on aged nine and Royal Derbi, the runner-up, did not quite have the credentials to win the race aged eight. Young pretenders included Vintage Crop, Montelado and Tiananmen Square from Ireland, Carobee, Spinning and Roll A Dollar.

She was to have a further seven races after her Wetherby run before the Champion, which was as many if not more than any of her rivals. As the opposition fell by the wayside Flakey Dove's form became more and more solid. Increasingly she began to put her best efforts together over two and half miles, three having proved beyond her.

At Ascot she wasn't beaten far by King Credo off levels. In the Bula Hurdle in December she was beaten twelve lengths into fourth by Staunch Friend. Halkopous and Muse filled the other minor places. I'd managed to deck Granville Again. It was a moderate performance by her standards and was put down to her being slightly below the weather. Her next outing saw her united with Norman Williamson for the first time and back on form she finished a good second to Absalom's Lady at Windsor in the New Year's Day Hurdle.

My first ride on Flakey Dove was at Haydock that January 1994 in the Haydock Park Champion Hurdle Trial where she beat the big Champion hope Tiananmen Square by twenty lengths. Sybillin was third. It was a procession. I was told to sit in, get a good lead and not to hit the front too soon. I took it up going to the second last, which was sooner than I wanted but I had little choice, and she won very, very easily. My first reaction was that she was a serious Champion Hurdle contender although the press overlooked it by focusing more on the disappointment of Tiananmen Square who finished lame. She still beat Sybillin thirty-two lengths though.

She was a straightforward ride, who jumped efficiently and well. There wasn't much complicated about her, she was a real professional. The only thing I'd been told was that she tended to idle a bit in front but a lot of horses do that.

A week later I rode her again in the Cleeve Hurdle over two miles and five furlongs at Cheltenham and again she bolted up from Sweet Duke whom she beat by six lengths. Mole Board was third and Absalom's Lady was last of the six finishers. That was my thousandth winner. The 66–1 once available about her for the Champion Hurdle was now long gone and she went to Newbury the 5–2 favourite to win the Tote Gold Trophy.

It was a great race and the first three in it, Large Action, Oh So Risky and Flakey Dove, were to go on to finish first, second and third in the Champion – albeit in reverse order. Unfortunately I had to go to Uttoxeter that day to ride for Martin Pipe, for whom I was now first jockey, and Norman got back on her.

I was convinced she would win but Large Action, getting 1st 6lb from Oh So Risky, prevailed – just. It was one of the great Tote Gold Trophies. Large Action was passed on the flat but, all out, got up in the dying strides to pip the brilliant but unlucky Oh So Risky. Flakey Dove was four lengths back in third.

I then got back on her for Newbury in early March for the Berkshire Hurdle. Again she absolutely bolted up. She was 2–1 on and only had Shujan, a game front-runner, to beat. He gave us a great lead to the second last and she won very comfortably by twenty lengths from Ivor's Flutter. The next outing was to be the Champion Hurdle.

That year I was banned from Cheltenham for putting Adrian Maguire out through a wing at Nottingham. A lot of people said I missed a Champion Hurdle winner but, to be fair, I would have been obliged to ride Granville Again, who finished seventh, or Valfinet. Norman Williamson was given the ride. However, nine days before the race he, too, received a two-day ban at Doncaster for careless riding on a horse called Cariboo Gold. It looked a harsh decision – it could have easily gone the other way. On Champion Hurdle day he stomped around the changing room like he'd seen a ghost, pale, almost white, in the belief that his best chance of ever winning the race had passed him by – little was he to know that the following year he would win both the Champion Hurdle and the Gold Cup.

Instead Mark Dwyer came in for the ride. He and she made it look so simple, so smooth. They made steady progress through the field from halfway. Up the hill she got her revenge on Oh So Risky and the novice Large Action. Like Norton's Coin, when he won the Gold Cup, Flakey Dove's Champion win was acclaimed as a triumph for the small man and the small owner-breeder. In National Hunt racing it can still happen. I heard about the result in Val d'Isère during my enforced skiing holiday.

Between then and Aintree she had a slightly unorthodox preparation when Richard Price ran her in a Flat race at Haydock which she won. For her last run of the season there was something of a hoohah because I jocked Mark off the mare. To be fair, I didn't jock him off; Richard wanted me to ride and I accepted. You can't say no if you're offered the Champion Hurdler whoever you might be upsetting and Mark had been in the business long enough to know that these things happen. You just have to thank your lucky stars that you rode the horse on the biggest day of its career.

Having won the Champion Hurdle at 9–1 on good with soft patches she was 9–4 for the Martell Aintree Hurdle on the heavy. She was tired from a long season and was entitled not to be 100 per cent. Although she had won on the soft at Haydock the first time I rode her I came in feeling this almost unraceable ground was too soft for her. Later that afternoon Miinnehoma won the National when only six finished which showed how soft it was. Danoli won the Aintree Hurdle beating Mole Board very comfortably by eight lengths. Flakey Dove finished fifth but beaten thirty-three lengths. I knew she was beaten turning out of the back straight. She hadn't really wanted to know about it on that ground, and that brought the championship winning season to an end.

Her last season began at Ascot in November when she finished third to Oh So Risky with Mark back on her. She returned to the scene of her greatest victory, at Cheltenham, for the Bula Hurdle in December and ran a good race finishing second to Large Action. She was favourite for the Christmas Hurdle after that but could only finish fifth, admittedly not beaten very far, to Absalom's Lady.

At Haydock in the soft she found Relkeel too good for her and he was installed as the new favourite to take her title from her. Now nine she had no answer for the turn of foot of a younger horse in the mud and went down by eight lengths. Her last run was in the Cleeve Hurdle at Cheltenham when she finished fifth to Mudahim. She returned home with a slight tendon strain and was retired to stud.

She is now on to her second career as a brood mare. Unlike the quick turnover of Flat racing, it will be some time before we know how good she is at this job.

I think she will be remembered as a very tough, genuine mare. When she was on song she was as good as any hurdler I've ridden and that included geldings and full horses. I would put her up there with Kribensis and Alderbrook. Very few mares are ever considered good enough to attempt

152

the Champion Hurdle let alone to win it, and Dawn Run was the last of her sex to win it before Flakey Dove. The only times she ran badly were when she had ample excuses. She won a Champion Hurdle and there was no fluke about it. She had a high cruising speed, quickened well off it and was a great jumper. Above all though she was exceptionally tough – whether her farm upbringing helped that I don't know – indeed she was a byword for toughness.

153

ALDERBROOK

14

ALDERBROOK WAS ONE OF THE MOST IMPRESSIVE CHAMPION HURDLERS THAT I SAW IN THE PRE-ISTABRAQ YEARS. Though his greatest moment came when he won the 1995 Champion for Kim Bailey with Norman Williamson up, I had three great races on him. We didn't quite manage to win the Champion Hurdle, however.

Unlike most horses that we ride over obstacles, Alderbrook was a full horse. When he was retired in the 1996–7 season without having run – he went to Newcastle for the Fighting Fifth Hurdle but Kim took him out because of the ground – it was early enough in the breeding year for him to have a full stud season and a full book of mares at Robin Knipe's Cobhall Court Stud at Allensmore near Hereford.

He is making a good sire of jumpers and, unlike so many stallions who become aggressive, Alderbrook, who always had a lovely character when he was racing, remains as laid-back as ever. Robin says you could send a child into his box without worrying and in my experience there are not that many stallions you could do that with.

Among the sixty-five mares he covered in his first season was Flakey Dove, another Champion Hurdler, and such a coupling must be almost unique. Others that he covered in his first season included the good race mares Springaleak, Winnie the Witch, Mariners Air and Arctic Oats and the proven broodmares Secret Keel (dam of Relkeel), Muznah (dam of Anzum) and Misty Sunset (dam of Percy Smollett).

He was by dual Ascot Gold Cup winner Ardross and out of a mare called Twine. Ardross, who died from a heart attack in 1994, did not set the world on fire as a stallion but he had bred a couple of useful performers on the Flat and over jumps before the best of his sons, Alderbrook, came to prominence. Flat horses Karinga Bay, Filia Ardross and Azzilfi were all by him and so was Avro Anson, sixth behind Lord Gyllene in the 1997 Grand National. Twine's half-sister was also the dam of Sybillin, so there was that jumping connection in Alderbrook's blood too.

He was bred by Jimmy Stone, an American from New Orleans, who kept Twine in Britain. Twine was subsequently sold to the Arabs. However, Mr Stone, who used to own horses with Henry Cecil including the 1981 Middle Park winner Cajun, sent the two-year-old Alderbrook to Henry's ex-wife Julie Cecil to train.

On the Flat he had twenty-four runs, won eleven of them and was placed eight times. He didn't run as a two-year-old as he was so backward and his three-year-old season did not have anyone dreaming of Champion Hurdles. He was not highly regarded at all. His first two runs were on the all-weather at Southwell over a mile and a half which, to be fair to the horse, was later to prove beyond his best distance of a mile and a quarter. He needed a cut in the ground and he was slightly slack in the pasterns which suggested he would, with a lot of racing, end up having problems with his legs. He was placed both times and then, very clearly, didn't stay a mile and three-quarters on turf in a Nottingham maiden. At Yarmouth back over a mile and a half it was the same and so Julie took him to Goodwood for a o–80 claimer (a pretty poor race in which you risk having your horse bought by a 'claim' whether it wins or loses.) It was in October and there was a bit more give in the ground than there had been mid-summer and, being hard ridden by Paul Eddery, he stayed on well to record his first victory. It was lucky, I suppose, for Julie that no one thought enough of the horse to claim him.

He ran a similar race first time in a o–70 handicap at Chepstow, running on to finish second, and he finished the season with a comfortable victory on the soft at lowly Folkestone in a race for similarly rated horses. A horse, no matter how moderate, can command a fair price at the horses-in-training sale if it is sound and if it has won a couple of races. Alderbrook's next port of call was the Newmarket horses-in-training sales where he was bought for 38,000 guineas by Middleham trainer Sally Hall for businessman Ernie Pick. Sally had him schooled and sent him to Newcastle that December 1992 for his first run over hurdles. Ridden by David Wilkinson he ran creditably enough, just weakening after three out,

to finish in the middle division in a juvenile hurdle won by another Middleham-trained runner, Bold Boss.

Alderbrook was still quite weak and light-framed. Sally did not want him to go hurdling any more that winter, feeling it would not benefit a Flat campaign the following summer. Mr Pick was keen to hurdle though and the end result was that he sent Alderbrook, who never did run over hurdles again that winter, back to Julie Cecil in the spring.

The winter had done him good and in April he kicked off where he had left off by winning another 0–70 handicap on the Flat at Folkestone. He then started to progress rapidly, winning 0–80 handicaps at Warwick and Nottingham, a 0–90 at Kempton and a 0–105 at Ascot's Heath meeting on the Saturday after the Royal meeting, where he beat Rambo's Hall two lengths. All were on good or softer ground and he had completed his sequence of five wins (six if you include his last win on the Flat the previous autumn) by the middle of June 1993.

His second of thirteen to Stoney Valley at York amounted to his best form all season. Julie had also withdrawn him from the Magnet Cup at York because of the good-to-firm ground. Though his last run was a little disappointing he had, nevertheless, shown considerable improvement all season and defied the handicapper for much of it.

Such was the improvement that his hurdling career remained on hold for another winter and he returned to the track at a rain-soaked Pontefract in April 1994, where he showed a nice turn of foot to beat Silver Wisp (the Derby third). Next time out he stepped up to Listed company when winning the Festival Stakes at Goodwood in May. In September he returned to Goodwood, a track on which he was never beaten on the Flat, where he displayed a great turn of foot to beat Lower Egypt and win his first Group Three, the Select Stakes, before finishing the season with a tremendously popular victory over Volochine and Frenchpark in the Group Two Prix Dollar at Longchamp on Arc day. When the question of hurdling again was put to Ernie Pick in the winner's enclosure at Longchamp, it seemed that he would rule it out.

However, he had a change of heart just after Christmas and with little more than two months to go before the Champion Hurdle he sent Alderbrook to Kim Bailey to be trained specifically for the race. The idea, he said, was that Kim, being a very successful jump trainer, would have a better chance than Julie of getting him ready for the race in such a short time. Julie was a top Flat trainer, he said, and could have him back for the Flat.

The dilemma Kim faced was to get the horse ready, which involved going out twice a day, without damaging his already fragile legs. Things were going so well that after he had schooled well for Norman the yard took a punt and backed him at 50–1 for the Champion Hurdle. That price was slashed when he went to Wincanton for the Kingwell Hurdle, a recognized Champion Hurdle Trial, towards the end of February 1995. Though I'd obviously noticed him winning on the Flat I wasn't really aware of how serious a hurdler he might be until Norman had said how well he had schooled and that he thought he'd win the race. There still wasn't much hype about the horse and Trying Again, who had been a good second in the Tote Gold Trophy at Newbury, seemed a worthy favourite ahead of Jazilah, my mount for Martin Pipe. Jazilah ran quite well but Alderbrook won extremely impressively. Even then I knew immediately that, despite his hurdling inexperience, he had some tough races under his belt on the Flat and providing he jumped he would be the horse they all had to beat in the Champion Hurdle. A lot of horses coming to jumping so late in their careers don't take to it at all but Alderbrook loved it.

Though his price was cut to about 7 or 8–1 for the Champion – he was 11–2 on the day – it still looked a stiff task for him with horses like Large Action, the Irish favourite Danoli, Fortune And Fame, Mysilv and Montelado in the field. I was on Jazilah again and he ran no sort of race in the 1995 Champion Hurdle but in spite of this, I think it was one of the best Champions I have ridden in. Alderbrook was always travelling really well for Norman. My clearest memory of the race was seeing how powerfully the horse passed me jumping the second hurdle down the back. He flew by me so quickly that I had hardly a moment to tell him to take his time! Norman judged his challenge to perfection. Alderbrook's Flat class left Large Action and Danoli in his wake as he galloped up the hill to win by a very impressive five lengths. It was, of course, a glorious week for Kim and Norman, who went on to win the Gold Cup with Master Oats two days later.

Because the ground dried up he didn't run again and went back to Julie for a spring campaign while he was still fit from hurdling. He went to Longchamp at the beginning of the month for his first run, in the Group Two Prix d'Harcourt, where he finished seventh of ten. This run demonstrated, as much as anything, the difference between hurdling and Flat racing at this level. Used to two miles at a relatively consistent pace over hurdles, he was made to look one-paced in the straight but the run clearly sharpened him up. At the end of the month he went to the same track again for the Prix

Ganay in which he finished a very good second to Paul Kelleway's Pelder. As Julie Cecil says, 'You go and stuff the French in their own backyard and your next-door neighbour called Kelleway comes and beats you.'

He ran his last trademark brave race on the Flat at Baden Baden in Germany at the end of May when he finished second to Freedom Cry in the Grosser Pries der Wirtschaft. Baden can dry out very quickly and it did that day, which probably cost Alderbrook the race. It was clear then, however, that if he was to have another season's hurdling he would have to have a rest during the summer and then an autumn campaign. His joints were showing significant signs of wear and tear.

During the summer I had a meeting with Julie and Ernie Pick at the Hilton Hotel in London. There was a lot of conjecture in the press about where the horse would be trained the following winter. People believed that Kim had had the horse only to prepare him in a rush for Cheltenham and that, with a longer preparation, he would remain with Julie. At the time I believe that is what Mr Pick intended to do. I was not sure why Norman was not keeping the ride but they wanted an agreement from me to the effect that if, as was expected, he'd stay the winter with Julie, I would be able to ride the horse. I couldn't give it. At that time I'd given my word to so many other connections to ride their horses that I was in danger of getting totally over-committed!

The long and the short of it was that he went back to Kim in the autumn and Kim's vets decided to carry out an arthroscopy on both his front joints. They found quite a bit of 'debris' in them and tidied them up as best they could but afterwards Alderbrook needed six weeks of nothing more strenuous than being walked in hand. The task of getting him fit for the defence of his title was going to be as challenging for Kim as it had been the year before, another race against time. Although he had slightly longer this time he was starting from scratch.

During the previous summer Kim had split with Norman. He hadn't really done much about fixing up a jockey for the horse until February 1996 because he wasn't sure if he would get Alderbrook on a racecourse again. Initially, Ernie and Kim chose Graham Bradley, who was asked to come and school the horse in Lambourn on a Sunday morning. Brad, who had been to a cracking party the previous evening, overslept and, much to Kim's fury, failed to turn up. The truth of the matter was that Graham's electric alarm clock had been stopped by a power-cut, so he had missed his call. Instead Jimmy McCarthy was summoned from the village and he popped him over a few hurdles. So Brad got the sack before he'd even sat on the horse and I got the call-up to ride Alderbrook in the Kingwell Hurdle at Wincanton. That meeting was frosted off but because the horse was an obvious attraction and we'd missed a couple of Champion Hurdle trials the race was rescheduled for Kempton the following Saturday.

I got on Alderbrook in the paddock and I couldn't believe how unsound he felt. I have never ridden anything that has moved so badly round the paddock. I then cantered him to the start. He was off the bridle and I was having to push him. I really thought he'd have no chance. Kim had said he would take a grip too.

In the race, though, he was quite keen and gave me a much better feel. They always reckoned at Julie's that if his head was slightly cocked to one side, his tongue was hanging out and he was taking a good grip then he was in good form. His jumping was very accurate and quick, amazingly so for a Flat horse having only his fourth-ever run over obstacles. He was a real professional. I kept him tucked in and turning into the straight I was running away. I pulled him wide over to the stands rail and going to the last I only had Mack The Knife to beat. We pinged it and he went away to win very comfortably, increasing his winning margin to three and a half lengths at the line. Kim had told me not to get to the front too soon because he was likely to idle but there was no question of him stopping at all.

So then we went to the 1996 Champion Hurdle. He was odds-on favourite, there were sixteen runners and basically everything should have been in his favour. The night before I watched the video of Norman winning the race on him and it was just about the worst thing I could have done because, in the race, he ran nothing like it. I jumped him off, got him nicely settled in and the plan was to creep gradually through the field, arrive there at the last and use his Flat speed to beat off any last-minute challenges. Everything was fine to halfway, Alderbrook was jumping well and travelling well and up the back of the hill, having just avoided Absolam's Lady who made a bad mistake, I pulled wide so as not to meet any traffic problems when we started going downhill towards the third- and second-last flights. As we turned down the hill Tony Dobbin on Chief Minister pulled out and took me wider than I wanted so I had to switch back in and it cost me half a length. Having landed over the third last I was then off the bridle, flat to the boards to the second last. I wasn't as close as I'd planned to be. I could see ahead of me that Brad on Collier Bay and Jamie Osborne on Mysilv, one of my main dangers, had kicked for home. Danoli and Squire Silk were also in front of me. I couldn't believe how badly Alderbrook was travelling. Because of his joints he hadn't come down the hill at all. He got a bit close to the second last and as soon as he met the rising ground from there on he really picked up and galloped. Saying that though, so did Collier Bay. We both galloped all the way to the line but the two and a half lengths I was behind him at the line was as close as we could get. We were six lengths clear of the third, Pridwell.

Predictably I was criticized for giving the horse too much to do. It made no difference. Collier Bay had beaten him fairly and squarely on the day. I was delighted for his trainer Jim Old and for Brad. Of course the irony of the result wasn't lost on anyone. Brad had been sacked from Alderbrook and, without a ride, picked up the spare on Collier Bay when Jamie Osborne, his regular rider, had chosen to partner Mysilv.

For my own peace of mind I've watched the race on video and timed certain points of it. I was 0.8 of a second behind the leader at the top of the hill. If you take 0.25 seconds as a length then I was never more than three-and-a-quarter lengths behind the leader from the top of the hill. I was three lengths off Collier Bay at the last and finished up two and a half lengths behind him at the line. I kept galloping. If I'd been a length down at the last I think I'd still have been beaten.

Kim didn't say anything about the performance at the time but he did about two days later. He, too, told me I'd given the horse too much to do. I disputed that then and I do now. If he had travelled downhill as well as he had done the year before, I'd have won. I am sure with an extra year's wear and tear on his joints he felt it more. He'd have been closer – but I was pretty much where I'd wanted to be at the top of the hill – closer, I think, than Norman had been the year before. Racing is all about opinions but if I'd thought I'd cost the horse, Kim and the yard the race I would have put my hands up and said so.

I was next to ride him in his last run of the season – and his career – in the Scottish Champion Hurdle about a month later. Fortunately for me, I managed to keep the ride. The ground came up soft enough for him to run. He didn't travel that well through the race: he kept coming on the bridle then going off it. However, when he turned into the straight he picked up and went into overdrive. He got to the front easily at the second last. I hung on to him a while longer and then let him quicken up. He won easily and was very impressive. I have rarely had a better feel over hurdles than I did over the last half mile of that race – it was electric. Rather than staying on like he had done at Cheltenham he quickened up really well and showed a lot of class. He was carrying 11st 7lb and giving weight to everything. Only Escartefigue and Land Afar, both carrying 10st 4lb and out of the handicap, gave him anything like a race and they were three and five lengths respectively behind us. Barring his victory in the Champion Hurdle, this was one of his best runs over obstacles.

He had the summer off and was brought back to run in the Fighting Fifth Hurdle at Newcastle in November. He even went up there in the horsebox and I went up to ride him instead of staying at Newbury to ride Challenger Du Luc in Coome Hill's Hennessy. Kim walked the course and reckoned it was too firm. I agreed. About a month later Kim, the owner and the vets got together and decided to call it a day and sent him to stud in time for the 1997 covering season.

I later spoke to Paul Eddery who had ridden Alderbrook in the majority of his Flat races. He also rode Kribensis on the Flat and he said that on the level Alderbrook was in a different class to Kribensis. Considering his problems he was a hell of a horse – as classy a horse as I have ever ridden. I also think that, judging by the way he walked around the paddock before a race, he must have been in a lot of discomfort. Kim must have worked wonders to get him to the course for those last three runs. He was an extremely brave horse to perform the remarkable way he did. Alderbrook stands at stud in Ireland and his best progeny are Sh Boom and Ollie Magern.

162

15

SOUND MAN

W HEN I PARTED COMPANY WITH MARTIN PIPE AFTER TWO YEARS AS FIRST JOCKEY AT THE END OF THE 1994–5 SEASON, I MADE IT CLEAR THAT I INTENDED TO RIDE A GREAT DEAL MORE IN IRELAND. Not only was I born in Northern Ireland but, having seen the light with regard to chasing my tail to win championships in Britain, I liked the pace of life over there and the fact that many cards in the summer would include a couple of Flat races so it was not all relentless jump racing all the time. You can't beat the fun and the hospitality of the Irish. Irish jockeys had been coming to England to ride for a living since time immemorial and I thought it might be an idea to reverse that trend a little.

It coincided with the time when Charlie Swan, the Irish Champion jockey, was committing himself even more to the burgeoning yard of Aidan O'Brien. That summer Edward O'Grady, whom I had ridden a lot for anyway, and Dermot Weld asked me to ride certain horses of theirs and I committed myself. Edward was particularly keen that I should ride his stable's flagship Sound Man while Dermot booked me up for the hurdlers Fortune And Fame and Vintage Crop, although I never got to ride the latter before he was retired.

Sound Man was a charismatic horse. Edward – who has sent out seventeen Cheltenham Festival winners over the years, which is one hell of a record and more than almost all the British trainers – started to concentrate on the Flat for a while before switching back to jumpers. When he switched back he pinned his hopes on one horse taking him back to the top – and that was Sound Man.

He bought him for the guts of £100,000 after the horse had won what he considered was the best winners' bumper he'd seen at The Curragh on Irish Guineas day in 1993. He asked bloodstock agent Brian Grassick to do the deal, which he did after falling in love with the horse himself. When Brian came to make out the bill he asked to whom he was to make it. Edward didn't have anyone in mind but fixed up the finance – never easy with horses – and said that to resurrect his National Hunt career after the Flat and remind people what he was about he needed a good horse badly. If he was the man he thought he was, he told Brian, he'd be able to find an owner for the horse.

He offered the horse to various people, including the legendary Irish gambler J.P. McManus, but had no joy. Then he decided he would try to put a syndicate of ten people together. He had takers for two shares and found a man who wanted to take half the horse which meant he then had only three shares to sell. However, he received a lengthy fax from the man who had wanted fifty per cent, giving a long list of reasons why he didn't now want the horse. Edward resumed the search to find people to take the remaining 80 per cent – and all the while Sound Man was costing him a lot of interest. After six weeks he spoke to J.P. again. J.P. wondered whether the horse was still unsold because Sound Man might be the horse for a new partnership he was setting up between himself, Dermot Desmond, John Magnier and David Lloyd, the British Davis Cup tennis player. 'Well, I've a little bit sold,' said Edward. 'Well,' said J.P., 'if it doesn't cause too much embarrassment your end we'll have the horse.'

Edward went to the two businessmen who had bought (but not yet paid for) two shares and told them his predicament. One was an accountant so he knew the score and both said that for Edward's sake he should sell the horse to the J.P. syndicate – which was kind and understanding of them.

Sound Man's first outing for Edward was at Navan in November 1994 and though he won well they'd hoped he'd be more impressive. He was then lame for a while, missed Christmas and came back in February at Fairyhouse where he was second over two and a quarter miles. Apart from the fact that he was still only 'November fit' because of his lay-off, the trip was probably just far enough for him at that stage of his career. There was a bit of disappointment in the Sound Man camp but in retrospect there needn't have been – he was beaten by a then virtually unknown novice, Dorans Pride. Others were more critical that day though. They thought Sound Man raised his head a little under pressure and swished his tail – a sign of an ungenuine horse. They could not have been further from the truth.

At Naas he won well in the heavy and he went to Cheltenham as favourite for the Citroën Supreme Novice Hurdle. The race was won by Arctic Kinsman and Sound Man finished tenth. He made a bad mistake at the second hurdle and Charlie Swan, who rode Cheltenham as well as anyone, blamed himself afterwards for trying to make up the ground lost at the hurdle too quickly. He followed that with a fair run at Fairyhouse where he was second to the bane of his steeplechasing career, Klairon Davis, and rounded off the season disappointingly at Punchestown, a track he never won around. Although he hadn't set the world on fire with his hurdling, Edward had bought him as a chaser and reckoned that anything he did over hurdles would be a bonus.

One trait Sound Man showed throughout his career was to jump obstacles with a flat back rather than arching it into a nice round shape. He could have jumped hurdles better than he did. If he got close to one he would crash through it or kick it out of the ground, like he did at Cheltenham, rather than be a bit clever and get himself out of trouble like a lot of horses would do by tucking up their undercarriage. He was schooled over fences by Jim Doyle, an Irish jockey who had ridden with reasonable success in England before returning home. Edward always tried to get him to arch his back by schooling him over in and outs and doubles just out of a trot. It never really altered the way he jumped though, and over fences he was always better when he was long at a fence rather than close to it.

He went to Roscommon in November 1995 for his first novice chase which he won well, beating another smart novice and subsequent Gold Cup winner, Imperial Call, into third. At Navan he fell – for the only time in his career – and he was beaten at Galway, where the track didn't suit him, by Eyelid. He never liked a very testing run-in. He also showed a preference for right-handed courses, which might also explain why he never won at Cheltenham.

At Naas he beat Imperial Call again but his best race as a novice was probably in the Drinmore Novice Chase at Fairyhouse in early December where he beat Coq Hardi Affair by eleven lengths after Charlie and Edward had decided to let him make the running, which Sound Man seemed to like.

The Guinness Arkle Trophy at Cheltenham in 1995 was one of the meeting's great races. I was riding the chancey jumper Dancing Paddy in the race and finished fourth after being nearly brought down at the first ditch by Graham Bradley on Sound Reveille. I think I managed to catch Graham and push him back into the plate! It was an all-Irish duel up front with Klairon Davis eventually getting the better of a great tussle with Sound Man to win by a length. He had two more runs that season. Ten days before the Power Gold Cup at Fairyhouse he had been lame, which required a week's walking, but Edward reckoned he would still be good enough to win. However, he met a tartar in Strong Platinum, a horse who looked like being very special but never really fulfilled his novice promise. The same horse beat him again at Punchestown a week later which shows just how tough Sound Man was and he reversed the form with Klairon Davis in that race, beating him by half a length, to round off a good novice chase season.

The following season is where I came into it. I had the benefit of all Charlie's hard work on the horse and Sound Man was bound to be better than he had been as a novice. I schooled him at Roscommon where the fences are quite small. Edward warned me that he jumped better long than short but he jumped well. We went to Navan, an undulating rectangular course, in October 1995 for our first outing together. He hacked up and did the same a few weeks later giving me a great deal of confidence in his jumping which was, at times, breathtaking. David Lloyd came over for one of these meetings and really enjoyed himself. He ended up playing golf with the other members of the syndicate for what J.P. and the others called 'units' per hole. He must have tied at that stage, probably to his benefit, because I don't think he ever discovered what a unit was worth. One night Edward and myself sat down and mapped a campaign for Sound Man, culminating in a crack at the Champion Chase. Edward was keen to take advantage of the fact that he went well on good ground and was superior in fitness to the English horses he would meet in the First National Bank Gold Cup at Ascot in November. It was a race for novices and first-season handicappers, which used to be sponsored by H. & T. Walker. Only one of the opposition had had a run earlier that season, which made life a little easier for us. It became a two-horse race between myself and Morceli and when the latter fell at the fifth last, Sound Man cruised home by a distance from Dancing Paddy.

Edward then brought him back for the Tingle Creek Chase at Sandown where he was to face the older generation and established stars of the two-miler brigade such as Viking Flagship, whom we knew usually needed his first run of the season, Storm Alert from the same stable, Travado and

Nakir. Sound Man was a very athletic horse and had tremendous power behind the saddle. He needed to have to keep coming up long at his fences and if I hadn't discovered that before, I certainly did that day. You had to be brave on him but in return he rarely let you down. At some fences he could be deer-like and he was spectacular in the Tingle Creek, especially considering that Sandown's railway fences can catch out horses. Anyway, he was in command by the time we got to the second last and I just had to nudge him out up the hill to beat Storm Alert five lengths. I won the Tingle Creek, the most important two-mile race before Christmas, five times but I never won the Queen Mother Champion Chase.

He then had a bit of a break and came back to England for the Comet Chase as a warm-up for the Champion Chase. He won very easily again although Coulton, our most serious opposition, fell and gave Jamie Osborne a really ugly crash at the fifth last. As it was over nearly two and a half miles I made less use of him than I had done in the past but he still did it nicely enough. Easy Buck was still upsides me at the second last and although fourteen lengths looked a handsome enough margin at the time I wasn't entirely happy with him. I didn't think he was as on-fire as he had been on his two previous visits.

Next stop Champion Chase. Yet another favourite to ride. This was the year I went there with Alderbrook favourite for the Champion Hurdle, One Man favourite for the Gold Cup and Sound Man 11–8 to win his race. As history now relates, I managed to get beat on all three of them. It just goes to show how unpredictable this sport can be.

169

I jumped him off handy, we didn't go a great gallop but he never quite used himself as well as he had done. Whether it was the occasion or the place or he was feeling his back I don't know. He made a bad mistake at the last on the first circuit and he'd never made a semblance of that sort of mistake with me before. I led at the water taking over from my old friend Dancing Paddy. Then Charlie Swan came upsides me on Viking Flagship. We jumped the ditch together. All I could hear was this almighty crash and Klairon Davis, who had been on the outside, disappeared from view. I thought that was him finished with. I assumed he had fallen, at best had made such a bad mistake that he was now out of contention. I kept trying to draw a little out of Viking Flagship.

At the third last Charlie and I both went long. Both horses put down and galloped through the fence. I was still in front at the next but we again got a shade too close to it and made another mistake. Turning in I had the rail and I pinged the last but resurrected Klairon Davis ranged alongside us on the outside. Viking Flagship also out-battled us. It seemed to be the story of my life in the Champion Chase – to jump the last upsides in front only to be passed up the run-in. I was obviously disappointed – a beaten favourite – and I know Edward maintains he probably didn't relish the hill there but we were only beaten five lengths and one and a quarter lengths and without those three mistakes I think he'd have been very close. But this game is all about jumping and on that particular day it didn't work out. He coughed on the way back to the winner's enclosure, whether it was 'kickback' caught in his throat, or something more serious, it cannot have helped him during the race either.

At Aintree he managed to reverse the form with a relatively flat Klairon Davis but not with Viking Flagship who was given a brilliant ride by Tony McCoy, riding him for the first time. Sound Man's jumping seemed worse still on that occasion. He hit the cross-fence and the second down the back very hard and was, even by his standards, flatter than usual at his obstacles. I thought his back might be worrying him. Needless to say Klairon Davis was back to his old self for Punchestown and he beat us ten lengths in the BMW Handicap Chase – giving us 4 lb. Sound Man did jump better until the third last when Klairon Davis ranged alongside and we hit it hard. I also asked him a question verging on the impossible at the second last and he did well to make it.

170

For his last season he started off at Tipperary. He was 4–1 on and wasn't convincing against a moderate bunch of horses. However, for him it was just a glorified school round. Next time out Norman Williamson rode him because I had to ride One Man at Wetherby. Also 4–1 on, he got beaten twenty lengths by Anabatic. He was still a bit on the gross side according to Edward, in the soft ground the fit as a flea Anabatic – who went on to run some good races that season – passed him at the second last and soon had him beaten. He blew hard afterwards.

I went back to ride him at Clonmel where it was heavy. Royal Mountbrowne and Belverderian, neither of whom were great jumpers, were in the race. I remember tracking their respective jockeys, Charlie Swan and Conor O'Dwyer, hearing them in deep discussion about my position and how much 'petrol' I had 'in the tank'. The second last is quite a difficult fence because it falls away a bit on landing. I was on Royal Mountbrowne's outer and he jumped violently across me causing Sound Man to 'miss' and make a mistake. For a few strides I thought I'd get beaten but we jumped the last well and he went on to win by a length, battling really well. Though he showed more determination than he had ever showed before, nevertheless you couldn't describe it as much more than a workmanlike performance.

His first visit of the season to England was for the Tingle Creek Chase. Edward says that Sound Man and Viking Flagship were like boys behaving badly that day. The Duke also had Storm Alert in the race and I jumped off behind him and Viking Flagship but going to the downhill fence I wasn't happy with my position. A small gap appeared between them and I tried to go through it but Adrian Maguire on board Viking Flagship wasn't happy about that and for a few strides I was the meat in the sandwich. Norman Williamson on Storm Alert nearly fell and Lord Dorcet, amazed by what was going on in front of him, did fall. Viking Flagship made several errors down the back, and I jumped reasonably well until we came to the Pond Fence, the third last. I went long on him when I should have gone short. It was, frankly, a pilot error and how he stood up I still don't know to this day. I went in a length up and stretching Viking Flagship but I came out of it three lengths down and at a standstill. I have never known a horse hit a fence as hard and still come out the other side. He must have broken it. Though he jumped flatly he always had his feet way out in front of him and they must have come to his rescue that day. He regularly came back from his races with birch scratches around his stifle and I expect there were a few on him after that. Somehow I managed to scramble back into the saddle and gave him a little bit of time to catch his breath. He flew the second last well and Viking Flagship, having his first race of the season, started to tie-up approaching the last. We overhauled him and eventually beat him five lengths. It was an exciting race to ride in and, I should think, exciting to watch, especially if you were connected to either the winner or second.

171

Edward's biggest regret during that season was not running him in the 1996 King George VI Chase at Kempton, which I won on One Man. Bred by Kemal, who produced many stayers including the Grand National winner Rhyme 'N' Reason, he should have got the trip on the good, fast ground, which it was in 1996. Apart from One Man it didn't appear the hottest contest on paper (Mr Mulligan, another runner, hadn't won a Gold Cup by then) and Sound Man was in good order after the Tingle Creek. He would have had a good shot at the race and I'm sure would have liked Kempton. Instead Edward kept him for the Comet Chase at Ascot in which I was committed to ride One Man, who was trying the shorter distance of two miles three furlongs to see if the Queen Mother Champion Chase was a viable alternative to the Gold Cup. It was decided that whoever rode him in the Comet Chase would ride him in the Champion Chase. I had to side with One Man, so Charlie Swan got back on Sound Man. During the race Sound Man made some mistakes and he eventually finished third to Strong Promise. He was sore afterwards but not for long and soon came sound again.

One Sunday morning shortly before Cheltenham, Sound Man was doing a couple of gentle canters on his own up a six-furlong strip of virgin turf at Edward's yard near Thurles. He had been up quietly once, his usual lad, usual canter, and as he neared his watching trainer doing no more than a hack canter for the second time he seemed to go lame. His lad had pulled him up by the time he reached Edward and they thought he had strained a muscle. By the time they got him home he was quite a bit lamer and when Edward took his boots off he discovered he had ruptured his deep flexor tendon. Throughout his racing career he had never appeared to have a problem in that area. Whether that was why he jumped like he did or whether it was the result of accumulated pressure on a weakness, no one knows. The irony of it was that he'd only been doing a gentle canter, not a gallop or jumping. The vet said there was no alternative but to put him to sleep. Edward was distraught – he loved the horse. For a while his career had depended on Sound Man and the horse hadn't let him down. It was like losing a member of the family for Edward. He was so upset about it that he didn't let anyone other than the connections know until the end of Cheltenham. He didn't want people coming up to him all through the meeting and saying how sorry they were and reminding him of it. It eventually leaked out on Gold Cup day.

He wasn't put down until Edward had left for Cheltenham and when he returned Sound Man had been buried beneath the spot where he stands to watch his horses work up the gallops. As Edward recalls the whole place was 'in tragedy street'. Sound Man did a lot for Edward's career and for my new freelance career and I loved riding him. He was a very special horse.

172

IT'S A SNIP

PARDUBICE, HOME OF THE VELKA PARDUBICKA, OR CZECH GRAND NATIONAL AS WE KNOW IT, IS A BIG TOWN ABOUT TWO HOURS' DRIVE EAST OF PRAGUE IN THE CZECH REPUBLIC. It is an ugly, flat, grey industrial area built, typically of post-war communism, without much character. Large factories and large blocks of flats interlinked by wide roads and rattling trams. Only the narrow, cobbled streets and hidden restaurants of the old town in the centre and the castle just out of town where the post-race reception was held remind you of a pre-Communist past and what it once must have been like.

Apart from the notorious Taxis fence in the race, Pardubice is known for being the world capital of Semtex, the town where the plastic explosive is made – I suppose it has to be made somewhere. It was in Pardubice early in 1997 that the inventor of Semtex committed suicide in style – by blowing himself up in the foyer of a sanitorium where he was a patient.

The Czech Republic in October is all pastels. The drive from the airport on a hill above the ancient and beautiful Prague is slow through the city, past the Charles Bridge over the Vltava River and past Wenceslas Square, named after the patron saint of the country and, symbolically, where the revolution against communism took place.

Norman Williamson and I were picked up by a Czech trainer called Tommy Jansa. That was a bit of a result in itself. The previous evening, a Friday, he had forgotten to pick up Charlie Mann, the trainer of It's A Snip, winner of the 1995 race as both trainer and jockey, and Charlie had had to hire a taxi for the two-hour trip. A year earlier he was a national hero in the Czech Republic, now he was virtually forgotten.

You can pick up as much speed as a Skoda allows when you get out in the country and start passing large prairie-sized fields of yellow stubble and the factory-sized farm buildings that used to be part of the farm collective systems. It is very different from the drive to Worcester.

I had flown there with Norman who was due to ride Irish Stamp for Ferdy Murphy in the race. It was a Saturday morning, the middle of October 1996, the National Hunt season was beginning to get going at home and, quite frankly, I was cold on the idea of riding in the race. I'd heard a lot about it, I still needed to lose a few pounds and, well, it's a bloody long way from home to go and fall on your head. I could have been riding in Ireland or at Worcester and, though I had committed myself to ride It's A Snip, I had tried unconvincingly to make excuses and to back out of it.

The Velka is an old race: the 1996 running of the four-and-a-quarter-mile chase over turf and plough and a variety of obstacles was the 106th. The course was bought from the town in 1848 by the Bohemian Horse Breeders' Union and by 1874 a committee had laid out a racecourse with 'uncommon obstacles'. For me it is a cross between Aintree, Badminton and a good hunt with my local pack at the time, the Old Berks Hunt.

The first Velka Pardubicka Steeplechase was run on 5 November 1874 and was won by a German stallion called Fantome ridden by an English jockey called Sayers. Since then it has become the biggest race in central Europe and there has always been a link between it and Britain, even in the darkest days of the Cold War when places like Pardubice were so inaccessible, you could still get to the race but if you won, as Chris Collins did in 1973, you couldn't get your prize money out.

Only one jockey, however – George Williamson – has ever won both this race and the Grand National. He won the Pardubicka in 1880 on Alphabet and in 1893 on Hadnagy. Towards the end of his career he won the 1899 Grand National on Manifesto, one of the handful of horses ever to have won the race twice and one of the few I know to have run in it more often than West Tip.

We arrived at the course. There was a basic, five-tier, white concrete grandstand, some stables which must have been built for the inaugural race and a hut for the changing room. I wasn't sure whether to laugh or cry and when It's A Snip failed the veterinary inspection – all horses have to trot up and down in front of a panel of vets – I was almost relieved. I'm not sure why because I would probably have been put on a local Czech runner instead. However, Chrissy Barnard, Charlie's travelling head lad, complained strongly for a re-inspection. When they trotted up It's A Snip again he was sound.

It was then from one camera to another. We hadn't been there long but it was already clear that the red carpet was being laid out for Norman and myself. There were not that many people there but they were already treating us like popstars, wanting our opinions and ideas. 'What do you think of the Taxis? How does it compare to the Brook of Captain Becher's?' and other questions in a stilted form of English. We hadn't even set foot on the course by the stage. There was also a large contingent of British racegoers, at least two hundred. Some had come on a Thoroughbred Breeders' Association tour, others on organized trips, some officers by car from Germany, some students on their gap year who were travelling Eastern Europe by car, and many with a connection to the two British runners, It's A Snip and Irish Stamp, and Sue Bramall's Valeda from Ireland. Most of us were in the same hotel, the Labe, in central Pardubice about a mile and a half from the course. It was the start of quite a weekend.

The course was like no other that Norman or I had set eyes on. I rode over fences in America, France and Sweden, Switzerland, and in Germany but I never encountered anything quite like Pardubice. The course is well kept, very tidy, surrounded by tall poplar trees with a wood in the middle. It is bisected by hedgerows and a wide, deep stream, which form the 'natural' obstacles. A third of it is arable farmland and in this October was light, dusty plough. (God knows what it's like in October when it's wet.) The grass was quite firm in places.

The route, well, that's another story. I suggest you go out there and walk it one weekend when the Pardubicka is being run. You are on the turn most of the time and cross your tracks at least six times while completing roughly one right-handed sweep of the inner area and two left-handed sweeps.

The first two fences are inviting hedges, the second of them with a small ditch on the landing side. The third fence is a 13-foot-wide open water known as a *prikop*. You then sweep round a right-hand corner in front of the stands to the Taxis, one of the biggest and most notorious fences in the world. The hedge is about five feet tall and five feet wide though, being a live and not desperately thick hedge, you don't have to clear the top of it.

The ditch on the landing side is 15 feet wide and used to be six feet deep. This has been filled in and since 1992 is only about three feet deep tapering up to the lip on the landing area. From take off to landing a horse needs to clear about 25 feet and the fallers are usually the ones that don't quite clear the ditch. For every faller at the modern Becher's Brook I would say there are four at the Taxis and photos of the runners landing over it often resemble a colourful battle scene – you could entitle it something like 'the Cavalry meets artillery for the first time'.

The next is a six-foot Irish bank, then it is on to the first field of plough to the sixth, a hedge and ditch, which is a bit like a right-handed Canal Turn. You then pass three gravestones (a bit ominous until you discover that they were soldiers killed in a car crash, but you only learn that after considerable research) before swinging right-handed again into a long line of hedges. All are different. The seventh is 10 feet wide, the eighth and ninth are a double over a road crossing with just a couple of strides in between, and the tenth is called the English Fence – it looks a little like an open ditch.

178

There is then another right-handed swing round an island marker in the middle of the field before you jump back over the same hedge line, crossing between the Taxis and Irish Bank to another hedge and then a hedge with a three-foot drop on it which is the twelfth. There's another island hedge, then a 180-degree turn to the smallest fence on the course, named in memory of a Captain Poplar, a great character from the race who died there in a fall. After hedge after hedge which you can, to a certain extent, get away with crashing through, this is a little bastard of a fence, about two and a half feet high so horses tend to ignore it but solidly constructed of white telegraph poles. It is the most solid fence on the course except for the wall. This is where Marcus Armytage had a crashing fall in 1991. His mount, Disco, treated it with disdain and turned a somersault. In the process he brought down the eventual winner Zeleznik, the Czech equivalent of Red Rum. Josef Vana, his jockey, remounted and set off a furlong behind. He caught up the field rapidly and went on to win for a record fourth time. It is that sort of race.

The next is a four-foot-drop bank and the sixteenth, in front of the stands, is a three-foot wall. We now swing left-handed over the Hadi Prikop, another wide, deep, open water and left again back over the same stream but further along. It's now back to hedges: the baby Taxis (only related by the fact that it forms part of the same hedgeline), back over the double, on across the plough to a small, open, dry ditch and a small rail and ditch, swinging left round the wood on to the outer track and off it almost as soon as you've got on to it, then another hedge, then another trick fence. It looks like a normal if slightly large hedge from the take-off but the landing side is about three feet higher than the take-off side. The horses, who by now have gone about three and a quarter miles, will be getting tired and casualties here tend to be caught out because they don't get their landing gear down in time.

There are just two more to be jumped inside the course now: a rail and ditch and the last hedge and ditch. It is then across the last stretch of plough and on to the hurdle course round the outside for the last three obstacles, the last of which, a flimsy hurdle, is in front of the stands and about a furlong from the winning post. It is an exhausting course to walk, an exhausting process to remember where the next fence is, so what the hell was it going to be like to ride? And what on earth was I doing there?

That Saturday evening we (the connections of It's A Snip, Valeda and Irish Stamp) went to a restaurant in old-town Pardubice and some went on to a nightclub afterwards. Dai Williams was also there. He had won the Czech St Leger at the course during the afternoon with a horse who had refused point blank to go on to the course during the few days she'd been stabled there. Charlie Mann intended to make a good weekend out of it but because of my weight I had an early night before getting up for a hot bath the following morning.

179

Norman and myself went to the racecourse mid-morning to walk the course again. There was already a good crowd there and we were again fêted like heroes, though we hadn't done anything yet. After numerous interviews we escaped to walk the course. It was a warm, sunny autumn day and, apart from having to ride in the race, all was well with the world.

I had ridden It's A Snip back in England and he was, to be frank, a little slow, but a safe jumper who would pop away in a race. He wanted a real test of stamina, four miles plus on soft ground. Charlie had bought him in 1994 at Doncaster sales where he had been sold by the RTE racing commentator, trainer and former jockey Ted Walsh. He had a good old-fashioned pedigree. His dam, Snipkin, was a half-sister to Drumlargan and his sire, Monksfield, had won the Champion Hurdle. Clients of Ted's had bought him and though he'd won a point-to-point as a five-year-old he was too slow to run in a bumper.

He ran straight over fences but wanted extreme distances. There are very few chases over three-and-a-half miles in Ireland and so, after he'd run well in the La Touche, a four-mile cross-country race at the Punchestown Festival, he offered him for sale. 'He was the sort of horse that if someone came to ride out on a Saturday morning you'd have no hesitation in sticking them on him,' says Ted. 'He wasn't a danger to anyone. As a racehorse he was never exciting.'

Charlie Mann had set up as a trainer in Lambourn and was doing remarkably well. I rode for him when I could. He had made a few reconnaissance missions to the Czech Republic and reckoned that the Velka, worth about £20,000 to the winner, wouldn't take much winning. An average British staying chaser that jumped would have every chance, and having seen that It's A Snip had jumped round the not dissimilar La Touche earlier in 1994, he bought him in August 1994, two months before the race. There wasn't enough time to get him fit and give him a run before setting off on the two-day journey by road to the Czech Republic.

Charlie decided he would ride It's A Snip himself. He hadn't ridden in a race since breaking his neck in a fall over hurdles at Warwick at the end of the 1988–9 season and he had been told he could not reapply for a licence to ride from the Jockey Club. He obtained one instead from the Arab Horseracing Society, believing that it would be sufficient.

It's A Snip first rode the Velka Pardubicka in 1994 and finished second, but Charlie had subsequently been fined £1000 for misleading the Arab Horseracing Society to get his licence. On the form was a question whether he had ever been turned down for a licence and he said no. Technically, he had not been turned down by the Jockey Club: they just told him not to bother applying. It turned out to be part of the adventure.

The following year, It's A Snip won. When the runners had come on to the hurdle track towards the end of the 1995 race, two Czech horses had gone early for glory and were so cooked by then that It's A Snip, who looked like he was flying, stayed on past them. He was, in fact, just plodding on at his normal pace while the other two had come to a grinding halt after jumping the last. Even when he hit the front he spooked at the crowd and did his best to throw it away, stopping to a virtual halt like he does at home on the gallops when he sees something he's not sure about. That, though, was It's A Snip's greatest hour.

I'm not sure where Charlie got his rider's licence from in 1995; maybe Japan or somewhere like that. I know he's quite cagey about it. However, on that famous winning note – the first Englishman to win the race since Chris

Collins on Stephen's Society in 1973 – Charlie, now a serious trainer, hung up his boots. Since then, it had been an agreement that I would ride him in the 1996 race.

The British racegoers became part of one large family over there and they all attached themselves to one or other of our runners. Norman, Ken Whelan who was riding Valeda II, Guy Lewis who was riding a Czech horse named Double Odds, and I changed in the same room.

There was an eccentric French amateur there whom Marcus had last seen when they had fallen together at the Taxis in 1992. André Bocquet was having a massage at the time – a heart massage, that is – and being loaded into an ambulance. He was clinically dead but the massage clearly did the trick and after being air-lifted to Prague where he spent the next five days in a coma he had made a full recovery. When I saw him it struck home that the least of our worries were the obstacles – it was the other riders. With a few exceptions they were a danger to themselves and us. A lot of them looked like they were related to the Russian jockeys of the sixties who had been promised a car by the authorities if they completed the course. To that end they used to tie the reins to their wrists so that when their horses invariably fell they didn't disappear loose. Had It's A Snip tipped up then I'd have quietly shooed him away to avoid the Central European mark of bravery (the British mark of stupidity) – remounting. Some of the other jockeys wore motorbike helmets. If I said a few rode like policemen I might never again be invited to the Silver and Blue (Metropolitan Police) Race Club. Few had body protectors.

It's A Snip is not a big horse but he pops away at his fences and I had been much encouraged watching the video of Charlie winning. Jiri Schindler, the great Czech starter, quite often likes to employ an element of surprise with his starts – a bit like stopping the music in musical chairs. This time he was rushed by the field and had little option but to let us go.

It is a crazy, amazing race. We set off fast, It's A Snip towards the back on the inside, Norman behind us, over the first two hedges which are about the same size as the first two fences at Aintree though you can brush through these. Across a sand track, on to the first water which all the horses skip over. It is easy for horses to drop their hind feet in this.

It is a tradition, I think, that the Czech jockeys quicken up the pace going to the big Taxis. The 40,000 crowd is roaring – or is it baying? – and, quite simply, they believe that the key to clearing the obstacle is speed. Consequently a lot of horses are on what I'd call the forehand. I, Norman,

Ken and Guy sought the steadier approach, trying to get our horses on their hocks. It's A Snip pinged it but was nearly taken out by a casualty getting to its feet in front of us. He swerved out right-handed on to the plough to avoid it. On the other side of the track out of my vision Guy Lewis came down, one of four casualties. It is quite like Becher's without the drop. It catches out more horses than Becher's and is only jumped once but I think a field of Cheltenham jockeys might have a slightly better record over it. There would certainly be fewer cabs called.

At the bank we lost Monsieur Bocquet. It's A Snip went into the obstacle in about tenth and came out in third. There seemed to be a traffic jam on top with horses hesitating to jump off it and we sneaked through a gap. By now the field had slowed down to a hack canter from the fast early pace to the Taxis. The plan was to make the running and make it a test of stamina. Charlie had also fitted him with blinkers to make my job easier.

For the next two miles we shared the lead with the Czech horse Libk and his jockey who seemed to know the way. I dare say It's A Snip knew his way round there too and I was fairly confident I knew mine. I had walked the course, knowing I might have to make the running. The Velka is more of a mental marathon than a race like the Grand National or the Gold Cup is. At somewhere like Cheltenham one thing you don't have to think about is where the next fence is, whether you turn left or right after jumping it, or which of three numbered and flagged fences in the same hedgerow is yours.

At the tenth we were already spread out over a furlong, concertina-ing round the sharp bends. Libk made the odd mistake but was doing a good job leading us. Ken Whelan was just behind me in third, Norman just behind him. By the time we got to the fourteenth I was really beginning to enjoy myself. It was just like hunter-trialing as a child.

At the wall we were in front and the crowd were cheering again. I was keen to keep stretching them along, not least of all to sap the stamina out of Irish Stamp whom I regarded as my biggest danger. Back over the double of hedges Irish Stamp had made a mistake at the water. At the twenty-fourth Veleda, who was travelling very well behind me, in fact as well as anything, over-jumped and rolled on Ken who had been in buoyant mood all weekend. That put an end to his party – briefly.

It's A Snip now had an eight-length lead. We'd done all the difficult bit as far as finding our way was concerned but we were being caught as we raced back on to the course with three-quarters of a mile left. At the third last, Cipisek, a huge local horse, trained by Josef Vana and ridden by a Russian, came past and so did Norman. I had expected Norman to but not Cipisek. 'Go on, that's useless,' I said to Norman as he passed to give him encouragement. I knew he wouldn't get past Cipisek, though, who was travelling far too well.

It's A Snip had given his best and I was resigned to third as Norman drove Irish Stamp after Cipisek. In the end – I think British stewards might have had a word in his ear over his use of the whip – he was a gallant two and a half lengths second. We were a distance away in third. I was physically and mentally exhausted. It was the most testing ride I had during the 1996–7 season: ten minutes of hard concentration.

And that, in many ways, was only the start of it. Norman and I were still treated like heroes. If they had wanted to know our opinions beforehand they now wanted documentary-length interviews on what we thought of their great race, how the Taxis compared to Becher's and The Chair, and which was the tougher race?

The Velka and the Grand National are two very different races but both are national institutions. When It's A Snip ran in the National in 1995 – he was allotted something like 7st in the long handicap. You need a very much better horse to win the National and while the National winner could win the Velka it will be some time before a Velka winner is good enough to win the National. Take nothing away from Cipisek. Irish Stamp beat It's A Snip to within about a pound of their respective handicap marks and Cipisek, who broke the course record by ten seconds, would be capable of winning some long-distance handicap chases in Britain I'm sure. It was a much better race in 1996 than it had been when It's A Snip won in 1995.

183

Norman and I weren't allowed to go and change for ages and at the press conference afterwards the winning jockey Vladislav Snitkovskij hardly got a look in. We signed more autographs there in a day than we normally signed in a season here. The buzz was as great, if not greater, than the National and that is saying something. We all got a hell of a kick out of it. I have not been given a greater reception anywhere – not even after winning a National.

André Bocquet, it turned out, was delighted to have got as far as fifth. His four previous attempts had all come unstuck at the Taxis and for him this was a major triumph. He was as chuffed as Norman or I. Ken was disappointed: he had been going so well and had fallen at an innocuous fence. Guy was not too despondent after his fall at the Taxis. He was, after all, uninjured.

last, Cipisek, a huge local horse, trained by Josef Vana and ridden by a Russian, came past and so did Norman. I had expected Norman to but not Cipisek. 'Go on, that's useless,' I said to Norman as he passed to give him encouragement. I knew he wouldn't get past Cipisek, though, who was travelling far too well.

It's A Snip had given his best and I was resigned to third as Norman drove Irish Stamp after Cipisek. In the end – I think British stewards might have had a word in his ear over his use of the whip – he was a gallant two and a half lengths second. We were a distance away in third. I was physically and mentally exhausted. It was the most testing ride I had during the 1996–7 season: ten minutes of hard concentration.

And that, in many ways, was only the start of it. Norman and I were still treated like heroes. If they had wanted to know our opinions beforehand they now wanted documentary-length interviews on what we thought of their great race, how the Taxis compared to Becher's and The Chair, and which was the tougher race?

The Velka and the Grand National are two very different races but both are national institutions. When It's A Snip ran in the National in 1995 – he was allotted something like 7st in the long handicap. You need a very much better horse to win the National and while the National winner could win the Velka it will be some time before a Velka winner is good enough to win the National. Take nothing away from Cipisek. Irish Stamp beat It's A Snip to within about a pound of their respective handicap marks and Cipisek, who broke the course record by ten seconds, would be capable of winning some long-distance handicap chases in Britain I'm sure. It was a much better race in 1996 than it had been when It's A Snip won in 1995.

Norman and I weren't allowed to go and change for ages and at the press conference afterwards the winning jockey Vladislav Snitkovskij hardly got a look in. We signed more autographs there in a day than we normally signed in a season here. The buzz was as great, if not greater, than the National and that is saying something. We all got a hell of a kick out of it. I have not been given a greater reception anywhere – not even after winning a National.

André Bocquet, it turned out, was delighted to have got as far as fifth. His four previous attempts had all come unstuck at the Taxis and for him this was a major triumph. He was as chuffed as Norman or I. Ken was disappointed: he had been going so well and had fallen at an innocuous fence. Guy was not too despondent after his fall at the Taxis. He was, after all, uninjured.

For pure spectacle and atmosphere there are few races to match the Velka Pardubicka, run on the second Sunday every October. It is a colourful mix of amateur and professional, good fortune and bad luck, the feeling of a mountain to be climbed at the start and a sense of relief at its completion among the oohs and ahhs and catcalls of the 40,000 crowd. Each obstacle is so different from the previous one it is like starting a new day. We should have had this chapter sponsored by the Czech Tourist Board because if you want an amusing, fun weekend racing abroad look no further than the Semtex capital of the world.

As for It's A Snip, his two victories in handicap chases in this country were nothing short of miraculous. He did win one of them on National day but it was at Hereford and not Aintree. He ran his last race in the Sporting Index Chase at Cheltenham – a cross-country race – in 1996, a month after the Velka. He had given me another exciting ride, until slipping a tendon off his hock and he was retired by Charlie Mann who'll give him a home for life. He has had an active retirement and still does the odd show in Wiltshire.

He is a character and, despite Ted Walsh's assertion that he was harmless, he spooked so often going up the gallops that he dropped more lads that season than any other in the yard. He was and remains a character. I think he was trained with considerable foresight by Charlie Mann. He won ten times what he paid for him, though mainly in Czech florins, very little in English quid. Without those trips we would never have heard of him and his owners, the Icy Fire Partnership, would never have had such fun.

We had a great night after the race. A civic reception was held in the nearby castle after which we were taken back to Prague to catch a flight home early the next morning. We stayed up with some other English racing people in the bar of our Prague hotel until the staff kicked us out and sent us to bed at 4.00 a.m. The party continued upstairs.

That morning the flight was delayed from 8.00 a.m. until lunchtime, which meant missing four rides at Roscommon. Norman and I had had such a good weekend that we were quite pleased. We slept for most of the five-hour delay on benches in the departure lounge of Prague Airport dreaming of fearsome obstacles, and even more fearsome rivals!

VIKING FLAGSHIP

17

I T IS NOT EASY TO COMPARE ALL THE HORSES I RODE WITH EACH OTHER. WEST TIP, FOR EXAMPLE, WAS AS IMPORTANT TO ME AT THE START OF MY CAREER AS DESERT ORCHID WAS IN THE LATER STAGES. They were both, in their own way, very good horses, though on a park course it is unlikely that West Tip would ever have beaten Desert Orchid. Both were tough but neither was as tough as Viking Flagship. When I left the Duke's to join Martin Pipe at the end of the 1992–3 season the one horse I most regretted not being able to ride the following year was Viking Flagship. This regret was never deeper than when I witnessed the Mumm Melling Chase at Liverpool in 1995 when he beat Deep Sensation in one of the races of the year. Martha's Son was a close third. If you had to nominate a dozen races that stood out in the last twenty years, that would be there among them, nearer the top of the list than the bottom.

David Nicholson says he was the toughest horse he ever trained. When you saw him storming up the hill at Sandown or Cheltenham you may not appreciate that Viking Flagship also ran four times as a two-year-old and fourteen times as a three-year-old – without success and providing little in the way of hope for the future over trips ranging from seven furlongs to a mile and three-quarters. Over fences he ran thirty-five times, won twenty and was unplaced only three times.

Viking Flagship was by Viking, a horse who was by Northern Dancer and out of an Irish Oaks winner. Viking, who won four races in America but nothing important, was not a popular sire and was exported to Denmark in 1988. His dam, Fourth Degree, never ran.

Graham Roach's Prideaux Boy had provided me with one of my first decent winners when he won the Mecca Hurdle at Sandown in my youth. Graham never normally buys named horses or horses out of a yard but the one exception was Viking Flagship. In the early nineties, the Irish jockey John Shortt rode for Graham, who trained his own horses at home in Cornwall. Graham had a call one day from John who asked him if he might be interested in buying a horse belonging to Tony Holdsworth, the chap with whom he lodged.

Viking Flagship's hurdling career with Martin Pipe didn't get off to the most promising of starts when he fell in a three-year-old hurdle with Dean Gallagher at Wolverhampton on Boxing Day. Martin then took him to Newton Abbot where he showed considerably more promise by finishing second of sixteen. That preceded a run of four wins, all over two miles. The first two were at Lingfield, the second of them on the all-weather. He beat me into second on both occasions. The first time I could never get to him but on the all-weather I decided to take him on and I had him struggling, off the bridle four out. Mine then weakened and was, as many others were to be later on in Viking Flagship's illustrious career, out-battled. He beat me four lengths.

It was about this time that Graham began to take an interest. He'd told John to get Tony to give him a ring if he was serious about selling and Graham had received the call on his way to Cardiff Arms Park one Saturday. He nearly drove off the road when Tony said he wanted £100,000 for the horse. Graham nearly crashed the car. He stressed that he never bought made horses, nor had he ever paid anything like that for a horse. 'You've got the wrong bloke,' he said. Tony pointed out that the horse was soon to run at Sandown and that he would go well. Viking Flagship ran there and skated up, 'But still wasn't worth £100,000,' says Graham.

His next outing was at Chepstow on a day that Graham was flying back into the country from abroad. He went straight from Heathrow to Chepstow to watch the race. It was very soft ground, Viking Flagship carried 12st and won in a time only a second and a half slower than the Welsh Champion Hurdle. Contrary to all his rules, Graham eventually agreed a price, closer to what he wanted to pay for the horse. He sent the vet to Martin's to inspect Viking Flagship. Martin hadn't realized the horse was for sale or he probably would have bought him himself. When the vet saw him he failed him as lame. He returned two days later and passed him.

Graham still trained his own horses at this point, but then business commitments persuaded him to give up and send his horses to the Duke the following season. Viking Flagship did have an entry at Punchestown, though, and Graham sent him there for his last run of the season.

After his summer break he joined David Nicholson, whose immediate worry was how to improve on a horse that had been trained by Martin Pipe. It did look like the Duke was on a hiding to nothing. Having run up a sequence of hurdling victories Viking Flagship was not particularly well handicapped and he would have to end up taking on some of the best handicappers in the country. It took the Duke a while to work out Viking Flagship and he admits it took four runs to get him fit. He was always a very stuffy horse at home, quite thick-winded, and, though he managed to win first time out, he usually took a race or two to get fit. His best runs were often shortly after a hard run somewhere else. Warren Marston rode him for his first couple of runs and I took over at Ascot in January 1992, when he finished fourth in the Teal and Green Hurdle. He was still blowing his head off at the end of the race. The comment in my rides file is that he pulled up stuffy. I also said he would be better going left. He must have hung to the left a bit during the race. He was not an over-big horse but jumped his hurdles well and it may have been a mistake in those first three races to try to make all and gallop the others into the ground.

As he had still blown hard after his third run of the season, the Duke decided to take him to Taunton five days later and, for once, we didn't try to make the running. If ever there was a horse who could take two quick races it was Viking Flagship and this was the first hard evidence we had of it. He was still a bit thick-winded but not nearly so stuffy and the track suited him. Worth £5,602, the Unity Farm Holiday Centre Handicap Hurdle was quite a valuable race by Taunton's standards. Norman Williamson led on a horse called Rusty Roc until we took over two out, holding Martin Pipe's Galway Star to win by a couple of lengths.

In February the Duke got a bit more ambitious with Viking Flagship and decided to run him in the Tote Gold Trophy at Newbury off 10st 5lb. It is always a competitive handicap and off this weight Viking Flagship was made third favourite behind Native Mission and Kibreet. He didn't run very well and eventually finished tenth, beaten thirty lengths by Rodeo Star who had also beaten him at Ascot earlier in the season. Once again he was very stuffy and having been very handy to a fast pace I probably burst him. I thought at the time that he may have sulked a little and I told the Duke that he needed his own way. In retrospect, I don't think that was quite right!

At Nottingham next time I decked him. (It was one of those weeks when I was having more falls than usual. You got into those ruts sometimes and I think it probably got through to the horses. I'd already been brought down in a hurdle earlier that afternoon.) This was my fault. The winner, Tomahawk, had made all the running, I'd tried to close him down and had succeeded in getting to him but I was beaten. In a vain effort to rescue the race I asked Viking Flagship for a very long one and ended up in putting him on the floor.

He then ran a good race in the Imperial Cup at Sandown to finish fourth to King Credo. Rodeo Star also finished in front of us. Viking Flagship had a good gurgle on pulling up which was further evidence of his thick-windedness. Somewhere, somehow, the air was not getting through quite as it should, but it didn't seem to be stopping him in his races. The Imperial Cup is five days before the County Hurdle at the Cheltenham Festival and the Duke decided it would do Viking Flagship no harm if he were to run in both. He ran a very gutsy race. I was always handy, led over the last, but he just tied up in the last hundred yards. He ran a cracking race to go down by just under two lengths to Dusty Miller and Bank View. It was his best race to date.

The improvement did not stop there either. Next stop was Aintree for the Cordon Bleu Handicap Hurdle where he ran another great race behind Flakey Dove. I made the running on him and the mare and Cheerful Times just did me for a bit of foot. He made just one mistake. He was a real professional hurdler, very quick in getting from one side to another, and the hurdles tended just to get in his way occasionally. It was a satisfactory end to a good season and Viking Flagship, without winning anything major, had established himself as one of the more reliable and useful handicap hurdlers of that season. He just found one too good for him over hurdles.

I had my doubts about Viking Flagship being a good chaser. I certainly didn't think he would be much better at chasing than he had been at hurdling. Though thoroughly genuine he wasn't very big and I thought he might struggle with his jumping. At this stage I certainly didn't think he would ever be a Champion Chase winner.

Though the ground at Liverpool had been good, Viking Flagship managed to jar his tendons. He was treated while on holiday with his owner in Cornwall. As a consequence his chasing career did not begin in earnest until the following February, 1993. When it did, it began, like his hurdling one had, on the deck. Those tendon problems never showed

themselves again but the Duke decided that he would be better off that season missing Cheltenham and Liverpool because of the fast ground.

It was at Nottingham that we let him loose over fences. He led and jumped pretty well on the whole although he was a bit flat at the last ditch. I gave him a breather five out. At the last, and we were some way clear, we had a difference of opinion. I went long and he put down on me and fell. He would have won very easily but the record books show that Bibendum, a decent horse owned by Robert Waley-Cohen, won the race. Viking Flagship never looked back.

At Wolverhampton he jumped very fluently to beat Dis Train. At Leicester he gurgled again and took a few novice-like liberties with his fences but still beat Antonin fifteen lengths. At Wincanton he jumped left quite markedly but still won. The Duke then took him out of the Arkle and Grand Annual because of the ground. The same thing happened at Liverpool – it was too firm to risk such a promising chaser and he was re-routed to Chepstow where it was soft. He was very stuffy, not having run for seven weeks. Even so he won by a distance after the only other reasonable member of the opposition, Atlaal, fell at the last.

The Duke was a big supporter of the Punchestown Festival. The prize money is very generous there and the ground is often good, which is a real incentive to keep good horses going a little longer, particularly on this side of the Irish Sea. Besides that the meeting is a real craic and I think owners enjoy themselves out there, win, lose or draw. Races are certainly not easy to win there and in 1993 the British came away with just three wins – two of them provided by Viking Flagship.

191

The plan was to run Viking Flagship on the first day and, providing he was all right, again on the third day. News had just broken about my moving to Martin Pipe's following Peter Scudamore's retirement. Viking Flagship was to be my last big ride for the Duke for the foreseeable future. I had already revised my opinion about how far he could go as a successful chaser and was regretting the fact that I would not be on board the following season.

The Duke had thought there was decent handicap chase in Viking Flagship while he was still a novice and so it proved in the BMW Drogheda Chase, worth £22,000 to the winner. He had only 10st 7lb but they made him favourite. He made a couple of mistakes, mainly because he was so keen to get on with it and get to the landing side. It looked like Foulksrath Castle might have the measure of us at the third last but I knew Viking

Flagship well enough. He likes nothing better than a good scrap. However, victory was sealed by virtue of two very good jumps at the second last and the last. The win was part of a first-day treble for me at the meeting.

Viking Flagship pulled out well and fresh on the Wednesday so the Duke decided to let him take his chance again in the Bank of Ireland Colliers Novices Chase on the Thursday. Ireland had a good bunch of novices around and they confidently expected to keep this race at home with either Soft Day or How's The Boss, the country's two best novice chasers. That clash ended early when Soft Day fell and broke a leg at the second; How's The Boss injured a shoulder at a later stage of the race. Antonin, whom we had already beaten, made the running and we got to him just before the last and beat him four lengths. Viking Flagship felt much clearer in the wind running for the second time in three days and also jumped much better than he had two days before. It was, I thought, quite a feat, and bode well for Adrian Maguire for the following season.

Despite winding up the season as one of the top two-mile novice chasers, and even though he had missed Cheltenham and Liverpool, David Nicholson planned to start Viking Flagship in handicaps in the 1993–4 season. He was still six at the start of that season and it was not until his third run, in the Victor Chandler Chase, that he won. Adrian had ridden him in his first two starts and had, like myself the previous season, found a horse who needed an incredible amount of work to get fit.

This particular Victor Chandler Chase marked something of a landmark in British racing history as it was the first time a major chase had been abandoned and rescheduled at another meeting. Ascot, where it was usually held, was unraceable and so the Victor Chandler Chase went to Warwick, at the suggestion of Channel Four Racing who covered the meeting. The same thing happened the following month when the Greenalls Gold Cup – won by Master Oats – was moved from Haydock to Newbury. It was a tremendous bonus for the top horses, many of whom have such limited chances anyway.

The race, luckily for me, attracted four runners, including the Duke's other good two-mile chaser Waterloo Boy, Adrian's choice, so that I was reunited with Viking Flagship. Had he chosen Viking Flagship, the final totals in the jockeys championship at the end of the season would have been different. If he had won this one and I had lost it, I would have won the championship by only one. As it was it went to the last meeting at Market Rasen and I won by 197 to 194. It would have been a difficult decision for Adrian because the Duke steered you and you couldn't argue!

It was desperately heavy ground and we were third-favourites behind Waterloo Boy and Egypt Mill Prince. Viking Flagship and Egypt Mill Prince drew clear from three out but I looked beaten at the second last until Viking Flagship rallied like a hero and wore down the other horse, a horse who was more often bridesmaid than bride, who came in second, beaten two lengths. Though Viking Flagship didn't mind the very soft ground, it could catch him out if he wasn't particularly clear in his wind and therefore extremely fit. It brought him right back into the public's mind with thoughts on the prospects for the Queen Mother Champion Chase.

Adrian then rode him in the Game Spirit Chase at Newbury, a race named after the Queen Mother's great old chaser. It looked a real good Champion Chase trial with Egypt Mill Prince, Deep Sensation, Sybillin and Wonder Man in the field. He looked to be the first off the bridle but that counts for little with a horse as game and as tough as he is. At the last it still looked like Sybillin and Deep Sensation had the better of him but, terrier-like, he out-battled them to win by a couple of lengths.

The Queen Mother Champion Chase was to prove the best and most exciting race of the 1994 Cheltenham Festival. It contained three previous winners in Katabatic, whose moment of triumph had come in 1991, Remittance Man, the brilliant winner from the following year who appeared to be back to his best after a lengthy absence through injury, and the enigmatic 1993 winner Deep Sensation. The race also contained three of the best novices from the previous season: Travado who had won the Arkle, Sybillin from the north and the up-and-coming Viking Flagship. It was the year I spent the Festival – due to a long ban – having my own little festival in the ski resort of Val d'Isère. Three out Remittance Man fell, which left a front line of three abreast at the second last: Viking Flagship on the inside, Travado on the outer and Deep Sensation, who tended to pull himself up in front, the meat in the sandwich. They all rose as one at the last and Jamie Osborne, who had ridden Travado, later confessed to being confident of victory. He didn't count on the toughness of Viking Flagship and his jockey who threw everything at the horse and was met with a terrific response. Adrian won with a neck to spare, with Deep Sensation back in third a length away. In defeat Jamie described Viking Flagship as a 'very tough horse'; in victory Adrian described him as the 'toughest' he had ever ridden – so that makes two of us.

His last race of that great season was at Liverpool where he again ran a

brave race but he was unable to give 2olb to Sybillin's stable companion Uncle Ernie.

His reign as Champion two-miler lasted two seasons. The following year I sadly didn't get to ride him at all. Adrian rode him to win his first two races, the 1994 Tingle Creek at Sandown, which contained the first four home in last season's Champion Chase, and the Castleford at Wetherby. Adrian had been delayed by fog that day and Peter Niven had been on standby to ride, although Adrian made it just in time in the end. I thought it an incredible training performance to get him to win first time out.

I don't think he can have been right in the middle of the season when he was beaten, carrying 12st in the Victor Chandler at Ascot a long way by Martha's Son. There had been rumours that all was not well with him before this race, which had caused some bookmakers to suspend ante-post betting on it. Then he fell in the Game Spirit Chase when he seemed to be in command. This presented the Duke with a problem because he knew another race was essential for the stuffy Viking Flagship if he was to have any chance of retaining his title at Cheltenham. So he went to Kempton for the Emblem Chase a fortnight later. There he appeared to have a very hard race to go down by a length to Thumbs Up on some pretty gluey ground. The ground was the Duke's excuse anyway, and he said that he was sure you didn't get that ground at Cheltenham, regardless of the weather.

194

Shortly before Cheltenham Adrian's mother died suddenly and he went back home to Ireland, missing the Festival. By that stage I was already committed to Travado and I couldn't get off him. The ride on Viking Flagship, who had not been in the best of form since January, went to the Irish Champion jockey and Cheltenham hero Charlie Swan. Travado ran a terrible race and made a couple of serious blunders but Viking Flagship returned to his very best. He was even more convincing than he had been the previous year. Again it was Deep Sensation who chased him home with Nakir, the previous season's Arkle winner, back in third. It was part of a treble on the second day of that Festival for the Duke, a feat not achieved since Charlie Rogers did it in 1946. Charlie Swan described him as the best chaser he had ever ridden. He had also become only the eighth horse to win the Queen Mother Champion Chase twice.

It was, however, his run in the Mumm Melling Chase that he shall be remembered for that season. There were only four runners and the race was set up by the fourth, Southolt, who set out in front. At the last Martha's Son, who went on to win the 1997 Champion Chase, landed marginally in front, but the race developed into a classic between Deep Sensation and Norman Williamson and Viking Flagship and Adrian. As so often was the case, Viking Flagship looked beat but rallied in the dying strides to snatch victory from Deep Sensation, who had also fought every yard of that run-in. I didn't have a ride in that race and watched jealously from the weighing room. I was gutted not to have been part of one of the greatest races ever run over jumps during my career.

In the 1995–6 season Viking Flagship was out to equal Badworth Boy's record of three Champion Chase victories. He failed gallantly. This season started off in the Tingle Creek when Graham Bradley rode him because Adrian was injured. I rode the winner Sound Man. Viking Flagship would have needed the race but the Duke was not very complimentary about Brad. It was his last ride for the Duke. I rode him then in the John Bull at Wincanton where he made a terrible noise with his wind. He did, however, show some spark, which was encouraging for although the Duke blamed Brad for his being tailed off at Sandown he did just wonder if the many miles on Viking Flagship's clock were not beginning to take their toll. We thought he would come on a lot for the race and so it proved in the Game Spirit with Adrian back in the saddle. He then hacked up in the Emblem Chase ahead of Cheltenham and three wins in the Champion Chase looked possible.

195

Adrian was injured with a broken collarbone just prior to the Festival and Charlie Swan was back in the saddle for Cheltenham. The race was won by Klairon Davis and Frankie Woods, who came from off the pace to beat Viking Flagship as well as me on Sound Man. Charlie and I were blamed for getting our horses into a long drawn-out battle in which we effectively cut our throats and allowed Klairon Davis to win. I rode my race and, knowing Viking Flagship's wind, tried to stretch him down the hill but, in saying that, I was doing it on the bridle. Klairon Davis made mincemeat of the last ditch. Viking Flagship and Sound Man also made a mess of the third last but neither of us had an answer for Klairon Davis, who liked the track having won the Arkle there the previous year.

Viking Flagship did round the season off with another win in the Mumm Melling Chase at Aintree under Tony McCoy when Sound Man finished second. He jumped very well for Tony, indeed I have rarely seen him jump better. Tony was injured for the Mira Showers Chase at Cheltenham in April so I took over again. I was beaten three-quarters of a length by Gales Cavalier who jumped like a buck that day. I suspect we might have been unlucky to meet Gales Cavalier in such good form and though I got to him at the second last I couldn't get past him. I had no excuse for Viking Flagship other than his wind, which was again quite thick even though he had been running regularly.

The next season he ran six times and again never finished out of the first four. I beat him on Sound Man in the Tingle Creek in which only two of us were really left in the contest from the downhill fence. We both made mistakes but at the pond fence I made a valiant effort to wrestle Sound Man to the floor. As it was his first run I knew that he would be thick-winded and if I kept persevering I'd get back to him and might even beat him. Sound Man rallied well, with a run already under his belt, to beat him five lengths. In the Victor Chandler at Ascot he didn't run particularly well behind Ask Tom, another young pretender to the title.

He suffered a set-back following that race when he bruised a foot and had to miss the Game Spirit so again he went to the Emblem Chase in which he hacked up once more despite a couple of mistakes. His main rival that day, Martha's Son, fell at the second.

Adrian had been desperately unlucky for three consecutive seasons to miss Cheltenham: in 1997, it was because of a bad break to his upper arm. Now that I was freelancing I was available to ride Viking Flagship again. He was, once again, one of the favourites. He jumped well and with a rare run up Norman Williamson's inner on Strong Promise I actually thought I was finally going to win the Queen Mother Champion Chase. It was a great feeling. I committed myself at the second last but going to the last I saw Martha's Son's head and I could see he was running away with Rodney Farrant. Ask Tom, whom I had passed at the second last, also came back past me but it was still one hell of a performance to go down to Martha's Son by only three lengths.

I rode him again at Liverpool but he gave me no feeling that day. He got very warm beforehand. Rodney had injured himself so Carl Llewellyn came in for the ride on Martha's Son. They did their utmost to come unstuck at the first but they went on to win very impressively again and confirm Martha's Son's position at the top of the two-mile chasers. I made a bad mistake at the third last where I'd pulled out to follow Strong Promise. It cost me my chance.

I think the Duke then wanted to give Richard Johnson, his promising young jockey and, after all, the stable's second, the chance to ride Viking Flagship. I was committed to ride Gales Cavalier but by then I think Viking

Flagship was over the top. He finished third behind Strong Promise and Gales Cavalier.

He was a real battler and I don't think he ever threw in the towel. He wasn't in just one of the most exciting races seen in many years, but several of them, and I don't think he ever lost a photo finish. He was retired in 1998 and, sadly, having survived so many battles on the racecourse, was put down two years later after breaking a leg while turned out in a paddock.

197

18 ONE MAN

I F I COULD HAVE INTERVIEWED ONE HORSE IN THIS BOOK IT WOULD HAVE BEEN ONE MAN. If only they could talk we would know so much more about them. Everyone involved in jump-racing has their theories about One Man's two runs in the Tote Gold Cup at Cheltenham. Each time he looked the winner turning in with two fences left to jump, each time he hit an invisible wall, scrambled over the last like you'd expect someone asked to negotiate an obstacle at the end of a marathon, and virtually walked up the hill. Did he fail to get the trip or was something internal stopping him?

In 1996 I have rarely felt so confident about winning a race but he went from hero to zero in two strides. In 1997, well, we were expecting it but I was even more confident with two to jump that we would wear down Mr Mulligan. He had carried me a hundred yards further than he did the previous year. It was still not quite far enough. I'm convinced something hurt him or that he was afraid of something hurting him. Possibly the biggest clue to those Gold Cup performances came at Liverpool in 1997 when he burst a blood vessel. One of my theories is that it was the manifestation of the problem that was preventing him win a Gold Cup. It is only a theory though. Vets could not find a single physical reason for it but I doubt anyone will be able to prove or disprove it.

One Man had originally been bought from Tom Costello in Ireland by the late Arthur Stephenson. Tom has a yard at Newmarket-on-Fergus in County Clare and has always been one of the best judges of a jumper in Ireland. He bought One Man, who had been bred by Hugh Holohan, as a three-year-old at the Derby sales for IR 4,000 guineas. 'He was a good mover, not too big,

199

not too small,' he recalls. 'He had a good pedigree and a nice horse like that can go a long way.'

He was broken in, schooled and trained for a point-to-point at Briarstown which he would have won easily had his rider not gone the wrong side of the winning post, resulting in his disqualification. 'I was sending him to David Nicholson,' he added, 'but in the end he went to Arthur.' Tom and Arthur had a deal whereby Tom would send over a load of horses on a horsebox, Arthur would have a good look at them and return the ones he didn't want.

His first run for Arthur and his main owner, a Swiss businessman called Peter Pillar, was at Hexham the following autumn when, ridden by Chris Grant, he finished tenth to Apache Brave. He looked a little bit backward and was in the rear of the fifteen runners for a long way before making up some ground, only to tire as they turned to come up the steep hill. It was a good education for him.

Second time out he finished second to Valiant Warrior over two and a half miles at Wetherby. Although he was never at any stage going to beat the winner he stayed on well to pass his more one-paced rivals from the second last. He kept progressing and won his third race, the Burghley Novice Hurdle at Newcastle, on 21 October 1992. Ridden closer to the pace by Chris he hacked up this time, beating Highlandman by a very comfortable ten lengths. It might not have been the greatest race to bless Gosforth Park but the ease with which he won suggested they had a good horse on their hands.

Having won over two-and-a-half miles, Arthur stepped him up to three and a quarter at Cheltenham, a trip that always haunted him, in November. The race was turned into a procession by Nigel Twiston-Davies's good mare Gaelstrom, who beat me on Musthaveaswig by ten lengths. We were twenty in front of One Man and Chris who weakened about three out (this was his first attempt at the Gold Cup trip and, aged four, you could forgive him for not staying the trip.) It was a tip in itself that Arthur thought a good deal of the horse by sending him to Cheltenham.

Arthur kept him fairly busy and a fortnight later sent him to Newcastle again on Fighting Fifth Hurdle day. Back over two and a half miles it proved to be a hot contest won by High Altitude. Trainglot, who went on to become a Cheltenham winner, was third in the race. One Man was just struggling with the pace two out when he tipped up with Chris. Shortly afterwards Arthur died and the horses ran in the name of his nephew Peter Cheeseborough.

Though I had ridden against One Man at Cheltenham, he had not really caught my eye as anything out of the ordinary until Nottingham in January

1993. I was due to ride the favourite Master Jolson for David Nicholson in a novice handicap hurdle and thought he was a good thing. All the conditions were right for him. I held him up at the back where Chris had One Man. He went a bit sooner than I did but I followed him through. Chris hit the front on him going to the last. Master Jolson stayed on but One Man beat us by a length and a half under strong driving from Chris. The third horse was twenty lengths behind us. When I said 'Well done' to Chris he remarked what a gutsy horse he was and what a lovely novice chaser he would make for the following season.

After that he won again, this time very easily at Ayr over two and a half miles again in February. He slightly disappointed at Aintree on the day of the void Grand National when he finished a distant third of three behind Lemon's Mill and Leotard but he redeemed himself with a good effort to finish second to Aahsaylad at Ayr's Scottish National meeting in April.

Arthur had always been quite a good mate of Gordon Richards and when they had talked about the grey Arthur had always said, 'Wait 'til this one sees the black ones [fences].' At the same time John Hales had bought a four-year-old with Gordon who wasn't going to be ready to do much for a couple of years. Being a little impatient, he told Gordon he should buy him something ready to run in the autumn. They were sent the catalogue for the Stephenson Dispersal Sale and the first horse they both picked out was One Man. When they arrived at Crawleas Farm near Bishop Auckland on 9 May 1993, their heads were turned towards another horse called Spanish Fair. They joined the bidding. Everyone else had dropped out except Sue Bramall who eventually secured him for 70,000 guineas. He was the top lot. When One Man came in Gordon and John were determined to buy him and they went up to 68,000 guineas. Sue Bramall was underbidder this time. As the horse was knocked down to John Hales he met Neale Doughty, Gordon's jockey, for the first time. 'I'll win his first five novice chases on him,' he said to John, who regrets that Doughts's prediction had not been the first six.

Now in the hands of Arthur's friend and heir apparent in the north, Gordon Richards, One Man's chasing career began as he had hoped it would, with a facile victory over three miles and a furlong at Ayr in November 1993. Doughts was in the saddle. Though he beat nothing at Ayr and barely had a work-out, he went to Haydock five days later and beat Monsieur Le Cure, who went on to win that season's Sun Alliance Chase by an easy ten lengths. Front Line and Reve de Valse were third and fourth.

In December he returned to Haydock again and this time, in slightly softer ground, he beat Lo Stregone an impressive three and a half lengths. Rapidly he was becoming the leading novice chaser in the north. It was a similar story at Wetherby on Boxing Day and no different when Gordon brought him down to Ascot for the Reynoldstown Chase over an extended three miles. He won pulling the proverbial cart, by three lengths to Mailcom, with Lusty Light and Mudahim back in fourth and fifth respectively.

His unbeaten sequence – extending to Doughts's predicted five runs – came to an end, ominously for the future, at Cheltenham in Monsieur Le Cure's Sun Alliance Chase. The 3–1 favourite, Doughts had him near the front for most of the way, he took it up at the thirteenth, lost the lead when he made a mistake at the next, the ditch, and was still in with a chance when he rapidly began to weaken at the third last. He was still in fourth but had no chance when he walked through the last, and Doughts just let him hack home a very tired horse to finish ninth of the twelve finishers. It was the only blot on One Man's landscape. He did, however, return home from Cheltenham with a twisted back, which Gordon assumed he had done when making his first mistake and which was the reason they gave themselves for his failure to get the trip.

That summer Neale Doughty retired and Tony Dobbin, who had been a highly promising conditional jockey in the north, took over as stable jockey. It was a big step up the ladder for Tony who was relatively inexperienced for such a job but it was a wonderful opportunity he just could not turn down.

His first ride in public on One Man was a doddle. The six-year-old hacked round over two and a half miles at Ayr in November 1994 as a prep race for the Hennessy Cognac Gold Cup for which he appeared thrown in on 10st.

I thought Tony gave the horse a cracking ride in the Hennessy. I was riding Lord Relic who had had very little racing and a difficult preparation, but if anyone was going to have him fighting fit for the race it was Martin Pipe. One Man only beat me two lengths but I never felt I was ever going to catch him. He travelled exceedingly well and once he'd settled down he began to ping his fences. Tony had let him go coming to the last ditch and he flew it. He could have beaten me further and people were now talking about the second coming of Dessie.

His career then suffered a couple of set-backs. First of all at Wetherby on Boxing Day in the Rowland Meyrick where he was an odds-on favourite to beat a previous Hennessy winner, Cogent, and a previous Gold Cup winner, Jodami. It was one of those peculiar races that prove that there is no such thing as a racing certainty. One Man made a right mess of the last fence down the back straight at Wetherby and unseated Tony. It was an impossible

202

mistake to sit on. Then at the next, the first in the straight, Jodami fell when upsides Cogent. This left the former Hennessy winner and amateur Chris Bonner to come home in their own time. Mark Dwyer remounted Jodami and finished a long time after the winner.

One Man was again made favourite to redeem himself in the Racing Post Chase at Kempton in February 1995. A good run here would have seen him a warm favourite to win the Gold Cup, for although he'd won the Hennessy it was off a low weight and he still had something to prove. But it was back to the drawing board after Kempton. Martin didn't have a runner so I watched this from the changing room on television. One Man was travelling well in second place but they'd just gone a circuit when he took a crashing fall, compounded by his falling broadside to the other runners which brought down Amtrak Express. The race went to the French challenger Val D'Alene who beat Southolt by a country mile to make François Doumen's Kempton record even more impressive.

One Man took a long time to get to his feet. For a moment John Hales thought he had lost the horse. Amazingly, he was sound when they trotted him up in the racecourse stables but such a heavy fall was a shock to his system and they roughed him off there and then. He didn't come back into training until August when John's daughter Lisa started schooling One Man indoors trying to get him to engage his brain instead of rushing the showjumps.

203

Gordon brought him back to Ayr in November with a view to having a second crack at the Hennessy. He scored an impressive victory beating Jodami, running his best race for a while, by seven lengths, although he was still getting 1st 2lb from the former Gold Cup winner. Tony was then injured badly in a fall at Catterick and Gordon rang to ask me to ride One Man in the Hennessy. I had already given a commitment to Jim Dreaper to ride Merry Gale at Punchestown in Ireland so I had reluctantly to turn the ride down and Mark Dwyer came in for it instead. I was frustrated that Friday evening before the Hennessy thinking I'd turned down the winning ride but that night the heavens opened. It rained all night and for most of Saturday. Eventually Gordon decided he wouldn't run him on very soft ground and though One Man had arrived there he withdrew him. I missed nothing, and in Ireland Merry Gale won his race after the first-fence fall of Imperial Call.

Mark did get his chance to ride him at Haydock the following month in the Tommy Whittle Chase when he beat Monsieur Le Cure by eleven lengths. Tony was still injured and, unfortunately for him, under Mark he put up an exhibition show. It was an impressive warm-up for the King George VI Chase and his jumping was back to his brilliant best. He stood off the second last a mile and a lot of people said it was reminiscent of Pendil.

The build-up to Kempton's Boxing Day showpiece centred on the controversial booking of me to ride One Man in the race. Tony is a popular jockey and had done nothing wrong on One Man but John Hales, his owner, and Gordon had a problem. They had the red-hot favourite for the race, Tony would have been back only a week from his injury and at that stage he did not have much big-race experience. Tony had not won the Grand National then and his fitness, after the fall, was in doubt. Adding to the problem from Tony's point of view was the fact that I, who had won the race twice, was without a ride in the race.

It was a difficult situation. The public felt sorry for Tony because they saw his big opportunity taken away from him. Others thought that if he was first jockey to Gordon then he should ride everything. I was without a mount in the race and, having been offered the ride, I could not refuse. If I didn't ride him then someone else would have and Tony would still have lost out. We've all been jocked off and one day it's one way; the next, it's the other. Indeed, Tony didn't start the 1996–7 season riding Lord Gyllene and yet he ended up winning the National on him. I must say, however, that throughout he was very good about it.

204

The whole rides business is now so much more competitive than it ever used to be. Everything is done through agents. To stay competitive I had no choice but to employ an agent back in the 1986–7 season. Some amateurs even have them now. When Adrian Maguire broke his arm before Cheltenham in 1997 about four agents were on to David Nicholson before Adrian had even had his arm X-rayed. When I started riding, jockeys tended to have their own rides and got really shirty if you ever tried poaching them. Except for a few yards which retain jockeys it's virtually a free-for-all now, a more cut-throat business. In this respect jumping has caught up with the Flat. On the Flat it wasn't considered quite so important if a jockey had never ridden a particular horse before because without any jumps to manage you don't have to build up quite the same partnership with the animal. I think it's sad that jumping's getting more like the Flat and it takes away from the sport but it's big business now.

We arrived at Kempton on Boxing Day. I'd never sat on One Man before. I met John and Gordon and we walked the course. There had been a hard frost and the racecourse was very keen to hold the race – it is Kempton's most profitable day of the year – but it was touch and go. There were some patches that weren't raceable and they didn't thaw in time. Happily for us the King George VI Chase was re-arranged for 6 January 1996 at Sandown, the same day as the Antony Mildmay/Peter Cazalet Memorial Chase, although Gordon hadn't been able to get much work into him between times because of the bad weather.

Having made a mistake at the first, he soon picked up and travelled strongly. He was very good. I remember going up alongside Adrian Maguire on Barton Bank and saying, 'We're not going very fast, are we?', but Adrian was flat to the boards.

He jumped to the front a little earlier than I'd hoped for at the first down the back. He came up a bit long at one and at another I lengthened him up and he put down on me but he was extremely clever in doing it. Bearing in mind that Gordon had been held up by the weather I was, all the while, trying to save a bit. The horse had been spot on for Kempton and he had told me he thought he was not quite 100 per cent.

On the first circuit Book of Music got killed in a fall at the second of the railway fences and when we came to it a circuit later it was dolled off. There are three fences in very close succession at this point of the course and I thought having to weave round the outside of the middle one might put him off because it was so tight, but he was fine. Behind me the field had all concertina-ed, distracting Monsieur Le Cure who walked through the fourth last fence with Jason Titley.

One Man was still travelling very well going to the Pond fence (the third last) and I'd have been surprised if anything had got to us going any better than we were. At the second last we were beginning to go clear and though I could feel him tiring going to the last he did not stop to a walk like he was to do later in his career. Monsieur Le Cure, who had recovered well from the mistake, was back in second, fourteen lengths away, with Master Oats showing signs of a return to form a further three lengths away in third. I thought it was a breathtaking display, considering he had needed the race. He was entitled to get tired having galloped the others ragged.

Everyone then began to look forward to the 1996 Gold Cup. One Man was to go straight there without another run. He did have a well-publicized gallop at Carlisle one morning when we jumped three fences and galloped over two miles in front of the cameras and he had impressed me there with his fitness. I certainly had no wish to swap him for anything else in the race.

He was a ridiculously short price for a Gold Cup at 11–8. Second favourite was the young Irish chaser Imperial Call, trained near Cork by the great character Fergie Sutherland. As a seven-year-old he was the most progressive horse in the race. He had won the Irish Hennessy Gold Cup in very good style and was attracting a great deal of support from the large Irish crowd at the Cheltenham Festival. The other popular bet was Captain Tim Forster's Dublin Flyer, a front-running course specialist ridden by Brendan Powell. Otherwise you could take your pick. Rough Quest had been in good form winning the Racing Post Chase with me on board; Couldn't Be Better was, like One Man, a Hennessy winner; Barton Bank and Young Hustler were old regulars in the race; Monsieur Le Cure had good form at the course having won the Sun Alliance two years earlier, and the wide outsiders included Lord Relic, who had had his problems since coming second in the Hennessy and King Of The Gales, the second Irish runner who looked out of his depth in this company.

The race went to plan – initially. We were popping away, One Man's jumping was quick and economical and we were creeping our way through the field, led for a circuit at a good pace by Dublin Flyer who weakened very quickly once he was headed at the fourteenth.

Couldn't Be Better and Imperial Call were alternating the lead and apart from pecking when we got a fraction close to the fifth last I got to Imperial Call pretty easily. I looked round then across to Conor O'Dwyer on Imperial Call and said, 'It's between the two of us now.' It was a straight two-horse race as far as I was concerned. I knew it wasn't in the bag – I had a lot of respect for Imperial Call – but I was travelling very well and prepared for a dogfight up the hill over the last two fences.

At the third last I sneaked another look over my shoulder. I didn't see Rough Quest and Mick Fitzgerald – they were the only ones whose tactics involved a stalk of the leaders – and it reaffirmed my view that it was just between the two of us. Two strides off the bend the petrol gauge went from full to empty. I wished Mick good luck when he passed me on Rough Quest. In a matter of a few yards I'd gone from thinking I've got a good chance to nothing. I fired him at the second last and bravely he came up for me but what was left in the tank disappeared with that leap. Then he absolutely walked, was drunk. He was shattered.

Pulling up crossed my mind but he was still in third going to the last and a lot of people were probably still depending on him. In a less important race I might have pulled up but you don't have much time to make those decisions and once you commit a tired horse and yourself to jumping a fence to pull out at the last moment would have added to the problems. He clambered over the last, he never looked like falling and then it was a hell of a long way up

206

that hill. We were passed by all the stragglers and eventually finished sixth of the seven finishers. The Irish were already celebrating Imperial Call's four-length win over Rough Quest when I was still halfway up the run-in.

It was very disappointing but I've had worse things happen. It had felt like my best chance of winning the race since I'd won it on Charter Party. But I'd given the horse every chance of winning. We'd crept into the race and only really joined the battle at the fifth last. If I could have ridden the race again I would have done exactly the same, and I've analysed the race a thousand times since. I talked to Gordon about it, I discussed it with John Hales and lots of people. People say he didn't stay, but he came up the hill at Sandown without any trouble and Sandown can be quite testing. He never stopped galloping when he won the Hennessy but kept going all the way to the line with Tony Dobbin and that was over the same trip. Some people blamed the course, others blamed the horse. I thought there was some physical reason, some internal problem, possibly his lungs or heart that stopped him dead – but I'm no vet. A psychological reason had not crossed my mind at this stage. John's daughter, who knows the horse well, thought he looked out of sorts in the pre-parade ring beforehand. The only other time she felt the same was when he was second to Strong Promise at Ascot in February 1997. Gordon also felt he wasn't right but had he been under the weather I don't know whether he would have travelled quite so well with me during the race.

207

That was it for that season. He had a long summer off and came back at Wetherby for the Charlie Hall Chase in November. With just four runners, us, Young Hustler, Barton Bank and Scotton Banks, it looked like the ideal reintroduction. The quality of the opposition was enough to ensure he had a good blow-out without being (from our point of view) invincible. We'd beaten them all except Tim Easterby's Scotton Banks before.

He was odds-on again to start the season with victory and looked on great form in the paddock. He was on song during the race, trying to tank with me up the straight the first time. He jumped well and I tracked Barton Bank and Young Hustler. Scotton Banks had rapidly dropped out of it. At the fourth last One Man jumped to the front but conscious of what had happened at Cheltenham I tried to hang on to him for as long as possible. He pinged the last again but apparently idled up the run-in. I was riding him as vigorously as I could without resorting to the whip. He held on to win by seven lengths from Barton Bank. Had anything come to me I'm not sure he'd have found much.

You could have excused him – he looked a little big for this first outing of the 1996–7 season – but I was now beginning to wonder whether or not it was a mental thing: the barrier he hits could be in his mind. I always wonder if at Sandown, back in January when he won his first King George VI Chase, he went to the extreme. I know he gave his all. He was very tired and blew hard afterwards. Maybe he went to his limits that day and just maybe he wasn't that keen to go there again. He was an intelligent enough horse to know where the limit was.

Then came his second King George VI Chase (in a year). There were only five runners in the race and the other four were Mr Mulligan, Rough Quest, Barton Bank and Strong Promise, a field short on quantity but quite long on quality. The race was to raise doubts again about how One Man would handle Cheltenham's three and a quarter miles.

We dropped in at the back as Tony McCoy and Mr Mulligan set off at a tremendous gallop. The plan, after Wetherby, was to hold up as long as possible so that he was involved in a race for as little time as possible. I was having to squeeze him up through the race but we made steady headway and got a lead off Mr Mulligan, who appeared to be feeling the effects of the pace he had set, to the third last. I still kept hold of One Man in front, wary about letting him go, and he pinged the second last. I knew there was a horse not far behind me, which I supposed was the tiring and beaten Mr Mulligan. I loosened his head going to the last, he again pinged it, but I hadn't heard Mr Mulligan fall. Instead of looking round to see what danger there was I picked him up to ask him to go away and win his race. He immediately came off the bridle and was desperately hard work, all the more so because I thought I was being caught by Rough Quest, who I feared might creep into the race more gradually than me and then stalk me up the run-in. Had I looked round, seen the situation and won by a cosy five lengths pulling up, everyone would have been highly impressed and largely forgotten about Cheltenham and Wetherby. As it was people still asked questions – did he idle in front or had he come to the end of his stamina reserves on this easy track? Either way it was something to argue about. I thought he didn't warrant any criticism having just broken the course record. It was my record fourth win in all – all on grey horses. As far as I was concerned, he was entitled to get tired, and as we now know with the benefit of hindsight overhauling Mr Mulligan was no easy task.

Gordon, too, had his doubts about Cheltenham and the trip. He didn't rule out the idea of running him in the Queen Mother Champion Chase. To test one theory – that it was the course he didn't like – he sent him to Cheltenham

208

for the Pillar Chase. The plan was just to get round and take up the lead as late as possible, with the emphasis on 'late'.

Adrian Maguire, who had been out for long periods in recent seasons with injury, rode a brilliant race on the rejuvenated Barton Bank. He went quick enough to test One Man's stamina and yet saved enough in reserve for the hill. I always knew he would keep galloping up the hill so I couldn't give him too much leeway and was only a length off him at the second last. I jumped it well; Barton Bank jumped it superbly. We both pinged the last and I was waiting, waiting, holding on, holding on. We went half a length up with fifty yards to go – you can't wait much longer than that – and all of a sudden the petrol gauge dropped on to empty again. I was doing everything within my power except hitting him to win the race. Sometimes when you're on a horse that ties up like One Man does, the sooner you use the stick the sooner they stop and I didn't want to use it.

It was a difficult race to analyse. Barton Bank was a very good horse on his day and had been given a tactical gem of a ride by Adrian. So I wasn't too worried and he had at least broken the hoodoo of being unable to win round the place.

Gordon was still not convinced about the trip. The Pillar Chase is over three miles and a furlong, marginally shorter than the Gold Cup. He decided to take him to Ascot ten days later for the Comet Chase to see if, by dropping him back to two and a half miles, the Champion Chase at Cheltenham might not be a better option. Ten days later was too soon for One Man. Outside of Cheltenham and the races in which he had fallen it was his first chasing defeat. (There was a bit of a muddle over rides beforehand because I also had an agreement to ride Sound Man for the season and the two horses were clashing in this race. Edward O'Grady said that whoever rode Sound Man in this race would ride him in the Champion Chase, which was totally fair, so Charlie Swan came in for the ride.)

We decided to make the running with him this time. One Man didn't jump quite like he could, he put down on me a couple of times, and although he looked like he was going very easily on the bridle he didn't travel like he could do, either. At the last ditch we were short and Strong Promise jumped past him in the air. That's all right, I thought, he can do some of the donkey work up the straight, but I was soon hard at work. However, when I gave him a couple of taps he responded and galloped. People had been saying all season that he didn't battle but he did and he proved it that day. He battled hard but was on the losing side. We were beaten a length.

The thing I liked about One Man this day was that he was still galloping when he went past the winning post. Strong Promise, on his day, was a very good horse and had we been stopping he would have drawn clear of us and beaten us a great deal further than a length. However, because he had been beaten, Gordon decided to have another crack at the Gold Cup. One Man should be given another chance, it was the preferred option and he would freshen him up beforehand.

This time there were no big racecourse gallops in front of cameras – the media had new heroes to follow in the build-up – and Gordon sent him hunting to give him a change of scenery. The same thing worked wonders for Master Oats at the same time. He went to Cheltenham well in 1997 and with a great chance at a much more realistic price. He had his ground, we would ride him to get the trip and at the third last there were plenty of people who would have willingly taken the 7–1 as he loomed up to the front-running Mr Mulligan.

Coming down the hill I reckoned I had Mr Mulligan covered. If he finished like he did at Ascot I'm going to win it, I thought. I was more confident than I had been a year before when we were upsides Imperial Call. But he weakened rapidly going to the last, used all his remaining energy to get over it and again it was a long way up the hill. He eventually finished sixth, beaten about thirty-five lengths. He had gone 100 yards further than he did the previous season. Gordon said he was fine the next day and was convinced that One Man did not stay three and a quarter miles round a stiff track that's hilly like Cheltenham. John thought he got about three miles and half a furlong in a race like the Cheltenham Gold Cup.

I am still of the opinion that something was hurting him and he didn't get the trip. If going through the pain barrier at Sandown hadn't hurt him then Cheltenham a year earlier certainly had. He wasn't drunk this time but it was almost like he was saving himself as well.

He came out of the Gold Cup so well that Gordon decided that he would have a go at the Martell Cup at Aintree three weeks later. Barton Bank, who had run his best race for ages to finish second in the Gold Cup under David Walsh, and Merry Gale were the main dangers. He was travelling well but made an uncharacteristic mistake down the end of the back straight with a circuit and a half still to run. Back in the home straight Jason Titley on Rouyan shouted over: 'You've burst, you've burst.' I looked down to try to get a look at his nostrils several times. There was blood on my breeches but I thought it was possible the blood had come from Merry Gale who had a red tongue-

tie which looked at first glance as if it could be blood. It is when a horse breaks a blood vessel and part of his lungs fills with blood that he can go 'drunk' on you. One Man was still travelling this time. The commentator noted that not all was right with us and after jumping the eleventh fence I could see he was bleeding from the nose – not that I didn't believe Jason but I just wanted to make sure – I pulled him up in front of the stands.

It was the only time One Man had shown externally that there might be a problem internally. The drunkenness at the end of races, in my experience, is more often found in horses who have broken a blood vessel rather than horses who have failed to get the trip. Horses who fail to get the trip tend to peter out rather than stop like they have been shot. The vets cannot confirm this though. It was possible in One Man's case that he was stopping himself before he burst, who knows.

The following season, he ran a terrible race in the King George and came trailing in behind for no obvious reason. Tony Dobbin rode him next time in the Comet Chase at Ascot when he dropped back to just under two-and-a-half miles. He won, beating his old rival Strong Promise – but Norman Williamson assured me he wouldn't win a Champion Chase after that performance. For the Champion I was committed to Arthur Moore's Klairon Davis, a previous winner of the race whose own jockey, Francis Woods, had been injured.

Tony Dobbin was injured on the first day of the Festival and the joke in the weighing room was that more jockeys were injured in the crush to get the ride on One Man. Gordon, however, put his faith in his second jockey, Brian Harding. They combined for a stunning, powerful victory. He never looked as if he would be beaten and I could see this from Klairon Davis 10 lengths back, in fourth.

I said in the past that One Man 'may yet prove a Champion at Cheltenham.' In that respect I was right, but his reign as Champion was tragically short. Three weeks later, again ridden by Brian, he was killed at the first fence down the down straight on the eve of the Grand National. There was a stunned silence in the grandstand as people looked away. The outcome was inevitable and the only thing you could say is that he would have felt little. It killed him instantly. Thus ended a career that, in many ways, mirrored Desert Orchid's – except that he went from long distances to short.

As for comparisons with Desert Orchid – they were both superb horses. One Man was a bit more compact and very athletic. He was possibly more agile than Dessie was and cleverer at a fence. He could get in close or stand off whereas Dessie was more flamboyant. Dessie would come up out of your hands more often and would keep coming up for you if you kept firing him in. The thing that struck you about Dessie was his fitness and the strength of his neck. As soon as you sat on him, you got a feeling of amazing power, which did not strike you immediately on One Man. Both were exceptional chasers and a clash between the two would have been worth travelling many miles to see.

PICTURE ACKNOWLEDGEMENTS

Ed Byrne Chpt 5 Kribensis; **Gerry Cranham** p1 bottom, p2, p3 bottom, p5 top, p6 bottom, p9 bottom, p10, p11 bottom, pp14-15, Chpt 4 Very Promising, Chpt 8 Morley Street, Chpt 17 Viking Flagship; **John Crofts** Chpt 3 Charter Party; **CTK** Chpt 16 It's a Snip; **E. L. Gibbs** p7; **Empics** Chpt 9 Florida Pearl; **Liam Healy** p9 top, Chpt 11 Rushing Wind; **Les Hurley** p11 top; **Alan Johnson** Chpt 1 West Tip, Chpt 10 Remittance Man; **Trevor Jones** p5 centre, p6 top, p8, Chpt 12 Miinnehoma; **George Selwyn** p1 top, p3 top, p4, p5 bottom, pp12-14, p16, Chpt 2 Desert Orchid, Chpt 6 Waterloo Boy, Chpt 7 Highland Bud, Chpt 13 Flakey Dove, Chpt 14 Alderbrook, Chpt 15 Sound Man, Chpt 18 One Man.